Lecture Notes in Computer Science 7555

Commenced Publication in 1973
Founding and Former Series Editors:
Gerhard Goos, Juris Hartmanis, and Jan van Leeuwen

Editorial Board

Hao Hu   Xiaoning Shi   Robert Stahlbock
Stefan Voß (Eds.)

Computational Logistics

Third International Conference, ICCL 2012
Shanghai, China, September 24-26, 2012
Proceedings

 Springer

Volume Editors

Hao Hu
Shanghai Jiao Tong University
School of Naval Architecture, Ocean and Civil Engineering
1954 Huashan Road, Shanghai 200030, China
E-mail: hhu@sjtu.edu.cn

Xiaoning Shi
Robert Stahlbock
Stefan Voß
Universität Hamburg
Institut für Wirtschaftsinformatik
Von-Melle-Park 5, 20146 Hamburg, Germany
E-mail: {shi,stahlbock}@econ.uni-hamburg.de; stefan.voss@uni-hamburg.de

ISSN 0302-9743   e-ISSN 1611-3349
ISBN 978-3-642-33586-0   e-ISBN 978-3-642-33587-7
DOI 10.1007/978-3-642-33587-7
Springer Heidelberg Dordrecht London New York

Library of Congress Control Number: 2012947229

CR Subject Classification (1998): F.2.2, H.4.1-2, D.2.2, I.2.8, I.6, J.1, J.7, C.2, F.1

LNCS Sublibrary: SL 1 – Theoretical Computer Science and General Issues

Typesetting: Camera-ready by author, data conversion by Scientific Publishing Services, Chennai, India

Printed on acid-free paper

Springer is part of Springer Science+Business Media (www.springer.com)

Preface

Computational logistics refers to the planning and implementation of logistics tasks using computations and advanced decision support. It covers significant work regarding theory and application of systems and methodologies for advancing planning and operations in logistics. It is applied in various areas including the flow and storage of goods or services as well as related information from their source to their destination. Typically, optimization models and algorithms are developed, verified, and applied for planning and executing complex logistics tasks, e.g., for finding the most efficient scheduling/plan for the transport of passengers or goods. These models and algorithms are integrated with advanced information and communication technology (IT) to obtain satisfactory results in appropriate time even for large-scale problem instances and providing interactivity, visualization, etc. for a better understanding, problem solution, and decision support. Furthermore, computational logistics involves the use of information systems and modern IT tools for the design, planning, and control of logistics networks as well as the complex tasks within them.

The International Conference on Computational Logistics (ICCL) provides an opportunity for researchers and practitioners in the field of computational logistics to present their latest results and findings in a fruitful and open-minded environment. This volume of Lecture Notes in Computer Science consists of selected papers presented at the 3rd International Conference on Computational Logistics, held at the Shanghai Jiao Tong University in Shanghai, China, September 24–26, 2012.

The ICCL 2012 was the third of its kind. The first was held in 2010, also in Shanghai, and the second one in Hamburg, Germany (see Volume 6971 of the LNCS). The idea of inviting participants to go back to Shanghai was motivated by the fact that computational logistics has become very visible in Shanghai with continuous developments to be seen in action. As a port city, Shanghai has moved from record to record, e.g., regarding container turnover, making it the largest port worldwide in that respect. For instance, Yangshan Deapsea Water Container Terminal upgraded its ranking in the world, increasing research interests to a great extent; Zhenhua Port Machinery Corporation (ZPMC) has developed advanced terminal handling systems based on information system design, matching very much the scope of the ICCL. Moreover, Hongqiao Airport Terminal II has applied advanced engineering management mechanisms, inspiring further research on computational logistics; an underground logistics system has been researched in Shanghai for a few years and is expected to be implemented in the near future. Technical excursions to these places, together with the academic submissions included in this special issue, brought the participants the flavor of the state of the art of computational logistics and its scientific outputs and implementations as well as applications.

The contributions presented at the conference as well as the papers in these proceedings show that computational logistics are gaining more and more importance in various areas. Academics as well as practitioners are deeply involved in the development of the field, which is going from strength to strength. This is well reflected in the advances seen in the contributions presented at the conference as well as the selected papers in these proceedings. Following the focus of the papers accepted, we grouped the contributions into four parts as follows:

- Part I: Maritime Shipping
- Part II: Logistics and Supply Chain Management
- Part III: Planning and Operations
- Part IV: Case Studies

While we believe that these proceedings provide insights into the state of the art of the field, we also hope and know that the story is never-ending. That is, new advances on different levels are expected, taking into consideration innovations in all areas of computational logistics, building upon what we have developed.

Organizing a conference and publishing the proceedings is a task that relies on the help and support of many people in various roles. Many thanks go to all the authors and presenters for their contributions. In addition, we greatly appreciate the valuable help and cooperation of the members of the international program committee and the referees. While preparing the conference and compiling the proceedings we also received enthusiastic support from Julia Bachale (IWI Hamburg) as well as the team of local organizers in Shanghai.

September 2012

Hao Hu
Xiaoning Shi
Robert Stahlbock
Stefan Voß

Organization

Organization Chair

Hao Hu   Shanghai Jiao Tong University, China
Stefan Voß   University of Hamburg, Germany

Organization Committee

Xiaoning Shi   Shanghai Jiao Tong University, China, and
     University of Hamburg, Germany
Robert Stahlbock   University of Hamburg, Germany, and
     FOM University of Applied Sciences,
     Essen/Hamburg, Germany

Program Committee and Referees

Jürgen W. Böse   Hamburg University of Technology, Germany
Buyang Cao   Tongji University Shanghai, China
Marco Caserta   IE Business School Madrid, Spain
José Ceroni   Pontificia Universidad Catolica de Valparaíso,
     Chile
Marielle Christiansen   Norwegian University of Science and
     Technology, Norway
Joachim R. Daduna   Berlin School of Economics and Law, Germany
Kjetil Fagerholt   Norwegian University of Science and
     Technology, Norway
Janusz Granat   National Institute of Telecommunications
     Warsaw, Poland
Hans-Otto Günther   TU Berlin, Germany
Kai Gutenschwager   University of Applied Sciences Ulm, Germany
Hans-Dietrich Haasis   ISL Bremen, Germany
Richard F. Hartl   University of Vienna, Austria
Geir Hasle   SINTEF Applied Mathematics Department of
     Optimisation, Norway
Sin C. Ho   Aarhus University, Denmark
Rune Møller Jensen   IT University of Copenhagen, Denmark
Herbert Kopfer   University of Bremen, Germany
Gilbert Laporte   HEC Montréal, Canada
Hoong Chuin Lau   Singapore Management University, Singapore
Janny Leung   Chinese University of Hong Kong, China

Hong K. Lo	Hong Kong University of Science and Technology, China
Arne Løkketangen	Molde College, Norway
André Ludwig	University of Leipzig, Germany
Belén Melián-Batista	University of La Laguna, Spain
João Lemos Nabais	Setúbal School of Technology, Portugal
Rudy Negenborn	Delft University of Technology, Netherlands
Dario Pacino	IT University of Copenhagen, Denmark
Helena Ramalhinho Lourenco	Universitat Pompeu Fabra, Barcelona, Spain
Juan José Salazar González	University of La Laguna, Spain
Silvia Schwarze	University of Hamberg, Germany
Hans-Jürgen Sebastian	RWTH Aachen, Germany
Xiaoning Shi	Shanghai Jiao Tong University, China, and University of Hamburg, Germany
Grazia Speranza	Brescia University, Italy
Robert Stahlbock	University of Hamburg, Germany
Wai Yuen Szeto	University of Hong Kong, China
David Woodruff	University of California (Davis), USA
Tsz Leung Yip	Hong Kong Polytechnic University, China

Table of Contents

Case Studies

The Liner Shipping Fleet Repositioning Problem with Cargo Flows

Kevin Tierney and Rune Møller Jensen

IT University of Copenhagen, Copenhagen, Denmark
{kevt,rmj}@itu.dk

Abstract. We solve an important problem for the liner shipping industry called the Liner Shipping Fleet Repositioning Problem (LSFRP). The LSFRP poses a large financial burden on liner shipping firms. During repositioning, vessels are moved between services in a liner shipping network. Shippers wish to reposition vessels as cheaply as possible without disrupting the cargo flows of the network. The LSFRP is characterized by chains of interacting activities with a multi-commodity flow over paths defined by the activities chosen. Despite its great industrial importance, the LSFRP has received little attention in the literature. We introduce a novel mathematical model of the LSFRP with cargo flows based on a carefully constructed graph and evaluate it on real world data from our industrial collaborator.

1   Introduction

Responsible for transporting over 1.3 billion tons of cargo in 2011 [10], liner shipping networks reliably and cheaply connect the world's markets. Vessels are regularly repositioned between services in liner shipping networks to adjust the networks to the world economy and to stay competitive. Since repositioning a single vessel can cost hundreds of thousands of US dollars, optimizing the repositioning activities of vessels is an important problem for the liner shipping industry.

The Liner Shipping Fleet Repositioning Problem (LSFRP) consists of finding sequences of activities that move vessels between services in a liner shipping network while respecting the cargo flows of the network. The LSFRP maximizes the profit earned on the subset of the network affected by the repositioning, balancing sailing costs and port fees against cargo and equipment revenues, while respecting important liner shipping specific constraints dictating the creation of services and movement of cargo. A unique feature of the LSFRP is the state-based nature of the activities in the problem. Many LSFRP activities span multiple physical locations and depend on where vessels are located at particular times in order to be performed. Automated planning techniques were used to represent a high-level version of the LSFRP that ignored cargo flows in [9]. Cargo flows, however, are an important aspect of the LSFRP that drive decisions on how vessels should be repositioned.

To this end, we present a novel model of the LSFRP with cargo flows using a mixed-integer programming (MIP) model on top of a detailed graph that embeds many LSFRP constraints. We solve our model using CPLEX and study the performance of our model

H. Hu et al. (Eds.): ICCL 2012, LNCS 7555, pp. 1–16, 2012.

on real world data from our industrial collaborator. Our instances contain two actual repositioning scenarios as well as several constructed scenarios to investigate the scaling performance of our model.

2   Liner Shipping Fleet Repositioning

Liner shipping networks consist of a set of cyclical routes, called services, that visit ports on a regular, usually weekly, schedule. Liner shipping networks are designed to serve customer's cargo demands, but over time the economy changes and liner shippers must adjust their networks in order to stay competitive. Liner shippers make adjustments by adding, removing and modifying the services in their network. Whenever a new service is created, or an existing service is expanded, vessels must be *repositioned* from their current service to the service being added or expanded. Vessel repositioning is expensive due to the cost of fuel (in the region of hundreds of thousands of dollars) and the revenue lost due to cargo flow disruptions. Given that liner shippers around the world reposition hundreds of vessels per year, optimizing vessel movements can significantly reduce the economic and environmental burdens of containerized shipping, and allow shippers to better utilize repositioning vessels to transport cargo.

The aim of the LSFRP is to maximize the profit earned when repositioning a number of vessels from their initial services to a service being added or expanded, called the goal service. We focus on the case where a new service is being added to the network because expanding a service can be seen as a special case of adding a new service, in which vessels are repositioned from the service being expanded to itself along with extra vessels from elsewhere in the network.

Liner shipping services are composed of multiple *slots*, each of which represents a cycle that is assigned a particular vessel. Each slot is composed of a number of *visitations*, which represent a specific time when a vessel is scheduled to call a port. A vessel that is assigned to a particular slot sequentially sails to each visitation in the slot. Figure 1 shows a schedule of an example service that contains three slots and visits five ports. The service requires three weeks to complete a cycle, and therefore needs three vessels in order to maintain weekly frequency. Each line (black, dark gray, light gray) represents a slot, and each dot is a visitation at a port at a particular time.

Vessel sailing speeds can be adjusted throughout repositioning to balance cost savings with punctuality. The bunker fuel consumption of vessels increases cubically based on the speed of the vessel. *Slow steaming*, in which vessels sail near or at their minimum speed, therefore, allows vessels to sail cheaper between two ports than at higher speeds, albeit with a longer duration. We linearize the bunker consumption of each repositioning vessel in order to more easily model the LSFRP.

Phase-out & Phase-in.   The repositioning period for each vessel starts at a specific time when the vessel may cease normal operations, that is, it may stop sailing to scheduled visitations and go somewhere else. Each vessel is assigned a different time when it may begin its repositioning, or *phase-out* time. After this time, the vessel may undertake a number of different activities to reach its goal service at low cost. In order to complete the repositioning, each vessel must *phase in* to a slot on the goal service before a time set by the repositioning coordinator. After this time, normal operations on the goal service are set to begin, and all scheduled visitations on the service are to be undertaken. Figure 1 shows a phase-in service with a phase-in deadline at port c in week 2. The solid lines connect all the visitations that must be undertaken, whereas the dashed lines connect visitations that will only be carried out if they are profitable during the repositioning.

Within a *tradezone*, which is a contiguous geographical area, vessels may sail freely from their initial service to goal service, as well as back from the goal service to the initial service. However, if two ports lie in different tradezones, vessels may only sail between them when going from the initial service to the goal service. Tradezone restrictions ensure cargo is not brought to places that would violate the law, as well as help keep vessels from experiencing unexpected delays.

When a port is visited that is not in the initial or goal service, or is visited out of order, it is called an *inducement*. If a port on the initial or goal service is left off of the repositioning vessel's schedule, it is called an *omission*. Figure 2 shows a vessel's repositioning (solid line) from its initial service (dashed) to its goal service (dotted) within a tradezone. Although FXT is on both the goal and initial services, it is omitted from the repositioning. Note also that the ports RTM and BRV are induced into the repositioning path. This is only possible because the induced ports are in the same tradezone as LEH and AAR.

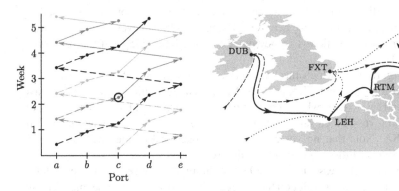

Fig. 1. A service time-space graph   **Fig. 2.** An example repositioning

Cargo and Equipment.   Revenue is earned through delivering cargo and equipment (empty containers). We use a detailed view of cargo flows. Cargo is represented as a set of port to port demands with a cargo type, a latest delivery time, an amount of TEU[1] available, and a revenue per TEU delivered. We subtract the cost of loading and unloading each TEU from the revenue to determine the profit per TEU of a particular cargo demand. In contrast to cargo, which can be seen as a multi-commodity flow where each demand is a commodity with a start and end port, equipment can be sent from any port where it is in surplus to any port where it is in demand. Ports which have an equipment surplus or deficit can be considered to have an infinite amount of supply

---
[1] TEU stands for *twenty-foot equivalent unit* and represents a single twenty-foot container.

or demand for a particular type of equipment. This is reasonable since the amount of extra containers on-hand or that are required tends to be much greater than the size of a vessel. Each piece of equipment brought from a port where it is in excess to a port where it is needed earns a small revenue. The revenue earned is an estimation of how much money was saved by bringing the equipment on a repositioning vessel instead of moving the equipment through other, more expensive means.

We consider both *dry* and *reefer* (refrigerated) cargo. Dry containers are standard containers with no specific handling requirements. Reefer containers, in contrast, must be stowed on a vessel in a location with a plug in order to keep the refrigeration unit running. Some ports have equipment, but are not on any service visited by repositioning vessels. These ports are called *flexible* ports, and are associated with flexible visitations. The repositioning coordinator may choose the time a vessel arrives at such visitations, if at all. All other visitations are called *inflexible*, because the time a vessel arrives is fixed.

Sail-on-Service (SOS) Opportunities. While repositioning, vessels may use certain services to cheaply sail between two parts of the network. These are called *SOS opportunities*. There are two vessels involved in SOS opportunities, referred to as the *repositioning vessel*, which is the vessel under the control of a repositioning coordinator, and the *on-service vessel*, which is the vessel assigned to a slot on the service being offered as an SOS opportunity. Repositioning vessels can use SOS opportunities by replacing the on-service vessel and sailing in its place for a portion of the service. SOS opportunities save significant amounts of money on bunker fuel, since one vessel is sailing where there would have otherwise been two. Using an SOS can even earn money from the *time-charter bonus*, which is money earned by the liner shipper if the on-service vessel is leased.

Consider Figure 3, in which the AC3 service is offered as a SOS opportunity to the vessel repositioning from CHX to Intra-WCSA. The repositioning vessel can leave CHX at TPP, and sail to HKG where it picks up the AC3, replacing the on-service vessel. The repositioning vessel then sails along the AC3 until it gets to BLB where it can join the Intra-WCSA. Note that no vessel sails on the backhaul of the AC3, and this is allowed because very little cargo travels on the AC3 towards Asia.

When a repositioning vessel uses an SOS opportunity, the on-service vessel is either laid-up or leased out, freeing a slot on the service. The repositioning vessel may join the freed slot in any of the *starting visitations* and may leave the slot in one of the *ending*

Fig. 3. A subset of the case study we performed with our industrial collaborator

visitations. There are two ways for repositioning vessels to start an SOS: *transshipment* and *parallel sailing.* When starting an SOS by transshipment, all cargo loaded on the on-service vessel is transshipped (moved) to the repositioning vessel. Each TEU transshipped has a fee roughly equal the cost of loading a TEU. Transshipment is not always possible, due to *cabotage restrictions,* which are laws preventing foreign flagged vessels from offering domestic cargo services in certain markets. Cabotage rules can be legally worked around using a *parallel sailing,* in which both the repositioning vessel and the on-service vessel visit ports in tandem. The repositioning vessel only loads cargo, and the on-service vessel only discharges cargo. Although parallel sailing is expensive, since fuel consumption is doubled, it is sometimes cheaper than performing a transshipment when the transshipment fees at a port are high.

2.1 Literature Review

The LSFRP has received little attention in the literature and was not mentioned in either of the most influential surveys of work in the liner shipping domain [3,4]. Although there has been significant work on problems such as the Fleet Deployment Problem (FDP) [8] and the Network Design Problem (NDP) [1], neither captures the movement of vessels through the network inherent in the LSFRP.

Although tramp shipping problems, such as [7], maximize cargo profit in the face of sailing costs and port fees as in the LSFRP, they lack liner shipping specific constraints, such as phase-in requirements and strict visitation times. Airline disruption management [5,6], while also relying on time-based graphs, differs from the LSFRP in two key ways. First, airline disruption management requires an exact cover of all flight legs over a planning horizon. The LSFRP has no such requirement over visitations or sailing legs. Second, there are no flexible visitations in airline disruption management.

Martin W. Andersen's PhD thesis [2] discusses a problem similar to the LSFRP, called the Network Transition Problem (NTP). No mathematical model or formal problem description is provided, so it is difficult to exactly ascertain what the NTP solves in comparison to the LSFRP. However, it is clear that the NTP lacks cost saving activities like SOS opportunities, empty equipment flows and slow steaming.

The primary previous work on the LSFRP in the literature is [9], by the authors, which introduced Linear Temporal Optimization Planning (LTOP), a hybrid of automated planning and linear programming that performs a branch-and-bound search for repositioning solutions. The authors focus on an abstraction of the LSFRP without cargo/equipment flows and SOS parallel sailings. The hybrid method works well on a version of the LSFRP solved due to the state dependent nature of the activities in the LSFRP, and outperforms a MIP model. The LSFRP seems to reside on the border between automated planning and mixed-integer programming. On the one hand, vessels have important state information that must be taken into account. On the other hand, there is not so much state information such that embedding that information in a graph for the MIP explodes as in classical automated planning problems. Nevertheless, LTOP is not capable of handling cargo flows, as the automated planning actions used must either model only costs or only revenues. LTOP is, therefore, unable to handle our model of the LSFRP.

3   Mathematical Model

We model the LSFRP with cargo flows on a graph $G = (V, A)$, where V is the set of nodes and A the set of directed arcs between nodes. Each node in V represents a *visitation* of a vessel at a particular port[2], and each arc in A represents an allowed sailing between two visitations. The graph encompasses all of the activities each vessel may undertake during a fixed *repositioning period*, which is the period from the time the vessel is first allowed to leave its phase-out service until the time when normal operations must begin on the phase-in service. The path of each vessel through the graph represents the activities to be undertaken by that vessel, and we therefore require the paths to be node disjoint to prevent multiple vessels from performing the same activity. This is an important constraint because there is only space for a single vessel at the quay during a visitation. Note that flexible visitations, i.e. visitations without a prior fixed schedule, can be undertaken by multiple vessels, even simultaneously. For ease of modeling, we therefore replicate flexible visitations for each vessel and consider them as node disjoint. We give more details about this process (and justifications) later. We embed a number of problem constraints and objectives directly in the graph, including sailing costs, sail-on-service opportunities, cabotage restrictions, phase-in/out requirements, and canal fees, which are described in detail in the next section, followed by our MIP model over the graph.

3.1   Graph Description

The visitations in the graph are split into two sets, thus $V = V^i \cup V^f$, where V^i is the set of *inflexible* visitations, i.e. visitations associated with a specific port call time, and V^f is the set of *flexible* visitations, which are assigned a time only if a vessel performs the visitation. The set V^f contains visitations in which a vessel can pick up/deliver equipment or incremental cargo that are not on any phase-out, phase-in, or SOS service.

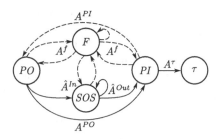

Fig. 4. A high level overview of the graph structure

Figure 4 shows a high-level view of the structure of the graph. The graph's visitations are classified into the sets PO, PI, F, and SOS, which contain the phase-out, phase-in, flexible and sail-on-service visitations, respectively. The node τ represents the graph sink. Vessels begin their repositioning in the PO visitations with the goal of reaching τ,

---

[2] We use the terms visitation and node interchangeably.

which can only be reached through the PI nodes in order to enforce constraints on how services are started. At any time during repositioning, each vessel is either performing a visitation, or sailing between two visitations. The vessel may sail to a visitation in a different set if an arc connects that set from the vessel's current visitation, with dashed lines indicating that the two visitations must be in the same tradezone, i.e. they must be geographically close to each other. We now formally define the graph of the LSFRP, using the following constants.

S	Set of ships, indexed by s.
L	Set of phase-in slots, where $|L| = |S|$, indexed by ℓ.
SOS	The set of SOS slots, indexed by o.
R_ℓ^{PI}	Set of visitations of phase-in slot ℓ.
R_s^{PO}	Set of phase-out visitations of vessel s.
$O_o^{\{P,TS,T,E\}}$	Sets of parallel, transshipment, transit, and end visitations.
V^R	Set of non-SOS inflexible visitations, $V^R = V^i \backslash (O_o^P \cup O_o^{TS} \cup O_o^T \cup O_o^E)$.
TZ	Set of trade zones.
$z_i \in TZ$	Trade zone of visitation $i \in V$.
$enter(i) \in \mathbb{R}^+$	Time a vessel begins inflexible visitation $i \in V^i$.
$exit(i) \in \mathbb{R}^+$	Time a vessel ends inflexible visitation $i \in V^i$.
$\tau \in V$	Graph sink, which is not an actual visitation.
$V' = V \backslash \tau$	Set of nodes without the graph sink.
$\Delta_{i,j}$	Minimum time required for any ship to sail from visitation i to j.
$A^{SD}(R)$	Set of arcs connecting subsequent visitations in the visitation set R.
A^{PO}	Set of arcs connecting phase-out slots to phase-in slots.
A^{PI}	Set of arcs from phase-in visitations to same tradezone phase-out visitations.
A^τ	Set of arcs from the phase-in to the graph sink.
A^f	Set of arcs connecting flexible visitations to other visitations.
$\hat{A}_o^{In}$	Set of arcs connecting to the start nodes of o.
$\hat{A}_o^{Out}$	Set of arcs extending from the end nodes of o.
$\hat{A}_o^{PTS}$	Set of arcs connecting the parallel nodes to transhipment nodes of o.
$\hat{A}_o^{TST}$	Set of arcs connecting transshipment nodes to transit nodes of o.
$\hat{A}_o^{TT}$	Set of arcs between transit nodes of o.
$\hat{A}_o^{EE}$	Set of arcs between sequential end nodes of o.
$\hat{a}_o^{TE}$	Arc from the latest transit node in o to its earliest end node.

We define the set of inflexible nodes as $V^i = \bigcup_{\ell \in L} R_\ell^{PI} \bigcup_{s \in S} R_s^{PO} \bigcup_{o \in SOS} (O_o^P \cup O_o^T \cup O_o^{TS} \cup O_o^E)$. The set of flexible visitations, V^f, contains all visitations that have equipment surpluses/deficits such that $V^f \cap V^i = \emptyset$. In order to formally define the set of arcs contained in the graph, let $follows(i,j) \in \mathbb{B}$ return $true$ if and only if visitation j is scheduled on any service to immediately follow visitation i, with $i, j \in V^i$. In addition, we let $can\text{-}sail(i,j) \in \mathbb{B}$ be $true$ if and only if $enter(j) \geq exit(i) + \Delta_{i,j}$, where $i, j \in V'$. This indicates whether or not it is possible to sail between two visitations at the fastest speed of the fastest vessel in the model. Note that all of the arc sets are disjoint. We now formally define all of the previously mentioned sets of arcs.

$$A^{SD}(R) = \{(i,j) \mid i,j \in R \wedge follows(i,j)\}, R \in \bigcup_{s \in S} R_s^{PO} \bigcup_{\ell \in L} R_\ell^{PI}$$

$$A^{PO} = \{(i,j) \mid i \in \bigcup_{s \in S} R_s^{PO} \wedge j \in \bigcup_{\ell \in L} R_\ell^{PI} \wedge can\text{-}sail(i,j)\}$$

$$A^{PI} = \{(i,j) \mid i \in \bigcup_{\ell \in L} R_\ell^{PI} \wedge j \in \bigcup_{s \in S} R_s^{PO} \wedge z_i = z_j \wedge can\text{-}sail(i,j)\}$$

$$A^\tau = \{(i,j) \mid i \in \bigcup_{\ell \in L} \operatorname*{argmax}_{i' \in R_\ell^{PI}} \{exit(i')\} \wedge j = \tau\}$$

$$A^f = \{(i,j) \mid \left((i \in V^f \wedge j \in V^R) \vee (i \in V^R \wedge j \in V^f)\right) \wedge z_i = z_j\}$$

$$\hat{A}_o^{In} = \{(i,j) \mid i \in \bigcup_{s \in S} R_s^{PO} \wedge j \in (O_o^P \cup O_o^{TS}) \wedge can\text{-}sail(i,j)\}$$

$$\bigcup \{(i,j) \mid i \in V^f \wedge j \in (O_o^P \cup O_o^{TS}) \wedge z_i = z_j \wedge can\text{-}sail(i,j)\}$$

$$\hat{A}_o^{Out} = \{(i,j) \mid i \in O_o^E \wedge j \in \left(\bigcup_{\ell \in L} R_\ell^{PI} \bigcup_{o' \in \{SOS \backslash o\}} (O_{o'}^P \cup O_{o'}^{TS})\right) \wedge can\text{-}sail(i,j)\}$$

$$\bigcup \{(i,j) \mid i \in O_o^E \wedge j \in V^f \wedge z_i = z_j \wedge can\text{-}sail(i,j)\}$$

$$\hat{A}_o^{PTS} = \{(i,j) \mid i \in O_o^P \wedge j \in O_o^{TS} \wedge follows(i,j)\}$$

$$\hat{A}_o^{TST} = \{(i,j) \mid i \in O_o^{TS} \wedge j \in O_o^T \wedge follows(i,j)\}$$

$$\hat{A}_o^{TT} = \{(i,j) \mid i,j \in O_o^T \wedge follows(i,j)\}$$

$$\hat{A}_o^{EE} = \{(i,j) \mid i,j \in O_o^E \wedge follows(i,j)\}$$

$$\hat{a}_o^{TE} = (\operatorname*{argmax}_{i \in O_o^T} \{exit(i)\}, \operatorname*{argmin}_{j \in O_o^E} \{enter(j)\})$$

The set of all arcs in the graph, A, is therefore defined by

$$A = \bigcup_{s \in S} \left(A^{SD}(R_s^{PO})\right) \bigcup_{\ell \in L} \left(A^{SD}(R_\ell^{PI})\right) \cup A^{PI} \cup A^f$$
$$\cup \hat{A}_o^{In} \cup \hat{A}_o^{Out} \cup A^\tau \cup A_o^{ST} \cup \hat{A}_o^{TT} \cup \hat{A}_o^{EE} \cup \hat{a}_o^{TE}.$$

Phase-out and Phase-in. Each vessel begins its repositioning at a pre-specified earliest phase-out visitation on its initial slot. The graph structure of the phase-out slots is fully described by $A^{SD}(R)$, $R \in \cup_{s \in S} R_s^{PO}$; A^{PO}; and $\hat{A}_o^{In}, o \in SOS$ since the only activities a vessel may undertake on its initial service slot are sailing between scheduled visitations in the slot, or leaving the slot for a flexible node, SOS opportunity, or the phase-in service.

The phase-in graph structure ensures that the goal service has a vessel in each of its slots. An example phase-in graph structure is given in Figure 5, which shows the graph for the service in Figure 1. Each sequence of visitations (colored light gray, dark gray, and black) represents a slot on the goal service. Each visitation is labeled with the

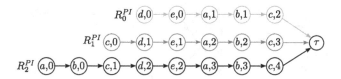

Fig. 5. The phase-in graph structure for the service in Figure 1

port and week that it is visited. The last node in each sequence corresponds to the on-time requirement (node $(c, 2)$) extended to each slot. After each of these visitations, the service begins normal operations, and is no longer under the control of the repositioning coordinator. This graph structure ensures that all vessels perform a legal phase-in, namely that each slot is assigned a single vessel. Each phase-in slot is guaranteed to be assigned a single vessel since there are as many slots as there are vessels (three), the graph sink τ only has a single incoming node from each slot, and the paths of vessels are node disjoint (except for τ).

Flexible Visitations. Flexible visitations are modeled by replicating the flexible visitation for each vessel in the model. If we did not replicate flexible visitations, only one vessel would be able to visit a flexible visitation, even though it is possible (and even desirable) for multiple vessels to undertake a single flexible visitation. This is because when a vessel visits a flexible visitation, the visitation must be assigned a time when it can take place. Therefore, we replicate the visitation and the node-disjoint paths of each vessel ensure two vessels do not use the same flexible visitation node. Since our instances generally do not contain many flexible visitations, this duplication does not significantly hinder the solvability of the instances. This opens the possibility that two vessels may visit the same flexible visitation at the same time. We do not consider this to be a problem since flexible visitations are at ports that will probably have the capacity to deal with multiple ships. Since flexible visitations do not have fixed entry and exit times, the time required for a vessel to visit them must be taken into account. The *piloting time* is the time required to maneuver the vessel in to, and out of, a port. The amount of cargo loaded or unloaded from the vessel at the port further extends the amount of time necessary for a vessel to stay at a flexible port, depending on the efficiency of the port at moving containers on and off the vessel.

SOS. Figure 6 shows the graph structure of an SOS opportunity. Vessels may enter the SOS either through parallel sailing nodes (O_o^P) or transshipment nodes (O_o^{TS}). Parallel sailings end in a transshipment, shown with graph arcs $\hat{A}_o^{PTS}$, in which cargo is moved to the repositioning vessel. Port p_1 does not allow any transshipments due to a cabotage restriction, necessitating a parallel sailing to carry cargo from the port.

The transshipment nodes then connect to the transit nodes (O_o^T), which represent the "normal" port calls of the SOS. The vessel calls each port of the SOS in sequence until it reaches an end port (O_o^E), where it may then leave the SOS. A single SOS opportunity may only be used by a single vessel, and since the paths of the vessels through the graph are node disjoint, the sequential nature of the end nodes ensures that only one vessel may traverse a particular slot in an SOS.

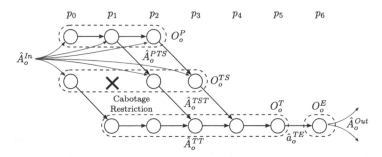

Fig. 6. The graph structure of an SOS opportunity

3.2 MIP Model

We now define the MIP model that guides the vessels through the graph, and controls the flow of cargo and equipment, using the following constants and variables to supplement the constants used to define the graph.

Constants

T	Set of equipment types. $T = \{dc, rf\}$.
$\sigma_s \in V'$	Starting visitation of vessel $s \in S$.
$V^{t+}, (V^{t-})$	Set of visitations with an equipment surplus (deficit) of type t.
V^{t*}	Set of visitations with an equipment surplus or deficit of type t.
V^{Goal}	Set of visitations corresponding to visitations on the goal service.
$In(i) \subseteq V'$	Set of visitations with an arc connecting to visitation $i \in V$.
$Out(i) \subseteq V'$	Set of visitations receiving an arc from $i \in V$.
$c_i^{Mv} \in \mathbb{R}^+$	Cost of a TEU move at visitation $i \in V'$.
$f_{s,i}^{Port} \in \mathbb{R}$	Port fee associated with vessel s at visitation $i \in V'$.
$d_{s,i}^{Mv} \in \mathbb{R}$	Move time per TEU for vessel s at visitation $i \in V'$.
$r_t^{Eqp} \in \mathbb{R}^+$	Revenue for each TEU of equipment of type $t \in T$ delivered.
$u_s^t \in \mathbb{R}^+$	Capacity of vessel s for cargo type $t \in T$.
A'	The set of arcs $(i, j) \in A$, where $i, j \in V'$.
$c_{i,j}^s$	Fixed cost of vessel s utilizing arc $(i, j) \in A'$.
$\alpha_{i,j}^s$	Variable hourly cost of vessel $s \in S$ utilizing arc $(i, j) \in A'$.
$\Delta_{i,j,s}^{Min}$	Minimum duration for vessel s to sail on flexible arc (i, j).
$\Delta_{i,j,s}^{Max}$	Maximum duration for vessel s to sail on flexible arc (i, j).
$(o, d, t) \in \Theta$	A demand triplet, where $o \in V', d \subseteq V'$ and $t \in T$ are the origin visitation, destination visitations and the cargo type, respectively.
$a^{(o,d,t)} \in \mathbb{R}^+$	Amount of demand available for the demand triplet.
$r^{(o,d,t)} \in \mathbb{R}^+$	Amount of revenue gained per TEU for the demand triplet.
$\Theta_i^O, (\Theta_i^D) \subseteq \Theta$	Set of demands with an origin (destination) visitation $i \in V$.
Θ_o^{SOS}	Set of demands corresponding to $o \in SOS$.

Variables

$y_{i,j}^s \in \{0,1\}$	Indicates whether vessel s is sailing on arc $(i,j) \in A$.
$t_i^E \in \mathbb{R}_0^+$	Defines the enter time of a vessel at visitation i.
$t_i^X \in \mathbb{R}_0^+$	Defines the exit time of a vessel at visitation i.
$t_i^V \in \mathbb{R}_0^+$	Defines the time spent at flexible visitation $i \in V^f$ loading and unloading cargo/equipment.
$w_{i,j}^s \in \mathbb{R}_0^+$	The duration that vessel $s \in S$ sails on flexible arc $(i,j) \in A^f$.
$x_{i,j}^{(o,d,t)} \in \mathbb{R}_0^+$	Amount of flow of demand triplet $(o,d,t) \in \Theta$ on $(i,j) \in A'$.
$x_{i,j}^t \in \mathbb{R}_0^+$	Amount of equipment of type $t \in T$ flowing on $(i,j) \in A'$.

$$\max \sum_{s \in S}\left(\sum_{(i,j)\in A'} c_{i,j}^s y_{i,j}^s + \sum_{(i,j)\in A^f} \alpha_{i,j}^s w_{i,j}^s\right) \tag{1}$$

$$+ \sum_{(o,d,t)\in\Theta}\left(\sum_{j\in d}\sum_{i\in In(j)}\left(r^{(o,d,t)} - c_o^{Mv} - c_j^{Mv}\right)x_{i,j}^{(o,d,t)}\right) \tag{2}$$

$$+ \sum_{t\in T}\left(\sum_{i\in V^{t+}}\sum_{j\in Out(i)}\left(r_t^{Eqp} - c_i^{Mv}\right)x_{i,j}^t - \sum_{i\in V^{t-}}\sum_{j\in In(i)}c_i^{Mv}x_{j,i}^t\right) \tag{3}$$

$$+ \sum_{j\in V'}\sum_{i\in In(j)}\sum_{s\in S} f_{s,j}^{Port} y_{i,j}^s \tag{4}$$

$$\text{s. t.} \sum_{s\in S}\sum_{i\in In(j)} y_{i,j}^s \le 1 \qquad \forall j \in V' \tag{5}$$

$$\sum_{i\in Out(\sigma_s)} y_{\sigma_s,i}^s = 1 \qquad \forall s \in S \tag{6}$$

$$\sum_{i\in In(\tau)}\sum_{s\in S} y_{i,\tau}^s = |S| \tag{7}$$

$$\sum_{i\in In(j)} y_{i,j}^s - \sum_{i\in Out(j)} y_{j,i}^s = 0 \qquad \forall j \in \{V' \setminus \bigcup_{s\in S}\sigma_s\}, s \in S \tag{8}$$

$$\sum_{(o,d,rf)\in\Theta} x_{i,j}^{(o,d,rf)} - \sum_{s\in S} u_k^{rf} y_{i,j}^s \le 0 \qquad \forall (i,j) \in A' \tag{9}$$

$$\sum_{(o,d,t)\in\Theta} x_{i,j}^{(o,d,t)} + \sum_{t'\in T} x_{i,j}^{t'} - \sum_{s\in S}\left(\sum_{t'\in T} u_s^{t'}\right) y_{i,j}^s \le 0 \quad \forall (i,j) \in A' \tag{10}$$

$$\sum_{i\in Out(o)} x_{o,i}^{(o,d,t)} \le a^{(o,d,t)} \sum_{i\in Out(o)}\sum_{s\in S} y_{o,i}^s \qquad \forall (o,d,t) \in \Theta \tag{11}$$

$$\sum_{i\in In(j)} x_{i,j}^{(o,d,t)} - \sum_{k\in Out(j)} x_{j,k}^{(o,d,t)} = 0 \qquad \forall (o,d,t) \in \Theta, j \in V' \setminus (o\cup d) \tag{12}$$

$$\sum_{i\in In(j)} x_{i,j}^t - \sum_{k\in Out(j)} x_{j,k}^t = 0 \qquad \forall t \in T, j \in V' \setminus V^{t^*} \tag{13}$$

$$\Delta_{i,j,s}^{Min} y_{i,j}^s \le w_{i,j}^s \le \Delta_{i,j,s}^{Max} y_{i,j}^s \qquad \forall (i,j) \in A^f, s \in S \tag{14}$$

$$t_i^E = enter(i) \sum_{s \in S} \sum_{j \in In(i)} y_{i,j}^s \qquad\qquad \forall i \in V^i \qquad (15)$$

$$t_i^X = exit(i) \sum_{s \in S} \sum_{j \in Out(i)} y_{i,j}^s \qquad\qquad \forall i \in V^i \qquad (16)$$

$$t_i^X + \sum_{s \in S} w_{i,j}^s - t_j^E \le 0 \qquad\qquad \forall (i,j) \in A^f \qquad (17)$$

$$t_i^X - t_i^E - t_i^V \le -pilot(i) \qquad\qquad \forall i \in V^f \qquad (18)$$

$$\sum_{(o,d,t) \in \Theta_i^O} \sum_{j \in Out(o)} d_{s,o}^{Mv} x_{o,j}^{(o,d,t)} + \sum_{(o,d,t) \in \Theta_i^D} \sum_{d' \in d} \sum_{j \in In(d')} d_{s,d}^{Mv} x_{j,d'}^{(o,d,t)}$$

$$+ \sum_{t \in T} \left(\sum_{i' \in \{V^{t+} \cap i\}} \sum_{j \in Out(i')} d_{s,i'}^{Mv} x_{i',j}^t + \sum_{i' \in \{V^{t-} \cap i\}} \sum_{j \in In(i')} d_{s,j}^{Mv} x_{j,i'}^t \right)$$

$$- t_i^V + M_i^s \sum_{j \in Out(i)} y_{i,j}^s \le M_i^s \qquad\qquad \forall i \in V^f, s \in S \qquad (19)$$

The objective consists of several components. The sailing cost (1) takes into account the precomputed sailing costs on arcs between inflexible visitations, as well as the variable cost for sailings to and from flexible visitations. Note that the fixed sailing cost on an arc does not only include fuel costs, but can also include canal fees or the time-charter bonus for entering an SOS. The profit from delivering cargo (2) is computed based on the revenue from delivering cargo minus the cost to load and unload the cargo from the vessel. Note that the model can choose how much of a demand to deliver, even choosing to deliver a fractional amount. We can allow this since each demand is an aggregation of cargo between two ports, meaning at most one container between two ports will be fractional. Equipment profit is taken into account in (3). Equipment is handled similar to cargo, except that equipment can flow from any port where it is in supply to any port where it is in demand. Finally, port fees are deducted in (4).

Multiple vessels are prevented from visiting the same visitation in (5). The flow of each vessel from its source node to the graph sink is handled by (6), (7) and (8), with (7) ensuring that all vessels arrive at the sink.

Arcs are assigned capacities if a vessel utilizes the arc in (9), which assigns the reefer container capacity, and in (10), which assigns the total container capacity, respectively. Note that constraints (9) do not take into account empty reefer equipment, since empty containers do not need to be turned on, and can therefore be placed anywhere on the vessel. Cargo is only allowed to flow on arcs with a vessel in (11). The flow of cargo from its source to its destination, through intermediate nodes, is handled by (12). Constraints (13) balance the flow of equipment in to and out of nodes. In contrast to the way cargo is handled, equipment can flow from any port where it is in supply to any port where it is in demand. Since the amount of equipment carried is limited only by the capacity of the vessel, no flow source/sink constraints are required.

Flexible arcs have a duration constrained by the minimum and maximum sailing time of the vessel on the arc in (14). The enter and exit time of a vessel at inflexible ports is handled by (15) and (16), and we note that in practice these constraints are only necessary if one of the outgoing arcs from an inflexible visitation ends at a flexible visitation. Constraints (17) sets the enter time of a visitation to be the duration of a vessel on a flexible arc plus the exit time of the vessel at the start of the arc, and (18) forces the enter and exit time at a flexible node to take into account the time the vessel spends in port, including piloting time. The time to load and unload cargo and equipment is reflected in (19), which sets the t^V variable to the cargo movement time.

The model forms a disjoint path problem in which a fractional multicommodity flow is allowed to flow over arcs in the paths, along with a small scheduling component in the flexible nodes. Flexible arcs could be alternatively represented using a discretized approach, however we forego a discretization because of the vast differences in timescales between port activities and sailing activities, which are on the order of hours and days, respectively. In order to achieve such a fine grained view of flexible arc activities, we would require numerous extra arcs and nodes for each flexible node.

3.3 Complexity

We reduce the knapsack problem to the LSFRP in order to show that the LSFRP is NP-complete. Given n items, each with a profit p_i and a size s_i, and a knapsack with a capacity C, the knapsack problem maximizes the objective $\sum_{i=0}^{n} p_i x_i$ where x_i is a binary variable indicating whether or not item i is in the knapsack, subject to the capacity constraint $\sum_{i=0}^{n} s_i x_i \leq C$.

Theorem 1. *The LSFRP with flexible visitations is NP-complete.*

We first note that the LSFRP is clearly in NP, as the total profit can be easily computed from the paths of the vessels through the graph. We initialize an LSFRP with a single vessel and no cargo or equipment demands. The problem instance contains a single phase-out visitation, ω, and a single phase-in visitation, λ. The port fees at both ω and λ are 0, and we let $enter(\omega) = exit(\omega) = 0$ and $enter(\lambda) = exit(\lambda) = C$. In other words, the timespan in which the repositioning must take place is limited to the capacity of the knapsack. For each knapsack item, we create a flexible visitation, f_i, which has a duration of exactly s_i, i.e. $pilot(f_i) = s_i$. The port fee for visiting f_i is $-p_i$, since the LSFRP maximizes profit (i.e. minimizes fees). All flexible nodes, as well as ω and λ, are in a single tradezone. Therefore, the specification of the LSFRP graph ensures that the phase-out node, ω, connects to all flexible nodes, all flexible nodes connect to each other, and all flexible nodes connect to the phase-in node, λ. The sailing time of the vessel between all nodes in the graph is set to 0.

Item i is included in the knapsack solution if and only if the vessel visits f_i during its repositioning. Since the vessel can only visit a single flexible visitation at a time, the duration of each flexible visitation is fixed to the size of the item it represents, and the phase-in visitation is fixed in time to the size of the knapsack, the capacity constraint of the knapsack must be satisfied. Additionally, according to the objective of the LSFRP, only the flexible visitations corresponding to the maximum profit knapsack items will be chosen. Therefore, the LSFRP with flexible visitations is NP-complete.   □

4   Computational Study

We created a benchmark set of instances containing two real world repositioning scenarios, with three and eleven vessels each. The rest of our benchmark set consists of

Table 3. Instance information and the time to solve each instance to optimality with CPLEX 12.4 and a timeout of one hour

ID	$\|S\|$	$\|V\|$	$\|A^i\|$	$\|A^f\|$	$\|\Theta\|$	$\sum_{t\in T}\|V^{t*}\|$	$\|SOS\|$	CPU Time (s)
1	3	49	214	0	72	0	1	0.12
2	3	60	227	0	115	0	2	0.2
3	3	61	200	0	81	0	3	0.1
4	3	68	201	0	108	0	2	0.17
5	3	70	351	0	81	0	3	0.18
6	3	84	218	0	146	0	4	0.24
7	3	86	612	0	99	0	3	0.54
8	3	113	864	132	138	6	3	42.05
9	3	113	864	132	138	10	3	50.52
10	4	61	542	0	99	0	0	37.51
11	4	65	542	42	99	6	0	CPU
12	4	77	630	0	134	0	2	311.87
13	4	83	651	0	146	0	4	115.72
14	4	83	651	0	146	25	4	139.34
15	5	74	381	0	251	0	0	0.74
16	5	109	428	0	398	0	5	1.32
17	6	112	1371	0	118	0	0	63.25
18	6	147	1913	0	128	0	4	CPU
19	6	147	1913	0	128	13	4	CPU
20	6	147	1913	0	128	37	4	CPU
21	6	160	1518	0	153	0	9	68.12
22	6	160	1518	0	153	42	9	45.01
23	6	172	1645	162	153	76	9	CPU
24	7	81	533	0	215	0	0	2.18
25	7	81	533	0	215	16	0	2.06
26	7	83	660	0	289	0	0	713.12
27	7	115	592	0	289	0	3	2.86
28	7	118	674	0	372	0	4	960.28
29	7	118	674	0	372	23	4	1345.34
30	8	119	1220	0	117	0	0	29.12
31	8	126	1621	0	337	0	0	127.43
32	8	161	1473	0	166	0	3	60.79
33	8	196	1495	429	168	50	3	CPU
34	9	317	11817	0	407	0	0	CPU
35	9	370	12004	40	777	124	4	Mem
36	9	377	12038	0	929	0	4	CPU
37	9	384	12099	0	1001	120	7	Mem
38	9	386	12038	40	929	132	4	Mem
39	9	392	12105	0	1057	0	7	Mem
40	9	392	12105	0	1057	124	7	Mem
41	10	257	8521	0	568	0	0	CPU
42	11	317	12438	0	781	0	0	CPU
43	11	325	12931	0	884	0	4	Mem

hypothetical repositionings crafted using real liner shipping data to examine the scaling behavior of the MIP. Our instances have graphs varying from as few as 49 nodes and 214 arcs up to 392 nodes and 12,105 arcs. Table 3 shows information about each instance in our dataset and the time it takes to solve each instance to optimality in seconds. The table gives the instance ID, number of nodes, number of inflexible and flexible arcs, number of demands, number of ports with equipment and number of SOS opportunities, along with the CPU time of each instance. Instances were alloted an hour of CPU time on an AMD Opteron 2425 HE processor and allowed 10 GB of RAM each. Instances that exceeded the maximum CPU time of one hour are marked with "CPU" and instances that ran out of memory are indicated with "Mem".

Instances 1 – 9 represent variations of the full case study shown in Figure 3. They are relatively easy to solve, even under the presence of flexible arcs for equipment. However, as the number of vessels grows, so does the size of the graph and the difficulty of the problems. Instances 42 and 43 correspond to another real world scenario, but neither can be solved in a reasonable amount of time using this model alone. In order to solve these problems to optimality, a more advanced technique, such as branch-and-price, will have to be employed.

There is no obvious way to characterize the hardness of instances. For example, instance 28 requires more than seven times the amount of time than instance 31, even though they have comparable graph sizes and almost the same number of demands. Additionally, instances 12 and 13 have similar graph structures, but instance 13 is solved in half the time of instance 12, perhaps because of the extra two SOS opportunities which may allow for better pruning. Overall, instances that do not timeout are solved relatively quickly, the slowest taking only 22 minutes. In fact, one third of our instances can be solved faster than a minute, including instance 30 with 8 vessels and 1220 arcs. On the instances where the MIP times out, not a single one is able to reach a gap of less than 10% with the linear relaxation, indicating the difficulty of such instances.

5 Conclusion

We presented a novel model of an important real-world problem, the LSFRP, using a MIP model and a constraint embedded graph. Our model takes into account all of the key aspects of the LSFRP, including liner shipping service construction constraints, cargo flows, empty equipment repositioning, cabotage restrictions, and sail-on-service opportunities, and maximizes the profit earned during repositioning. We proved the NP-completeness of the LSFRP, studied the performance of our model on two repositioning scenarios from our industrial collaborator, as well as on a number of instances crafted from real-world data.

For future work, we intend to use a branch and price framework to overcome memory issues and solve instances to optimality faster. In addition, we will investigate using heuristics to provide good solutions to the LSFRP in the low amount of time that would be required for a decision support system.

Acknowledgements. We would like to thank our industrial collaborators Mikkel Muhldorff Sigurd and Shaun Long at Maersk Line for their support and detailed description of the fleet repositioning problem. We would also like to thank David Pisinger and Björg Áskelsdóttir for their insightful comments and suggestions on this work. This research is sponsored in part by the Danish Council for Strategic Research as part of the ENERPLAN research project.

References

1. Álvarez, J.F.: Joint routing and deployment of a fleet of container vessels. Maritime Economics and Logistics 11(2), 186–208 (2009)
2. Andersen, M.W.: Service Network Design and Management in Liner Container Shipping Applications. PhD thesis, Technical University of Denmark, Department of Transport (2010)
3. Christiansen, M., Fagerholt, K., Nygreen, B., Ronen, D.: Maritime transportation. Transportation 14, 189–284 (2007)
4. Christiansen, M., Fagerholt, K., Ronen, D.: Ship routing and scheduling: Status and perspectives. Transportation Science 38(1), 1–18 (2004)
5. Clausen, J., Larsen, A., Larsen, J., Rezanova, N.J.: Disruption management in the airline industry–concepts, models and methods. Computers & Operations Research 37(5), 809–821 (2010)
6. Kohl, N., Larsen, A., Larsen, J., Ross, A., Tiourine, S.: Airline disruption management–perspectives, experiences and outlook. Journal of Air Transport Management 13(3), 149–162 (2007)
7. Korsvik, J.E., Fagerholt, K., Laporte, G.: A large neighbourhood search heuristic for ship routing and scheduling with split loads. Computers & Operations Research 38(2), 474–483 (2011)
8. Powell, B.J., Perakis, A.N.: Fleet deployment optimization for liner shipping: An integer programming model. Maritime Policy and Management 24(2), 183–192 (1997)
9. Tierney, K., Coles, A.J., Coles, A.I., Kroer, C., Britt, A.M., Jensen, R.M.: Automated planning for liner shipping fleet repositioning. In: Proceedings of the 22nd International Conference on Automated Planning and Scheduling (to appear, 2012)
10. United Nations Conference on Trade and Development. Review of maritime transport (2011)

An Accurate Model for Seaworthy Container Vessel Stowage Planning with Ballast Tanks

Dario Pacino[1], Alberto Delgado[1], Rune Møller Jensen[1], and Tom Bebbington[2]

[1] IT-University of Copenhagen, Denmark
{dpacino,alde,rmj}@itu.dk
[2] Maersk Line Operations, Global Stowage Planning, Singapore
Tom.Bebbington@maersk.com

Abstract. Seaworthy container vessel stowage plans generated under realistic assumptions are a key factor for stowage decision support systems in the shipping industry. We propose a linear model with ballast tanks for generating master plans, the first phase of a 2-phase stowage optimization approach, that includes the main stability and stress moments calculations. Our approach linearizes the center of gravity calculation and hydrostatic data tables of the vessel in order to formulate stability and stress moments constraints that can handle variable displacement. The accuracy level of these linearizations is evaluated when the displacement of the vessel is allowed to change within a small band.

1 Introduction

The past two decades have seen a continuous increase in containerized shipping. Liner shipping companies meet these demands offering a higher frequency of service and deploying larger vessels. As a consequence, the generation of stowage plans (assignments of containers to vessel slots) has become more complex and hard to handle manually, raising the interest of the industry toward computerized aids. Stowage plans are hard to produce in practice. First, they are made under time pressure by human stowage coordinators just hours before the vessel calls the port. Second, deep-sea vessels are large and often require thousands of container moves in a port. Third, complex interactions between low-level stacking rules and high-level stress limits and stability requirements make it difficult to minimize the makespan of cranes and, at the same time, avoid that containers block each other (overstowage). In a previous work, [7], we have developed a stowage planning optimization approach that, similar to the most successful current approaches (e.g, [9,5,1]), decomposes the problem hierarchically as depicted in Figure 1. First the *multi-port master planning* phase decides how many

Fig. 1. Hierarchical decomposition of stowage planning into master and slot planning

H. Hu et al. (Eds.): ICCL 2012, LNCS 7555, pp. 17–32, 2012.
© Springer-Verlag Berlin Heidelberg 2012

containers of each type to stow in a set of storage areas. Based on this distribution, a complete stowage plan is generated in the *Slot Planning* phase by stowing individual containers. The approach can generate representative stowage plans for up to 10.000 Twenty-foot Equivalent Units (TEU) vessels within 10 minutes (on a 2.0 GHz AMD Opteron), as required for practical usage by the industry.

All of the models present in the literature, however, are based on the assumption that the displacement of the ship (the total weight of the loaded vessel) is constant. Hydrostatic calculations, such as buoyancy, stability, trim and draft restrictions are based on non-linear functions of the ship's center of gravity and vessel displacement. Those can, however, easily be linearized and translated to bounds on the position of the center of gravity when considering a constant displacement. In reality ballast tanks are used by stowage coordinators to better handle the stability of the vessel and allow stowage configurations that are otherwise infeasible. Ignoring ballast water can become a great source of error, as it can constitute up to 25% of the ship's displacement. Including tanks in the mathematical models, however, brings forth a number of non-linear constraints due to the, now variable, vessel displacement. When variable displacement is taken into account, the above mentioned hydrostatic calculations become a function of two variables, center of gravity position and displacement. The previously trivial linearization has now become complex and difficult to handle efficiently. The intuition behind this complexity is simple. When the displacement is constant it is possible to pre-calculate the amount of water the vessel will displace. With variable displacement the amount of displaced water changes and causes the buoyancy forces to change non-linearly due to the curved shape of the vessel hull.

In this paper we introduce a linear model for the master planning phase that considers ballast tanks and deals with variable displacement. This model is concerned only with the seaworthiness of the vessel, but can easily be extended to optimize handling of the vessel at port. According to our industrial partner, it is possible for stowage coordinators to make an educated guess on the amount of ballast water that a vessel might need within 15% from the actual amount. We use this assumption to define a displacement range within which we are able to formulate a linearization of the stability constraints within an acceptable error. We analyse the accuracy of our model experimentally on 10 real instances provided by our industrial partner. Our analysis suggests that within 5% of the current displacement of the vessel, our calculations are accurate enough for the master plans to be seaworthy. The analysis also indicates a direct relation between the size of the variation in the displacement of the vessel and the error on the center of gravity and the linearizations depending on it.

The remainder of the paper is organized as follows. Section 2 describes the problem. Section 3 introduces related work. Section 4 presents our model. Section 5 and 6 present the analysis and conclusions.

2   Background and Problem Statement

ISO containers transported on container ships are normally 8' wide, 8'6" high, and either 20', 40', or 45' long. *High cube* containers are 9'6" high and *pallet wide* containers are slightly wider and can only be placed side-by-side in certain patterns. Refrigerated containers (*reefers*) must be placed near power plugs. Containers with dangerous goods (*IMO containers*) must be placed according to a complex set of separation rules. The capacity of a container ship is given in TEU. As shown in Figure 2, the cargo space of a vessel is divided into sections called *bays*, and each bay is divided into an *on deck* and a *below deck* part by a number of *hatch-covers*, which are flat, leak-proof structures. Each sub-section of a bay consists of a row of *container stacks* divided into *slots* that can hold a 20' ISO container. Figure 3 (a) and (b) show the container slots of a bay and stack, respectively. Stacks have max height limit and different weight limits. Two weight limits exists for each stack, one regarding the outer container supports and one regarding the inner supports. Limits on the inner supports are often the smallest as the vessel structure in the middle of a stack is weaker. The inner supports are used only when 20â containers are stowed as depicted in Figure 3 (b). When 20â and 40â containers are mixed in the same stack, only half of the 20â weight is considered to be supported by the outer supports, since the other half sits on the inner supports. Below deck, cell guides secure containers transversely. Containers on deck are secured by lashing rods and twist locks with limited strength. Thus, container weights must normally decrease upwards in stacks on deck. Moreover, lashing rods of 20' stacks must be accessible and stack heights must be under the vessel's minimum line of sight. 45' containers can normally only be stowed over the lashing bridge on deck.

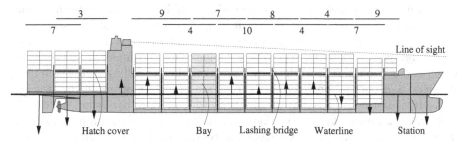

Fig. 2. Arrangement of container vessel bays. The vertical arrows show an example of the resulting forces acting on the ship sections between calculation points (stations). Single crane work hours for adjacent bays are shown at the top.

A container ship must sail at even keel and have sufficient *transverse stability*. Figure 3(c) shows a cross section of a ship. For small inclination angles, the volume of the emerged and immersed water wedges (shaded areas) and thus the distance GZ are approximately proportional with the angle such that the buoyancy force intersects the center line in a fixed position called the *metacenter*, M [8]. For an inclination angle θ, the ship's uprighting force is proportional to $GZ = GM \sin \theta$. GM is called the *metacentric height* and the center of gravity G must be on the center line and result in sufficient GM for the ship to be stable. Maximum and minimum draft restrictions apply due to port depths, working height of cranes, and the propeller. The *trim* is the difference between the aft

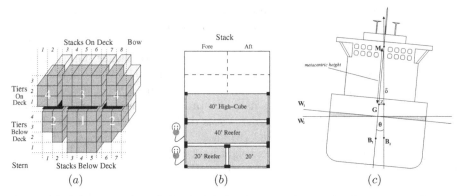

Fig. 3. (a) A bay seen from behind. (b) A side view of a stack of containers. Power plugs are normally situated at bottom slots. (c) Transverse stability.

and fore draft and must be kept within a given span. For a station position p, the *shear force* is the sum of the resulting vertical forces on vessel sections (see Figure 2) acting aft of p, and the *bending moment* is the sum of these forces times the horizontal distance to them from p. Both of these stresses must be within limits. The vessel also has transverse bending moment (*torsion*) limits. Given the displacement and longitudinal center of gravity (lcg) of a vessel, the metacenter, draft, trim, and the buoyancy of each section of the vessel can be derived from hydrostatic tables. Ballast tanks distributed along the vessel are used to modify displacement and center of gravity by pumping water in or out of the tanks, changing metacenter, draft, trim, and buoyancy of each section.

A container ship transports containers between ports on a fixed cyclic route. A *stowage plan* assigns the containers to load in a terminal to slots on the vessel and it is often sent to the terminal shortly before calling it. It is the liner shippers, and not the port terminals, that are in charge of producing stowage plans. It is impractical to study large optimization models that include all details of stowage planning. On the other hand, all major aspects of the problem must be modeled for the results to be valuable. For container types this includes 20', 40', and reefer containers. In addition, since stability, trim, draft and stress moment limits should not fully be ignored, some weight classes of containers must be introduced. It is also important to take into consideration the containers already onboard the vessel when arriving at the current port.

3   Literature Review

Even though several of the publications on stowage planning available in the past years address stability and stress moments, very few present Linear/Integer programming models that incorporate them as constraints or objectives. Additionally, none of them consider variable displacement due to ballast tanks. The most complete formulation of stability and stress moments as part of a Integer Programming (IP) model is introduced in [4]. Though their model is not solved in practice, due to its complexity, it constrains GM, transversal stability (heel angle), trim, shear forces, and bending moments. Linearizations depending on the displacement of the vessel, made variable due to the inclusion of the loading and unloading sequence of containers into the model, are suggested for the stability constraints. No evaluation of the impact of these linearizations is presented, probably due to the fact that their model was not used in practice. Shear forces and bending moments are addressed, but they disregard the impact of the cargo in the buoyancy force. The IP formulations introduced in [2,6] determine in which vessel slot to load each container in the loadlist. These models handle transversal stability and trim by constraining the weight difference between transversal (left and right) and horizontal (bow and stern) sections of the vessel to be within certain tolerance. The GM is constrained by not allowing heavy containers on top of light ones, a rule of thumb used in the industry for some vessels, but that does not necessarily generalize to all kinds of vessels. In [5], a model that distributes types of containers to sections of the vessel is introduced. This model constrains the center of gravity of the vessel with respect to precomputed constants to satisfy GM, trim, and transversal stability constraints. To the best of our knowledge, the only approach available in the literature that considers the use of ballast tanks is presented in [3]. A heuristic uses ballast water to bring the longitudinal center of gravity within a permissible range defined based on the trim desired. Later, a local search is used to fix the GM.

4 Stability and Stress Model with Ballast Tanks

The introduction of ballast tanks into the optimization model causes the displacement of the vessel to become variable. This makes the calculation of the center of gravity non-linear and thus, it is no longer possible to use the linearization of the hydrostatic data from our previous work.

4.1 Non-linearities of Variable Displacement

Two major non-linearities must be handled once variable displacement has to be modelled. First, the calculation of the center of gravity, and second the linearization of the hydrostatic data. Consider the calculation of lcg without ballast tanks: $\frac{LM^o + \sum_{l \in L} G_l^L v_l}{W}$, where LM^o is the constant longitudinal moment of the vessel, G_l^L is the lcg and v_l is the weight of a location $l \in L$, and W is the displacement given by $W = W^o + \sum_{l \in L} v_l$, where W^o is the constant weight of the vessel. Since all containers in the loadlist are loaded, the displacement is constant, which makes the calculation linear. Now consider the same calculation where we include ballast tanks as a variable: $\frac{LM^o + \sum_{l \in L} G_l^L v_l + \sum_{u \in U} G_u^L v_u}{W + \sum_{u \in U} v_u}$, where U is the set of ballast tanks, G_u^L is their lcg, and v_u is the variable defining the amount of water to be loaded in tank $u \in U$. Since the amount of water in the tanks is not known a priori, the displacement of the vessel is now no longer constant, and the calculation becomes non-linear. In order to deal with this, we propose the following approximation:

$$LCG = \frac{LM^o + \sum_{l \in L} G_l^L v_l + \sum_{u \in U} G_u^L (v_u + \Delta_u)}{W + W^T + \sum_{u \in U} \Delta_u} \tag{1}$$

$$\approx \frac{LM^o + \sum_{l \in L} G_l^L v_l + \sum_{u \in U} G_u^L (v_u + \Delta_u)}{W + W^T}, \tag{2}$$

where we model the stowage coordinator estimation error with the variables Δ_u, thus the total displacement becomes $W + W^T + \sum_{u \in U} \Delta_u$, where W^T represents the amount of water that we expect to remain constant. We then make a linear approximation of the vessel lcg by removing the allowed changes of ballast water from the denominator of the fraction resulting in equation (2). Given the total capacity of the tanks (W^T) and the fact that the constant weight of an empty vessel $W^o \approx 2W^T$ and that the weight of the cargo $W^C \approx 6W^T$, we can reasonably assume that the error in the approximation of the lcg, given that stowage coordinators can estimate the ballast within 15 percent accuracy, is less than $0.15W^T/(2W^T + 6W^T + W^T) = 1.7\%$. Note that the same approximation can be used to calculate the vertical and transversal center of gravity.

The assumption that the amount of ballast water lies within a given interval is useful for the linearization of the hydrostatic calculations. Hydrostatic calculations are in practice linear approximations of given data points. When the center of gravity and the displacement of the vessel are known, the linearization is very accurate. For the problem we are going to model, this is, however, not the case since both the center of gravity and the displacement can vary. Figure 4 shows a plot of the hydrostatic data for the trim and metacenter calculation. The functions are clearly non-linear. Notice that within a small displacement interval it is possible, however, to approximate the functions accurately with a plane. This is only true for displacement levels that are not at the extremes of the data tables, but it is reasonable to assume that the displacement of a stowage plan will be within these extremes. The planes described above can be defined by the limited ballast water change and thus be used in our model.

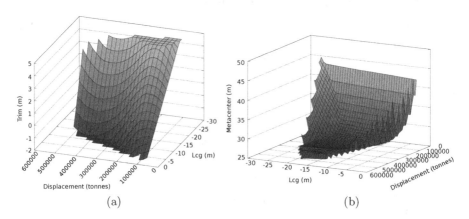

(a)   (b)

Fig. 4. (a) Trim as a function of displacement and lcg (b) Metacenter as a function of displacement and lcg

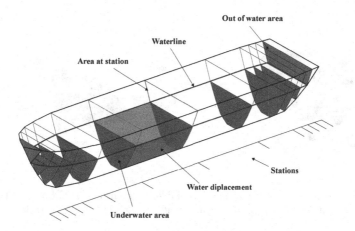

Fig. 5. Areas for buoyancy calculation and stations distribution

The buoyancy of a vessel is the volume of water that the vessel displace. In order to calculate this volume, it is necessary to know the shape of the vessel hull. For this purpose, the hydrostatic data tables provide the possibility of calculating the submerged area of a vessel at a specific point called a *station*. Figure 5 shows an example of such areas and how stations are distributed along the vessel. Given two adjacent stations, s_1 and s_2, the buoyancy of the vessel section between the two stations is approximated by $\frac{(A_{s1}+A_{s2})D(s_1,s_2)\delta^W}{2}$, where A_s is the underwater area at station s from now on called *bonjean*, $D(s_1,s_2)$ is the distance between the two stations and δ^W is the density of the water. As Figure 5 shows, stations are not evenly distributed along the vessel. A greater concentration is found at the vessel's extremities, where the hull changes the most. Figure 6 shows two plots of the hydrostatic data related to the bonjean of a station at bow and a station in the middle of a vessel. As expected, the function describing the hull at bow is highly non-linear since the hull greatly changes, which is not the case for stations in the middle of the vessel. Within specific displacement ranges, it is still possible to approximate the function linearly. Should one want to model displacement ranges that include the most non-linear parts, piece-wise linear approximations with a few binary variables can be used.

4.2   A Linear Model

Following the linear approximation described in the previous section, we propose a refined Linear Programming (LP) model for the master planning phase that includes ballast tank modeling. We constrain ourselves, without loss of generality, to analyse the model for one loading port and several discharge ports. Objectives that focus on efficiency of the master plan (described in [7]) are not included in the model under analysis as they do not have any influence on the seaworthiness of the vessel, and are thus irrelevant to this study.

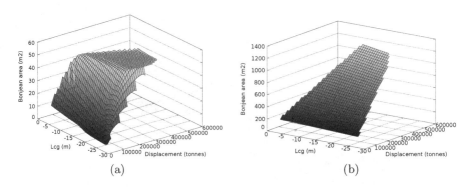

Fig. 6. (a) Underwater area as a function of displacement and lcg at a bow station (b) Underwater area as a function of displacement and Lcg at a middle station

The multi-port master planning phase assigns types of containers to subsections of bays (*locations*). Figure 3(a) shows four locations within a bay. Outer locations are symmetrically split (such as locations 2 and 4 in the Figure) to ease transverse stability calculations. For 20' and 40' containers, we consider a set of four mutually exclusive container types $T = \{L, H, RL, RH\}$, respectively light and heavy containers and light and heavy reefer containers. Notice that the container types T are only a classification and thus are not bound to fixed weight ranges. For each type $\tau \in T$ the average weight of the containers going to a specific discharge port $p \in P$ is calculated and represented by the constants $W_p^{20\tau}$ and $W_p^{40\tau}$, thus causing a more refined weight categorization than taking the average weight of the containers in each container class. We define two sets of decision variables, $x_{pl}^{20\tau}$ and $x_{pl}^{40\tau}$, representing respectively the amount of 20' and 40' containers of type $\tau \in T$ to be stowed in location $l \in L$ going to port $p \in P$, where L is the set of all locations. Given the set U of ballast tanks in a vessel, we define a set of decision variables, $x_u \in \mathbb{R}$, representing the amount of water present in the tanks. We then propose the following LP model:

minimize

$$\sum_{u \in U} y_u \tag{3}$$

subject to

$$\sum_{p \in P} \sum_{\tau \in T} \left(x_{pl}^{20\tau} + 2x_{pl}^{40\tau} \right) \leq C_l \quad \forall l \in L \tag{4}$$

$$\sum_{p \in P} \sum_{\tau \in T} x_{pl}^{\alpha\tau} \leq C_l^{\alpha} \quad \forall l \in L, \alpha \in \{20, 40\} \tag{5}$$

$$\sum_{p \in P} \sum_{\tau \in \{RL, RH\}} \left(x_{pl}^{20\tau} + x_{pl}^{40\tau} \right) \leq C_l^{RS} \quad \forall l \in L \tag{6}$$

$$\sum_{p \in P} \sum_{\tau \in \{RL, RH\}} \left(0.5x_{pl}^{20\tau} + x_{pl}^{40\tau} \right) \leq C_l^{RC} \quad \forall l \in L \tag{7}$$

$$\sum_{p \in P} \sum_{l \in L} x_{pl}^{\alpha\tau} = LD^{\alpha\tau}p \quad \forall \tau \in T, \alpha \in \{20, 40\} \tag{8}$$

$$\sum_{p\in P}\sum_{\tau\in T} W_p^{\alpha\tau} x_{pl}^{\alpha\tau} = v_l^{W\alpha} \quad \forall l \in L, \alpha \in \{20, 40\} \tag{9}$$

$$v_l^{W20} \leq W_l^{20} \quad \forall l \in L \tag{10}$$

$$0.5 v_l^{W20} + v_l^{W40} \leq W_l^{40} \quad \forall l \in L \tag{11}$$

$$v_l^{W20} + v_l^{W40} = v_l^{W} \quad \forall l \in L \tag{12}$$

$$\sum_{u\in U} x_u + \sum_{l\in L} v_l^{W} + W^o = v^{W} \tag{13}$$

$$x_u \leq C_u \quad \forall u \in U \tag{14}$$

$$(E_u - \epsilon) \leq x_u \leq (E_u + \epsilon) \quad \forall u \in U \tag{15}$$

$$\frac{\sum_{l\in L} G_l^L v_l^W + \sum_{u\in U} G_u^L x_u + LM^o}{W} = v^{Lcg} \tag{16}$$

$$\frac{\sum_{l\in L} G_l^V v_l^W + \sum_{u\in U} G_u^V x_u + VM^o}{W} = v^{Vcg} \tag{17}$$

$$\mathcal{L}^{Trim-} \leq A_T^W v^W + A_T^{Lcg} v^{Lcg} + A_T \leq \mathcal{L}^{Trim+} \tag{18}$$

$$\mathcal{L}^{DraftA-} \leq A_{DA}^W v^W + A_{DA}^{Lcg} v^{Lcg} + A_{DA} \leq \mathcal{L}^{DraftA+} \tag{19}$$

$$A_{DF}^W v^W + A_{DF}^{Lcg} v^{Lcg} + A_{DF} \leq \mathcal{L}^{DraftF+} \tag{20}$$

$$A_M^W v^W + A_M^{Lcg} v^{Lcg} + A_M = v^M \tag{21}$$

$$v^M - v^{Vcg} \geq \mathcal{L}^{GM-} \tag{22}$$

$$\delta^W D_{(i,j)} \frac{\sum_{s\in\{i,j\}} A_{Bs}^W v_{p0}^W + A_{Bs}^{Lcg} v^{Lcg} + A_{Bs}}{2} = v_{(i,j)}^B \quad \forall (i,j) \in S \tag{23}$$

$$W_f^\alpha + \sum_{l\in L} p_{lf}^\alpha v_l^W + \sum_{u\in U} p_{uf}^\alpha x_u - \sum_{s\in S} p_{sf}^\alpha v_s^B = v_f^{S\alpha} \quad \forall f \in F, \alpha \in \{Aft, Fore\} \tag{24}$$

$$M_f^\alpha + \sum_{l\in L} a_{lf}^\alpha p_{lf}^\alpha v_l^W + \sum_{u\in U} a_{uf}^\alpha p_{uf}^\alpha x_u - \sum_{s\in S} a_{sf}^\alpha p_{sf}^\alpha v_s^B = v_f^{B\alpha} \quad \forall f \in F, \alpha \in \{Aft, Fore\} \tag{25}$$

$$\mathcal{S}_f^- \leq w_f v_f^{sFore} + (1 - w_f) v_f^{SAft} \leq \mathcal{S}_f^+ \tag{26}$$

$$\mathcal{B}_f^- \leq w_f v_f^{BFore} + (1 - w_f) v_f^{BAft} \leq \mathcal{B}_f^+ \tag{27}$$

$$E_u - x_u \leq y_u \quad \forall u \in U \tag{28}$$

$$x_u - E_u \leq y_u \quad \forall u \in U \tag{29}$$

All the weight limits and capacities of the model have been reduced to account for onboard containers. The TEU capacity of each location, C_l, is enforced by constraint (4). Location specific capacity requirements regarding the length of the containers (C_l^{20} and C_l^{40}) are enforced using constraint (5). Constraint (6) and (7) limit, respectively the total number of reefer TEU (C_l^{RS}) and Forty-foot Equivalent Units (FEU) (C_l^{RC}) used. Constraint (8) ensures that all containers are loaded. With constraint (9), we define the variables v_l^{W20} and v_l^{W40}, holding respectively the weight of the 20'and 40' containers in location $l \in L$. Weight limitations for the 20' (W_l^{20}) and 40' W_l^{40} containers are guaranteed by constraints (10) and (11). Constraint (12) defines the auxiliary variable v_l^W representing the weight of location $l \in L$. The displacement of the vessel is represented by the auxiliary variable v^W with constraint (13) where W^o is the constant weight of the vessel. Note that the constant weight of the vessel also includes the weight of the onboard containers. Constraint (14) defines the capacity (C_u) of the tanks, while given E_u as the initial condition of the tanks constraint (15) defines the allowed ϵ ballast change. Variable v^{Lcg} represents the lcg of the vessel and is computed in constraint (16) using the approximation defined in (2). The constant LM^o is the constant longitudinal moment of the vessel, including onboard containers, G_l^L is the lcg of location $l \in L$, G_u^L is the lcg of tank $u \in U$, and W is the approximated constant displacement. The same approximation is used in constraint (17) for the calculation of the vertical center of gravity (vcg) represented by the variable v^{Vcg}. Constraint (18) represents the linearized hydrostatic calculation of trim. Given the displacement of the vessel v^W and its lcg v^{Lcg}, constraint (18) approximates the plane with the coefficients A_T^W, A_T^{Lcg} and A_T. The calculated trim is then kept within the limits $\mathcal{L}^{Trim-}$ and $\mathcal{L}^{Trim+}$. Changing the coefficients accordingly, constraint (19) and (20) approximate the draft aft and fore of the vessel. Both drafts are kept within the maximum limits $\mathcal{L}^{DraftA+}$ and $\mathcal{L}^{DraftF+}$. Due to the propeller it is also necessary to constrain the draft aft to be at a minimum depth $\mathcal{L}^{DraftA-}$. The metacenter is also calculated using the hydrostatic approximation and it is defined in constraint (21) by the variable v^M. The GM is then calculated in constraint (22) and kept above the security limit $\mathcal{L}^{GM}$. The buoyancy of the section of a vessel between two adjacent stations is defined in constraint (23) by the variable $v_{(i,j)}^B$. The set S is the set of adjacent station pairs (i,j), $D_{(i,j)}$ is the distance between the two stations, and δ^W is the density of the water. In the shear and bending calculations, we take into account the forces aft or fore of a frame. Since frames do not always coincide with the starting points of tanks, locations or buoyancy stations, it is necessary to know given a frame (a fixed calculation point) $f \in F$ the faction of weight that needs to be taken into account from a location l, tank u or station s. For this purpose the constant $p_{lf}^{Aft} \in [0,1]$ is used to denote the fraction of cargo to be considered from location $l \in L$ aft of frame $f \in F$ and p_{lf}^{Fore} for the fraction fore of the frame ($p_{uf}^{Aft}, p_{uf}^{Fore}$ for the tanks and $p_{sf}^{Aft}, p_{sf}^{Fore}$ for the buoyancy). Since the shear forces and bending moments are calculated per frame, errors from the linearization are accumulated the further away from the calculation frame that the weights are. This can become very problematic in the case of bending, where the forces are multiplied by the arm, increasing the approximation error substantially. Shear and bending calculations can be done for either fore or aft part of a frame. A more precise modelling of stress forces requires the calculation at both the aft and fore part of a frame, where the two resulting stresses are blended such that aft calculations are weighted more at the stern and less at the bow. Constraint (24) calculates the shear forces both aft and fore of each frame $f \in F$ and defines the shear variable v_f^S, and where W_f^α is the constant weight aft or fore of frame f. The final shear calculation, where the aft and fore shear are mixed using a scaling factor $w_f \in [0,1]$ (such that it is 1 for the first frame at bow and 0 in the first frame at stern) is kept within the limits $\mathcal{S}_f^+$ and $\mathcal{S}_f^-$ in constraint (26). The same calculation is made

Table 1. *Characteristics of the test instances.* Starting from the left the columns indicate: the ID of the instance, the total utility percentages in terms of TEU capacity used, thereof the percentage of containers in the release and in the loadlist. The next three columns indicate percentages of utilization in terms of weight, in total, for the containers in the release and in the loadlist. The initial displacement and the estimated ballast water are given by the last two columns.

ID	TEU (%)			Weight (%)			Displacement (10^3 tons)	Tanks (10^3 tons)
	Total	Release	Load	Total	Release	Load		
1	92	39	53	32	13	19	149	5
2	74	37	37	45	23	23	176	8
3	60	18	41	42	12	30	169	7
4	81	29	52	53	20	33	192	7
5	66	13	52	26	8	18	135	11
6	49	18	31	25	9	16	133	11
7	69	28	41	41	17	23	161	5
8	46	13	33	29	8	21	144	10
9	59	25	34	30	14	16	141	5
10	59	20	39	32	10	22	146	7

for the bending. The bending variable $v_f^{B\alpha}$ is defined in constraint (25), where $a_{lf}^{\alpha}, a_{uf}^{\alpha}, a_{sf}^{\alpha}$ are respectively the arm to frame $f \in F$ of location $l \in L$, tank $u \in U$ and buoyancy section $s \in S$ for both the aft and fore calculation. The constant moment of the vessel is given by the constant M_f^o and bending is kept within the limits $\mathcal{B}_f^+$ and $\mathcal{B}_f^-$ by constraint (27). Constraints (28) and (29) define the cost variable y_u quantifying the changes in tank configuration from the initial estimate. The accuracy of the approximations decreases with the extend of the change in ballast water. Thus, objective (3) minimizes this change.

5 Analysis of Model Accuracy

The model has been evaluated experimentally on a case study of 10 industrial stowage plans for a vessel of approximately 15.000 TEUs. The linear approximations used by the LP model for the generated solutions are compared with exact manual calculations. Table 1 gives an overview of the instances' characteristics.

We performed experiments allowing different changes in displacement and observed how the accuracy of the model changes accordingly. First we consider the linear approximation about the center of gravity of the vessel.

Figure 7 shows two graphs describing how the approximation of the longitudinal (a) and vertical (b) center of gravity behaves as the displacement changes. For both graphs, the horizontal axis represents the change of displacement in percentage, while the vertical axis represents the error in meters. Each point in the graph is generated by forcing changes in the ballast water of the 10 test instances. In Figure 7a it is possible to see, as expected, that when the displacement is unchanged, the value of the lcg is accurate and the more the displacement moves away from its true value the less accurate the approximation becomes. Note that for a displacement range of 5 percent, the calculation inaccuracy is at most 0.3 meters and is thus, still very accurate for practical usage. The calculations for the vcg are not as accurate (Figure 7b). Within the 5 percent range,

28   D. Pacino et al.

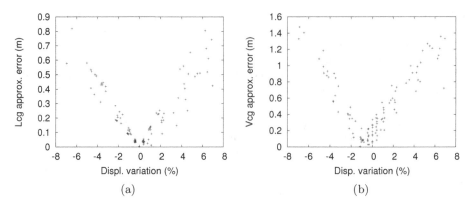

Fig. 7. (a) Error in the lcg. (b) Error in the vcg

the linearized value is, however, at most 0.8 meters from the correct one. This
was an expected result, as it is not possible to precisely estimate the vcg of, for
example, locations since we do not know where the containers will be stowed.
The accuracy error of the vcg is, however, still very small.

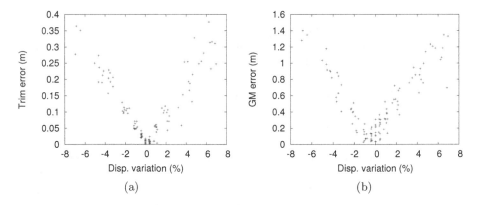

Fig. 8. (a) Error for the trim (b) Error for the *GM*

Now that we have shown that linearizations for the center of gravity are accurate, we focus on analyzing the accuracy of the hydrostatic data linearization.
In Figure 8 we use the same graph as before with the horizontal axis describing
the percentage displacement changes and the vertical axis the calculation error.
Figure 8a represents the error for the trim which, as it can be seen, is very small.
Within a 5 percent displacement range, the error is at most 15 centimeters. Figure 8b shows the same analysis for the calculation of *GM*. Notice that both for
the trim and *GM* calculations, an error is present even at constant displacement.
The error we see is due to the linearization of the hydrostatic functions. For *GM*
it also includes the approximation error of the vcg.

We now move our focus to the linearization of the bonjean areas which we expect to be the most inaccurate. Figure 9a shows the same analysis we have done so far for the bonjean areas. The graph shows the maximum error over all bonjean areas as a function of the displacement changes. As can be seen, the variation in displacement is not the main source of error. Most of the inaccuracy is due to the linearization of the hydrostatic data. Figure 9b shows how the bonjean error is concentrated at the extremities of the vessel where the hull changes most. The horizontal axis represents the position of the station on the vessel (where 0 is at bow) and the vertical axis is the bonjean error. Notice that the largest errors are found for stations at the bow. This can be explained by the fact that the range of drafts in our test data forces the linearization of these bonjean areas to be right by the inflection point of the hydrostatic curve (see figure 6a) where the linearization is most inaccurate. Better approximations can then be expected for larger drafts, as it is the case for the bonjean of the stations at the stern. The inaccuracy of the bonjean is, however, still quite small if we consider that the in the worst case, there is an error of only 4 square meters over an area of over 111 square meters.

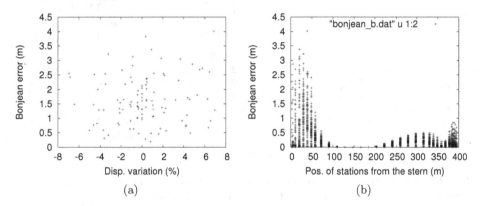

Fig. 9. (a) Approximation error of the total bonjean as a function of displacement change (b) Approximation error of the bonjean areas per station

Shear forces and bending moment calculations depend on the buoyancy of the vessel which in turn is calculated using the bonjean approximations. Figure 10a shows, in the same way as the other graphs, how the percentage error in the shear calculation (the vertical axis) behaves as a function of the variation of the displacement (the horizontal axis). As expected, the dominant error is not the approximation of the center of gravity of the vessel since the inaccuracy is more or less the same independently of how much the displacement changes. A more tight relation can be seen when the shear calculation is related to the error in the bonjean linearization. Figure 10b shows the percentage error of the shear force calculation as a function of the total error in bonjean area from the hydrostatic linearization. As depicted, the error in the shear calculation increases with the error in the bonjean linearization. The graph also groups the

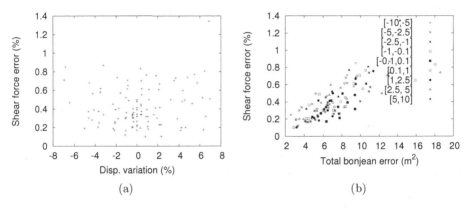

Fig. 10. Approximation error of the shear forces as (a) a function of displacement change, and (b) a function of the total bonjean error

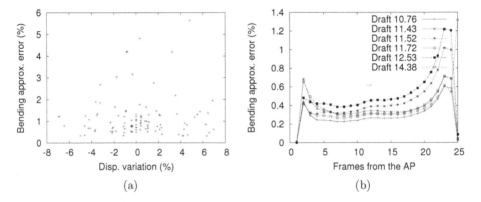

Fig. 11. Approximation error of the bending moment (a) as a function of displacement change, and (b) at each bonjean station for constant displacement

data points according to their displacement range, and for the data points with no displacement change we can see that the tendency remains the same. One must also take into account that the linearization error of the bonjean is amplified in the shear forces calculation by the fact that it becomes accumulated in the summation of the forces. This particular information is very important when analyzing the error in the bending moment calculation, since this accumulated error is multiplied by the arm of the moment and thus multiplies its impact.

Figure 11a shows the error in the bending calculation as a function of the changes in displacement. As expected, like for the shear force calculation, the main source of error is not the approximation of the lcg, but rather the error in the linearization of the bonjean areas. Due to the fact that the bonjean error is amplified by the multiplication of the arm, it is necessary to look at the error at each calculation frame in order to see how the error of the bending moment changes. We do this by forcing the displacement to remain constant, thus removing the error of the lcg approximation, and analyzing how the bending error changes at each calculation frame as the draft of each of the 10 test instances changes. The result is shown in Figure 11b, where the horizontal axis represents the frames of the vessel and the vertical axis is the percentage of error in the bending moment calculation. Each of the lines plotted in the graph represent one of the 10 test instances each of which has a different draft. As expected the bending moment is less accurate at the bow and stern due to the imprecision in the bonjean calculations. One more thing worthy of notice is that there is no direct relation between the bending error and the draft of the vessel. This is due to the non-linear shape of the hull. The bending error for constant displacement does not exceed 1.4 percent, however, when variable displacement is considered an error of up to 3.5 percent might be reached within a 5 percent displacement variation. We consider these approximations acceptable. Higher accuracy can be achieved by reducing the linearization error of the hydrostatic functions for bonjean.

6   Conclusion

This paper introduced an LP model including ballast tanks for the master planning phase of a 2-phase stowage planning optimization approach. Analysis of 10 real instances show that our model is successful at coping with variable displacement, a feature introduced by the ballast tanks, within an acceptable error tolerance. Within a 5% band of the current displacement, the master plans generated were seaworthy, with the error in stability calculations increasing proportionally to the variability of the displacement. In future work, we plan to introduce piece-wise linearizations on the bonjean hydrostatic data to reduce the error in the stress calculations in our model. This must be done carefully since it might be necessary to include Boolean variables that will negatively impact the performance of the solver. A study of the trade-off between the inclusion of piece-wise linearizations and the error reduction must be carried out.

Acknowledgments. We would like to thank Wai Ling Hoi, Andreas Hollmann, Kasper Andreasen, and Mikkel Mühldorff Sigurd at Maersk Line for their support of this work. This research is sponsored in part by the Danish Maritime Fund under the BAYSTOW project.

References

1. Ambrosino, D., Anghinolfi, D., Paolucci, M., Sciomachen, A.: An Experimental Comparison of Different Heuristics for the Master Bay Plan Problem. In: Festa, P. (ed.) SEA 2010. LNCS, vol. 6049, pp. 314–325. Springer, Heidelberg (2010)
2. Ambrosino, D., Sciomachen, A., Tanfani, E.: Stowing a conteinership: the master bay plan problem. Transportation Research Part A: Policy and Practice 38(2), 81–99 (2004)
3. Aslidis, A.H.: Optimal Container Loading. Master's thesis, Massachusetts Institute of Technology (1984)

4. Botter, R., Brinati, M.A.: Stowage container planning: A model for getting an op-timal solution. In: Proceedings of the 7th Int. Conf. on Computer Applications in the Automation of Shipyard Operation and Ship Design, pp. 217–229 (1992)
5. Kang, J., Kim, Y.: Stowage planning in maritime container transportation. Journal of the Operations Research Society 53(4), 415–426 (2002)
6. Li, F., Tian, C., Cao, R., Ding, W.: An Integer Linear Programming for Container Stowage Problem. In: Bubak, M., van Albada, G.D., Dongarra, J., Sloot, P.M.A. (eds.) ICCS 2008, Part I. LNCS, vol. 5101, pp. 853–862. Springer, Heidelberg (2008)
7. Pacino, D., Delgado, A., Jensen, R.M., Bebbington, T.: Fast Generation of Near-Optimal Plans for Eco-Efficient Stowage of Large Container Vessels. In: Böse, J.W., Hu, H., Jahn, C., Shi, X., Stahlbock, R., Voß, S. (eds.) ICCL 2011. LNCS, vol. 6971, pp. 286–301. Springer, Heidelberg (2011)
8. Tupper, E.C.: Introduction to Naval Architecture. Elsevier (2009)
9. Wilson, I.D., Roach, P.: Principles of combinatorial optimization applied to container-ship stowage planning. Journal of Heuristics (5), 403–418 (1999)

Scientometric Analysis of Container Terminals and Ports Literature and Interaction with Publications on Distribution Networks

Silvia Schwarze[1], Stefan Voß[1], Guohua Zhou[2], and Guoli Zhou[2]

[1] Institute of Information Systems, University of Hamburg,
Von-Melle-Park 5, 20146 Hamburg, Germany
schwarze@econ.uni-hamburg.de, stefan.voss@uni-hamburg.de
[2] Shanghai Jindun Industrial Group Co., Ltd, No. 365, Hengqiao Road,
Zhoupu, Pudong District, Shanghai, China, 201318
{hua_08,katharina_li}@web.de

Abstract. Ports and container terminals have been modernized and expanded world-wide in recent years. In particular under the aspect of recent developments based on the financial crisis and resulting intensified competition in global markets, modern techniques for structuring and operating of harbors and container handling are required. These needs are reflected in the increased research activity in the field of *container terminals and ports*. We apply scientometric means to study trends and developments within this area. Moreover, we investigate the interplay with *supply chain management in distribution networks* to visualize collaboration structures and interdependencies.

Keywords: Container Terminals, Ports, Supply Chain Management, Distribution Networks, Scientometric Analysis.

1 Introduction

Comprehensive surveys and compilations [1,14,18] illustrate the strong growth of harbors world-wide caused by increased container shipping. This leads to permanently changing requirements on organization and handling at container terminals. The need for efficient and sustainable process design has become a core aspect, in particular due to latest market developments, caused by the world-wide financial crisis. Severe competition and globalization of markets intensify the need for cost reduction and profitable management. A growing amount of research publications on *container terminals and ports* (CTP) reflects the increased need for planning and optimization tools in this field.

Scientometric studies should reflect this tendency. *Scientometrics* provides a view on a research field from a meta-level by applying quantitative means. Empirical measures like counting number of citations, frequent keywords, number of authors, etc. focus on understanding the development of an academic field and its collaboration structures. Scientometrics helps in measuring scientific activities and aims at

H. Hu et al. (Eds.): ICCL 2012, LNCS 7555, pp. 33–52, 2012.
© Springer-Verlag Berlin Heidelberg 2012

achieving a better apprehension of customs within a field of research like those of information sharing and development of scientific offspring.

Container terminals are essential elements in global supply chains. Efficient, flexible and robust design of these interfaces is a core issue of competitive distribution networks and, at the same time, an incentive for increasing research activities. As element of general supply chains, scientific work in CTP is naturally connected to research concerning *supply chain management* (SCM), in particular to *supply chain management in distribution networks* (SCMD). For instance, the subject "SCM Planning Operation, Distribution, Container Port" has been highlighted as relevant for SCMD by a scientometric study [13]. Similar to CTP, the research area SCMD reports an increased research activity in recent years. Moreover, the fields CTP and SCMD cannot be related explicitly to a single research field like business administration, sociology, engineering science, or macro economics [19]. Those aspects motivate a quantitative study of the development of the scientific fields SCMD and CTP by scientometric means. In particular, the interaction of both fields should be in focus of a respective study. A comprehensive scientometric study of SCMD is given by [13]. In this paper we carry out a related study for CTP and compare the results with those of SCMD. In particular, we study and describe interdependencies of both fields.

The paper is structured as follows. In Section 2 we introduce the research field CTP, in particular with a focus on the relation to SCMD. Afterwards, we analyze the development of publications per year and present top-keywords of CTP, as well as joint top-keywords with SCMD. Moreover, we study top-journals, top-authors, and top-articles, which we, again, compare to top-lists of SCMD. Section 4 is devoted to a study of collaboration structures for CTP. In Section 5 we focus on a joint analysis and present interaction of top-keywords and collaboration structures of top-authors for both fields. We close with some final remarks.

2   Terminals and Ports as Elements of Distribution Networks

Container terminals and ports are an essential interface of global supply chains. The scientific interest in container terminal processes, as well as in their design and optimization, has increased a lot in recent years. Comprehensive surveys of scientific work in CTP are provided by [17,18]. A container terminal can be considered as an open system of material flow with basically two external interfaces. The first is to the seaside and it is concerned with loading and unloading of container vessels. The second interface to the hinterland provides handling of road and railway traffic. After arrival, each container ship is assigned to a berth. On the ship, containers are stacked in bays that are cleared by cranes located at the quayside (*quay cranes*). Import and transshipment containers are transported to storage areas (*yards*) within the container terminal. At the yard, containers are stored until retrieval and further transport. Additional operations, like restacking of containers, might become necessary to generate a yard configuration optimized for future retrieval. Also, transports within the yard are carried out, to move containers to packaging or import/export-areas. From the hinterland, containers arrive via road or railway and have to be stored in export areas. Especially the handling of export containers is faced with the difficulty of stochastic or unknown arrival times. Relevant issues at container terminals are

- berth allocation, i.e., the location of container vessels at the quayside,
- crane scheduling, i.e., the assignment of quay cranes to ships as well as the control of loading and unloading activities,
- storage space allocation, i.e., the distribution of inbound containers to storage blocks and bays within the yard,
- transportation planning/vehicle dispatching, i.e., planning and control of transportation activities within the yard and of stacking operations.

In world-wide distribution networks, container terminals are important links that act as transshipment and storage points and as interconnection between different means of transportation like shipping, railway, and road traffic. Thus, container terminals play a crucial role in SCM as interfaces of intermodal traffic. Also in the wider context of supply chains as flows of not only goods, but also of information, service and finances, container terminals are important connections between supply chain entities. Consequently, the research fields CTP and SCMD overlap and interact with each other, justifying an analysis of the research areas under scientometric aspects.

3   Frequent Keywords, Authors, and Publications

The first scientometric work has been published by [10]. The term *scientometrics* (Russian: *Naukometriya*) was used mainly for the exploration of all aspects concerning science and technology literature [7]. Following the rapid development of scientometric research, more researchers joined this field world-wide. Some important (partly even earlier) publications are [4,5,9,15].

We distinguish the terms *citation* and *reference* as suggested by [16]. Consider two publications A and B, where A refers to B, i.e., B is contained in A's reference list. We say that A has a reference to B, but B receives a citation of A. Thus, the number of references an article provides is given by the number of entries in its bibliography. However, the number of citations an article receives is given by the number of publications, like journal papers, conference proceedings, and monographs that mention it.

A simple, but yet revealing tool of scientometrics refers to counting occurrences within citation databases. We take an insight into relevant keywords and study most frequent keyword clusters. Moreover, by counting citations as well as self-citations, we illustrate important journals, authors, and articles.

3.1   Relevant Keywords

A scientometric study is a pure quantitative analysis of a specific research area. Fundament of such a study is a collection of publications and corresponding citations. We generate a respective database by using the online citation source *Scopus* under the observation period 01/1996 – 08/2008. To obtain relevant publications in CTP, requests for the keywords "container terminal*" and "port*" (alternative: "harbor*" or "harbour*"), and "container terminal*" and "logistic*" (alternative: "transport*") are carried out in the fields *title*, *abstract*, and *keywords*. The asterisk acts as wildcard character in this query. We receive 651 source articles containing 8,324 references.

Among those sources, only 403 articles have a non-empty bibliography. Thus, we end up with an average number of 20.65 references per article.

The development of publications per year is presented in Figure 1 and measured against the publications per year in SCMD. Both areas show an increasing number of publications that illustrate the relevance of the topics. Notice that the last entry relates not to a complete year but only to eight months (January – August 2008).

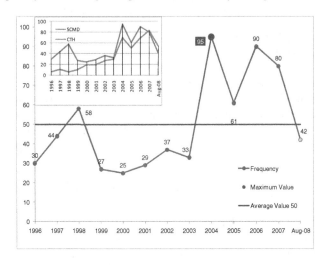

Fig. 1. Source articles per year in CTP and comparison to SCMD

To study top-keywords in CTP, 1,361 expressions are extracted from the keyword tag of the collected source articles. After excluding non-specific expressions, called *stopwords* (http://users.fmg.uva.nl/lleydesdorff/software/ti/index.htm), like "not", "as", or "if", we obtain 46 top-keywords with a frequency $f \geq 40$, see Table 1. The top-keywords make up 46.38% of the total frequency. Referring to the study on SCMD [13], there are 25 identical top-keywords found. Those expressions are marked in Table 1 by asterisks and illustrate the strong connection of the research areas.

A further analysis considers not only single, but groups of expressions. An analysis of top-keyword clusters has been carried out using the analytic tool *Wordsmith* (http://www.lexically.net/wordsmith/). The study provides 25 most frequent combinations providing a frequency f greater than or equal to 55 (see Table 2; R.: Rank).

3.2   Relevant Journals, Articles, and Active Authors

We measure the impact of journals in CTP by the number of citations a journal receives. Table 3 presents journals obtaining ≥29 citations. Those journals receive 54.05% of the total citations directed to journal articles. The list contains two A+, five A, ten B, and one C Journal regarding the JQ2-Rating of the VHB (German academic association for business research, http://vhbonline.org/service/jourqual/details2008/). Journals also being top-journals in SCMD [13] are marked by an asterisk.

Table 1. Top-keywords in CTP ($f \geq 40$)

Rank	Expression	f	in %	Rank	Expression	f	in %
1	CONTAINER	757	5.72	*24	LOGISTICS	83	0.63
2	TERMINAL	686	5.18	*25	ANALYSIS	81	0.61
3	PORT	612	4.62	*26	CONTROL	78	0.59
*4	TRANSPORTATION	412	3.11	*27	OPTIMIZATION	70	0.53
*5	SYSTEMS	219	1.65	28	ECONOMICS	68	0.51
6	HANDLING	157	1.19	29	DEVELOPMENT	67	0.51
7	CRANES	154	1.16	*30	METHODS	64	0.48
*8	MODELS	149	1.13	*30	PROGRAMMING	64	0.48
9	OPERATIONS	148	1.12	*32	PROBLEM	60	0.45
*10	SIMULATION	143	1.08	33	INTERMODAL	57	0.43
11	FREIGHT	138	1.04	34	RAILROAD	55	0.42
12	MATERIAL	123	0.93	34	SHIPPING	55	0.42
*13	PLANNING	118	0.89	*36	HEURISTIC	54	0.41
*14	SCHEDULING	108	0.82	*36	INDUSTRIAL	54	0.41
15	HARBORS	107	0.81	36	TRAFFIC	54	0.41
16	SHIP	102	0.77	*39	DESIGN	53	0.40
17	CARGO	101	0.76	*40	DECISION	52	0.39
*17	MANAGEMENT	101	0.76	41	EUROPE	50	0.38
*19	COMPUTER	100	0.76	*42	THEORY	49	0.37
20	STRUCTURAL	99	0.75	*43	STRATEGIC	45	0.34
*21	ALGORITHMS	90	0.68	*44	ALLOCATION	44	0.33
21	AUTOMATED	90	0.68	*45	GENETIC	41	0.31
*23	MATHEMATICAL	86	0.65	46	EURASIA	40	0.30

Table 2. Top-keyword cluster of length 3 ($f \geq 55$)

R.	Keyword cluster	f	R.	Keyword cluster	f
1	CONTAINER TERMINAL(S) PORT	621	14	SHIP CONTAINER TERMINAL	63
2	PORTS AND HARBORS	476	15	CONTAINER TERMINAL LOGISTICS	62
3	HANDLING CONTAINER TERMINAL	106	16	YARD CRANE SCHEDULING	61
4	CARGO HANDLING CONTAINER	96	16	CHINA EURASIA FAR	61
5	COMPUTER SIMULATION CONTAINERS	94	16	MULTI AGENT SYSTEMS	61
6	RAILROAD YARDS AND	86	16	AUTOMATED GUIDED VEHICLES	61
7	YARDS AND TERMINALS	85	20	MODELS PORT TERMINALS	60
8	EURASIA FAR EAST	83	21	BERTH ALLOCATION CONTAINER	56
9	TERMINALS PORTS AND	76	22	CONTAINERS FREIGHT TRANSPORTATION	55
10	DECISION SUPPORT SYSTEMS	70	22	MATHEMATICAL MODELS PORT	55
10	PROBLEM SOLVING SCHEDULING	70	22	AUTOMATED GUIDED VEHICLE	55
12	ASIA CHINA EURASIA	69	22	MARITIME CONTAINER TERMINAL	55
13	PORT TERMINALS PORTS	66			

Moreover, Table 3 illustrates self-citation. If a journal article refers to an older article published in the same journal, this is called *self-citation of journals*. We distinguish *self-citing* and *self-cited rates of journals* according to [8]. The self-citing rate is given by the ratio of number of self-citations of a journal and the total number of references provided by this journal. Thus, the self-citing rate can be controlled by adding further references. On the other hand, the self-cited rate of a journal is defined by the number of self-citations of this journal divided by the total number of citations this journal receives from other journal articles (including the self-citations) and is thus more significant in measuring self-citation. Note that column f in Table 3 reports the number of citations a journal receives in total, i.e., not only from journals, but from all considered means of publications, like monographs, conference proceedings, etc. However, the self-cited rate is computed based only on citations received from journals. An entry "-" in column *self-citation* reports "undefined", i.e., there are no source articles of the corresponding journal contained in the data collection. To study the relation between self-citation and productivity, a Pearson correlation analysis is performed. This proves no significant correlation between self-citing rate and productivity of journals ($r=0.440$, $p>0.05$), but a strong significant correlation between self-citing rate and citation frequency ($r=0.655$, $p<0.01$). Moreover, no significant correlation between self-cited rate and productivity ($r=0.026$, $p>0.05$), or between self-cited rate and citation frequency ($r=0.031$, $p>0.05$) can be proved.

Table 3. Top-journals in CTP ($f \geq 29$) with JQ2-rating and self citation

Rank	f	Journal	JQ2-Rating	Number of Articles	Self-citation	Self-cited rate	Self-citing rate
*1	355	EJOR (European Journal of Operational Research)	A	133	53	16.21%	9.12%
2	315	Maritime Policy and Management	-	143	50	16.29%	9.80%
*3	282	Transportation Research B	B	45	17	6.39%	13.39%
*4	166	OR Spectrum	A	35	94	61.04%	10.47%
*5	141	Transportation Science	A	69	3	2.16%	3.19%
*6	121	Int. Journal of Production Research	B	90	-	-	-
*7	110	Computers and Industrial Eng.	C	36	3	3.06%	4.84%
*8	99	IJPE (International Journal of Production Economics)	B	30	3	3.37%	5.45%
*9	90	Journal of Transport Geography	-	33	23	25.56%	9.16%
*10	86	Operations Research	A+	69	-	-	-
*11	83	Transportation Research A	B	35	15	18.52%	5.98%
*12	72	Computers & OR	B	33	0	0%	0%
*13	66	Naval Research Logistics	B	16	1	1.56%	1.30%
14	63	IJME	-	27	-	-	-
15	61	Marit. Econ. and Log.	-	30	7	11.48%	1.20%
*16	60	Journal of the OR Society	B	24	1	1.69%	1.61%
17	58	Simulation	-	15	3	5.45%	6.82%
18	52	J. Waterway Port Coastal and O. Eng.	-	18	-	-	-
19	46	J. of Advanced Transportation	-	4	0	0%	0%
20	43	IIE Transactions	A	23	-	-	-
*21	41	Transportation Research Record	-	26	16	40.00%	6.06%
*22	39	Management Science	A+	33	-	-	-
*23	37	Trans. Res. Part E Logistics	B	22	3	8.11%	2.26%
23	37	J. of Econometrics	A	19	-	-	-
25	36	Transportation Journal	-	28	17	47.22%	6.72%
25	36	OR Letters	B	7	-	-	-
27	32	Annals of Operations Research	B	24	0	0%	0%
28	31	Trans. Planning and Technology	-	9	9	29.03%	6.77%
29	29	Journal of Commerce	-	29	-	-	-

Next we focus on active authors considering all co-authors of a publication. Table 4 presents most cited authors and their citation frequencies ($f \geq 20$) as well as the number of publications from our data base. Moreover, self-citation, self-cited and self-citing rates of authors are given according to the analogous definitions for journals. An entry "-" in column *self-citations* indicates "undefined," i.e., our data collection does not contain source articles by this author. Three authors are given in bold as they have a self-cited rate $\geq 45\%$. First-rank author is Kim with 297 citations, 57 publications and a citation rate of 5.21. Considering only citation rates, the highest value is attained by Peterkofsky who has just a single publication receiving 30 citations.

A Pearson correlation analysis provides a significant correlation only between self-cited and self-citing rates ($r = 0.405$, $p < 0.01$). There is no significant correlation reported between productivity or citation frequency and self-cited or self-citing rates. Considering the research field SCMD, there are six joint authors found. Those authors are marked with asterisks in Table 4.

Table 4. Top-authors and self-citation rates ($f \geq 20$)

Rank	f	Author	Number of publications	Citation rate	Self-citations	Self-cited rate	Self-citing rate
1	297	Kim K H	57	5.21	26	8.75%	10.24%
*2	166	Daganzo C F	17	9.76	7	4.22%	22.58%
3	120	Imai A	17	7.06	35	29.17%	17.41%
4	96	Nishimura E	16	6.00	29	30.21%	15.59%
5	92	Papadimitriou S	13	7.08	27	29.35%	16.88%
6	90	Kozan E	16	5.63	31	34.44%	25.41%
*7	89	Notteboom T	39	2.28	11	12.36%	17.46%
8	67	Slack B	31	2.16	13	19.40%	5.94%
8	67	Kim K Y	7	9.57	0	0.00%	0.00%
10	65	Cullinane K P B	32	2.03	-	-	-
11	62	Park Y M	8	7.75	1	1.61%	2.86%
12	59	Vis I F A	8	7.38	8	13.56%	2.58%
13	57	Steenken D	10	5.70	9	15.79%	4.25%
13	57	Voss S	13	4.38	14	24.56%	3.01%
15	56	Hayuth Y	15	3.73	-	-	-
16	55	Ng J W C	11	5.00	18	32.73%	15.65%
17	52	Gambardella L M	13	4.00	5	9.62%	29.41%
18	49	Bish E K	7	7.00	9	18.37%	10.84%
19	48	Ryu K R	10	4.80	3	6.25%	7.14%
19	48	Rizzoli A E	10	4.80	2	4.17%	11.76%
21	47	De Koster R	5	9.40	1	2.13%	1.41%
*21	47	Simchi Levi D	10	4.70	5	10.64%	8.06%
23	46	Lim A	19	2.42	-	-	-
24	45	Tanchoco J M A	26	1.73	-	-	-
25	44	Song D W	24	1.83	13	29.55%	5.39%
26	42	Ottjes J A	24	1.75	13	30.95%	25.49%
26	42	De Castilho B	4	10.50	-	-	-
28	41	Li C L	7	5.86	2	4.88%	3.23%
28	41	Evers J J M	17	2.41	3	7.32%	16.67%
28	41	Linn R J	10	4.10	2	4.88%	4.44%

Table 4. (*continued*)

31	40	Zhang C	4	10.00	4	10.00%	8.89%
*32	39	Laporte G	19	2.05	4	10.26%	7.27%
32	39	Jula H	11	3.55	5	12.82%	10.00%
34	38	Ioannou P A	14	2.71	7	18.42%	17.95%
35	37	Legato P	13	2.85	10	27.03%	10.53%
35	37	Comtois C	17	2.18	6	16.22%	16.22%
35	37	Bae J W	10	3.70	0	0.00%	0.00%
38	36	Liu J	9	4.00	10	27.78%	10.31%
39	35	Zaffalon M	6	5.83	1	2.86%	5.88%
39	35	Taleb Ibrahimi M	2	17.50	-	-	-
39	35	Kim H B	4	8.75	1	2.86%	20.00%
39	35	Wan Y W	10	3.50	11	31.43%	11.34%
39	35	Stahlbock R	3	11.67	3	8.57%	0.65%
44	33	Preston P	5	6.60	6	18.18%	13.95%
45	32	Winkelmans W	13	2.46	3	9.38%	9.38%
46	31	Robinson R	12	2.58	4	12.90%	25.00%
47	30	Peterkofsky R I	1	30.00	-	-	-
48	29	Murty K G	11	2.64	11	37.93%	20.75%
48	29	Liu C I	11	2.64	5	17.24%	9.80%
48	29	Choi Y S	5	5.80	0	0.00%	0.00%
51	28	Duinkerken M B	14	2.00	7	25.00%	13.73%
51	28	Crainic T G	21	1.33	-	-	-
53	27	Henesey L	13	2.08	7	25.93%	10.61%
54	25	Van De Voorde E	12	2.08	6	24.00%	37.50%
54	25	Cheung R K	5	5.00	0	0.00%	0.00%
56	24	*Wang J J*	12	2.00	12	50.00%	6.09%
*56	24	*Rodrigue J P*	13	1.85	11	45.83%	15.28%
56	24	Lai K K	6	4.00	2	8.33%	10.00%
56	24	Egbelu P J	14	1.71	-	-	-
56	24	Baird A J	17	1.41	2	8.33%	6.25%
61	23	Hartmann S	10	2.30	9	39.13%	8.41%
61	23	Dekker R	10	2.30	2	8.70%	7.69%
*61	23	Brown G G	2	11.50	-	-	-
61	23	Lawphongpanich S	2	11.50	-	-	-
65	22	Meersman H	8	2.75	4	18.18%	25.00%
65	22	Gendreau M	16	1.38	-	-	-
67	21	Yun W Y	2	10.50	-	-	-
67	21	Noritake M	4	5.25	-	-	-
69	20	Tongzon J	8	2.50	7	35.00%	11.48%
69	20	Schmidt P	8	2.50	-	-	-
69	20	Heaver T	4	5.00	2	10.00%	12.50%
69	20	Charnes A	7	2.86	-	-	-
69	20	*Bruzzone A G*	15	1.33	11	55.00%	73.33%
69	20	Nagaiwa K	1	20.00	0	0.00%	0.00%

Scientometrics and performance indicators in academia seem a critical undertaking regarding various indices and data bases. While the settings of our study are well defined we mention that, once differently defined, considerable changes may arise. We underline this by some general remarks and an example.

Authors and editors have different objectives when choosing outlets and papers to publish; this might even be incorporated into game theoretical considerations between journal editors and authors [3]. With this, one might argue that academic networks neither affect the number of publications nor the quality of an author's papers but the number of an author's citations. This, however, reveals that different outlets are considered with varying importance in different communities. That is, one might even end up in getting citations in different outlets which belong to one community but are not visible in others. This is clarified by means of the h-index (Hirsch index) [6].

To compare our ranking with a general index, we add in Table 5 the h-index for the Top-authors of Table 4. An author has a h-index of h if h of his/her publications are cited at least h times each and the remaining publications are cited less than h times each. The data presented in Table 5 has been generated using *Scopus* (reference date 14.12.2011). The column *Number of cited publications (Scopus)* gives the number of publications that are recorded at the *Scopus* database. For the computation of the h-index, Scopus considers only documents that are published after 1995. The column *Number of publications considered for h-index* gives the according figure. Finally, the column *h-index* reports the respective figure computed within *Scopus* and column *Rank (h-index)* gives the corresponding ranking of the authors.

To clarify our above concern that 'once differently defined, considerable changes may arise' we calculate as follows (leaving the option for authors not mentioned that their papers and citations captured by other data bases would reveal a completely different picture). The h-index in our short interlude given here was taken on the set of documents available at Scopus, while in our general study we worked on a selection of articles having a relation to CTH. Thus, an author's impact in our study may differ from the impact reported by the general h-index. For instance, consider the author Hayuth who is among the top 15 in our study. However, this author has an h-index of 0 as there are no papers reported in *Scopus* after 1995. On the other hand, the two authors with Ranks 1 and 2 regarding the h-index, Laporte and Gendreau, have only Ranks 32 and 65 within our study. Another difficulty might arise in various other dimensions such as the use of special characters as is the case, e.g., regarding the different ways of writing the name of the author Voß in various papers and citations.

Considering top-documents in CTP, there are 30 publications with a frequency $f \geq 11$ extracted from the data base; see Table 6. To compare with a publicly available citation measure, we add a column f^G giving the citation count of *Google Scholar* (http://scholar.google.com, date: 01/07/10). Of course, this indicator has to be handled with care as it counts citations, regardless from which field they arise. In contrast, frequency f reported in Table 6 counts only citations arising from CTP literature.

Note that, although in CTP we have around 1,000 references less than in SCMD, here we introduce a stronger bound $f \geq 11$ than [13] for SCMD with $f_{SCMD} \geq 9$. Using a bound of $f \geq 9$ would result in a list of 67 top-documents in CTP while the study in SCMD yields just 31 top-documents given that bound. Thus, although considering fewer references in CTP, there is a larger number of articles attracting many citations. In addition, we note that there are no joint top-documents in CTP and SCMD although there are 210 identical documents found in the references of both fields. Rank one is taken by one of the older publications in the list of top-documents by Daganzo (Rank 2 in top-authors). The productivity of rank-one author Kim is reflected by his top-documents on ranks 4, 9, 13, 18, 19, 25, 35, 40, and 43.

Table 5. Top-authors and *h*-index (f ≥ 20)

Rh: Rank (h-index); ***h:*** h-index ; **# Sc:** Number of cited publications (Scopus);
 # Ph: Number of publications considered for the h-index

Rh	Author	# Sc	# Ph	h	Rh	Author	# Sc	# Ph	h
5	Kim K H	74	66	20	11	Liu J	50	47	16
10	Daganzo C F	139	63	17	28	Zaffalon M	42	42	10
14	Imai A	18	18	14	71	Taleb Ibrahimi M	0	0	0
16	Nishimura E	15	15	13	21	Kim H B	47	46	12
21	Papadimitriou S	16	16	12	39	Wan Y W	26	23	8
16	Kozan E	44	40	13	50	Stahlbock R	19	19	5
21	Notteboom T	40	40	12	58	Preston P	3	3	3
16	Slack B	46	32	13	67	Winkelmans W	9	2	1
5	Kim K Y	221	220	20	54	Robinson R	15	10	4
16	Cullinane K P B	51	49	13	71	Peterkofsky R I	2	0	0
21	Park Y M	25	25	12	34	Murty K G	46	18	9
39	Vis I F A	17	17	8	58	Liu C I	5	5	3
67	Steenken D	4	2	1	65	Choi Y S	2	2	2
12	Voss S	92	80	15	54	Duinkerken M B	9	7	4
71	Hayuth Y	12	0	0	12	Crainic T G	81	61	15
34	Ng J W C	18	16	9	58	Henesey L	9	9	3
3	Gambardella L M	87	84	24	50	Van De Voorde E	28	24	5
39	Bish E K	21	21	8	28	Cheung R K	27	27	10
50	Ryu K R	33	33	5	39	*Wang J J*	14	13	8
16	Rizzoli A E	54	51	13	28	*Rodrigue J P*	28	24	10
34	De Koster R	23	20	9	65	Lai K K	39	39	2
8	Simchi Levi D	75	55	19	21	Egbelu P J	72	33	12
9	Lim A	183	170	18	47	Baird A J	21	20	6
28	Tanchoco J M A	89	18	10	21	Hartmann S	13	13	12
34	Song D W	21	21	9	4	Dekker R	88	77	21
54	Ottjes J A	19	12	4	39	Brown G G	48	28	8
71	De Castilho B	0	0	0	45	Lawphongpanich S	37	28	7
14	Li C L	61	48	14	58	Meersman H	17	17	3
58	Evers J J M	12	6	3	2	Gendreau M	192	177	33
28	Linn R J	36	24	10	34	Yun W Y	43	35	9
54	Zhang C	4	4	4	67	Noritake M	11	1	1
1	Laporte G	310	248	34	47	Tongzon J	26	21	6
39	Jula H	12	12	8	28	Schmidt P	72	34	10
5	Ioannou P A	203	107	20	58	Heaver T	13	4	3
47	Legato P	12	10	6	58	Charnes A	99	3	3
45	Comtois C	24	15	7	50	*Bruzzone A G*	40	40	5
21	Bae J W	51	51	12	67	Nagaiwa K	1	1	1

Table 6. Top-documents in CTP (*f* ≥ 11)

R.	f	Publication	f^G
1	37	Daganzo, C.F. (1989) The crane scheduling problem. *Transportation Research B* 23(3): 159-175.	140
2	34	Peterkofsky, R.I. and Daganzo, C.F. (1990) A branch and bound solution method for the crane scheduling problem. *Transportation Research B* 24(3): 159-172.	118

Table 6. (*continued*)

3	33	Steenken, D., Voss, S. and Stahlbock, R. (2004) Container terminal operation and operations research - a classification and literature review. *OR Spectrum* 26(1): 3-49.	234
4	31	Kim, K.H., Park, Y.M. and Ryu, K.-R. (2000) Deriving decision rules to locate export containers in container yards. *EJOR* 124(1): 89-101.	114
4	31	De Castillo, B. and Daganzo, C.F. (1993) Handling strategies for import containers at marine terminals. *Transportation Research B* 27(2): 151-166.	83
4	31	Taleb-Ibrahimi, M., de Castilho, B. and Daganzo, C.F. (1993) Storage space vs. handling work in container terminals. *Transportation Research B* 27(1): 13-32.	90
7	29	Vis, I.F.A. and de Koster, R. (2003) Transshipment of containers at a container terminal: An overview. *EJOR* 147(1): 1-16.	159
8	28	Imai, A., Nishimura, E. and Papadimitriou, S. (2001) The dynamic berth allocation problem for a container port. *Transportation Research B* 35(4): 401-417.	120
9	27	Kim, K.H. and Kim, K.Y. (1999) An optimal routing algorithm for a transfer crane in port container terminals. *Transportation Science* 33(1): 17-33.	87
10	24	Imai A., Nagaiwa, K.-I. and Tat, C.W. (1997) Efficient planning of berth allocation for container terminals in Asia. *Journal of Advanced Transportation* 31(1): 74-94.	75
10	24	Nishimura, E., Imai, A. and Papadimitriou, S. (2001) Berth allocation planning in the public berth system by genetic algorithms. *EJOR* 131(2): 282-292.	95
12	23	Yun, W.Y. and Choi, Y.S. (1999) A simulation model for container-terminal operation analysis using an object-oriented approach. *IJPE* 59(1-3): 221-230.	100
13	22	Kim, K.Y. and Kim, K.H. (1999) A routing algorithm for a single straddle carrier to load export containers onto a containership. *IJPE* 59(1-3): 425-433.	60
14	20	Kozan, E. and Preston, P. (1999) Genetic algorithms to schedule container transfers at multimodal terminals. *International Transactions in Operational Research* 6: 311-329.	90
15	19	Bish, E.K., Leong, T.Y., Li, C.L., Ng, J.W.C. and Simchi-Levi, D. (2001) Analysis of a new vehicle scheduling and location problem. *Naval Research Logistics* 48(5): 363-385.	71
15	19	Gambardella, L.M., Rizzoli, A.E. and Zaffalon, M. (1998) Simulation and planning of an intermodal container terminal. *Simulation* 71(2): 107-116.	103
17	18	Legato, P. and Mazza, R.M. (2001) Berth planning and resources optimisation at a container terminal via discrete event simulation. *EJOR* 133(3): 537-547.	88
18	17	Park, Y.-M. and Kim, K.H. (2003) A scheduling method for berth and quay cranes. *OR Spectrum* 25(1): 1-23.	87
19	16	Bish, E.K. (2003) A multiple-crane-constrained scheduling problem in a container terminal. *EJOR* 144(1): 83-107.	73
19	16	Lai, K.K. and Shih, K. (1992) A study of container berth allocation. *Journal of Advanced Transportation* 26(1): 45-60.	47
19	16	Zhang, C., Wan, Y.-w., Liu, J. and Linn, R.J. (2002) Dynamic crane deployment in container storage yards. *Transportation Research B* 36(6): 537-555.	81
19	16	Kim, K.H. and Kim, H.B. (1999) Segregating space allocation models for container inventories in port container terminals. *IJPE* 59(1-3): 415-423.	64
19	16	Daganzo, C.F. (1990) The productivity of multipurpose seaport terminals. *Transportation Science* 24(3): 205-216.	23
19	16	Evers, J.J.M. and Koppers, S.A.J. (1996) Automated guided vehicle traffic control at a container terminal. *Transportation Research A* 30(1): 21-34.	65
25	15	Lim, A. (1998) The berth planning problem. *OR Letters* 22: 105-110.	67
25	15	Liu, C.-I., Jula, H. and Ioannou, P.A. (2002) Design, simulation, and evaluation of automated container terminals. *Intelligent Transportation Systems* 3(1): 12-26.	60
25	15	Kozan, E. (2000) Optimising container transfers at multimodal terminals. *Mathematical and Computer Modelling* 31(10): 235-243.	86
25	15	Daganzo, C.F. (1989) Crane productivity and ship delay in ports. *Transportation Research Record* 1251: 1-9.	29
25	15	Kim. K.H. (1997) Evaluation of the number of rehandles in container yards. *Computers and Industrial Engineering* 32(4): 701-711.	79

Table 6. (*continued*)

25	15	van Hee, K.M. and Wijbrands, R.J. (1988) Decision support system for container terminal planning. *EJOR* 34(3): 262-272.	46
31	14	Imai, A., Nishimura, E. and Papadimitriou, S. (2003) Berth allocation with service priority. *Transportation Research B* 37(5): 437-457.	76
31	14	Brown, G.G., Lawphongpanich S. and Thurman, K.P. (1994) Optimizing ship berthing. *Naval Research Logistics* 41(1): 1-15.	48
31	14	*Containerisation International Yearbook.* Containerisation International. London: National Magazine Company.	5
31	14	Kozan, E. (1997) Comparison of analytical and simulation planning models of seaport container terminals. *Transportation Planning and Technology* 20(3): 235 – 248.	45
35	13	Hayut, Y. (1981) Containerization and the load center concept. *Economic Geography* 57(2): 160-176.	110
35	13	Notteboom, T.E. and Winkelmans W. (2001) Structural changes in logistics: How will port authorities face the challenge? *Maritime Policy & Management* 28(1): 71-89.	104
35	13	Kim, K.H. and Moon, K.C. (2003) Berth scheduling by simulated annealing. *Transportation Research B* 37(6): 541-560.	90
35	13	Li, C.-l., Cai, X. and Lee, C.-y. (1998) Scheduling with multiple-job-on-one-processor pattern. *IIE Transactions* 30(5): 433-445.	46
35	13	Nicolaou, S. (1967) Berth planning by evaluation of congestion and cost. *Journal of the Waterways and Harbors Division* 93(4): 107-132.	22
40	12	Kim, K.H. and Park, Y.-M. (2004) A crane scheduling method for port container terminals. *EJOR* 156(3): 752-768.	87
40	12	Robinson, R. (1998) Asian hub/feeder nets: The dynamics of restructuring. *Maritime Policy & Management* 25(1): 21-40.	66
40	12	Grunow, M., Günther, H.-O. and Lehmann, M. (2004) Dispatching multi-load AGVs in highly automated seaport container terminals. *OR Spectrum* 26(2): 211-235.	62
43	11	Zhang, C., Liu, J., Wan, Y-w., Murty, K.G. and R.J. Linn (2003) Storage space allocation in container terminals. *Transportation Research B* 37(10): 883-903.	79
43	11	Bramel, J. and D. Simchi-Levi (1997) The logic of logistics: Theory, algorithms, and applications for logistics management, Springer	145
43	11	Kia, M., E. Shayan, and F. Ghotb (2002) Investigation of port capacity under a new approach by computer simulation. *Computers and Industrial Engineering* 42(2-4): 533-540	46
43	11	Kozan, E. (1997) Increasing the operational efficiency of container terminals in Australia. *Journal of the Operational Research Society* 48: 151-161.	31
43	11	Kim, K.H. and Kim, H.B. (1998) The optimal determination of the space requirement and the number of transfer cranes for import containers. *Computers and Industrial Engineering* 35(3-4): 427-430.	43

4   Collaboration in CTP by Co-citation Analysis

Given two authors, *co-citation analysis* measures the occurrence of joint appearance in reference lists of further publications. White and Griffith [20] describe co-citation as "someone cites any work by any author along with any work by any other author in a new document of his own." Co-citation analysis is suited to measure thematic connections within research fields and collaboration structures of authors and working groups. By considering only the first author of each publication we say that *pure first-author co-citation* takes place if a publication of first-author A appears together with a second publication of first-author B in the reference list of a third publication, where neither A nor B is co-author of the third publication.

On the other hand, we say that *co-author co-citation* takes place when publications of co-author A and co-author B appear in the reference list of another publication, where A and B might even be co-authors of the same article. Note that co-authors of a publication include also the first author. For further co-citation definitions see [12].

By a result of [21], the outcomes of pure first-author co-citation and co-author co-citation analysis differ. Thus, we carry out a survey for each variation. We consider 74 top-authors in CTP with citation frequency ≥20, excluding three authors that have a high self-cited rate; see Table 4. Regarding pure first-author co-citation analysis, seven authors have no connection to other first-authors, thus, we obtain a 64×64 co-citation matrix. Considering co-author co-citation, we generate a full 71×71 co-citation matrix. Using Pearson correlation coefficients [11] and factor analysis (in particular, principal component analysis with oblimin rotation [2]) we present results as two-dimensional maps. We visualize connections with an absolute factor value of 0.3 or higher (Figure 2). Authors are pictured by squares, factors are given as dots.

The highest impact is reported for the subject *container terminals and ports* where 50% of all top-authors are linked to this field. Note that this subject includes subfields like *crane scheduling, simulation, automated operation, storage and stacking logistics*, and *crane transport optimization*. The remaining eight subjects are *port competition, storage and stacking logistics, optimum berth capacity, AGV, berth allocation, container & port (development)*, and *(dynamic) berth allocation & port*. Figure 3 presents results of the co-author co-citation analysis. Three subjects have been already given by the pure first-author co-citation analysis including *container terminals and ports* (with 62% of the top-authors associated to the field) and *AGV*. Further subjects include *global port competition/European* and *berth allocation & container*. Compared to the study for the research area SCMD, it can be observed that the research in CTP shows a stronger focus on a smaller number of subjects.

A partition of research subjects into two, almost separated fields is observable in Figure 3. An explanation could be motivated by a separation of fields into "Quantitative/Engineering (Engin)" vs. "Qualitative/Economics (Econ)". Under thematic aspects, *global port competition/European* and *frontier production* are close to (Econ), whereas the remainder, given by, e.g., *container terminals and ports, AGV, storage stocking logistics/crane scheduling* could be associated to (Engin). As Figure 3 illustrates, *port competition/European* is totally isolated, while *frontier production* is loosely connected by one author. Studying Figure 2 under similar aspects, one could link, under thematic aspects, the fields *port competition* and *container & port (development)* to (Econ), while the remainder, e.g., *storage and stacking logistics, AGV*, and *berth allocation* could be associated to (Engin). Note that the authors of both studies (first-author as well as co-author co-citation), that are associated to (Econ) fields are identical, except for one case (Tongzon). One might suppose that we face two almost separated research communities within the field CTP. Indeed, checking the author's affiliations, it can be observed that authors related to (Econ) are in most cases associated to (applied) economics or geography institutes, whereas authors from (Engin) are in most cases affiliated with engineering, mathematics or business schools. Nevertheless, a clear distinction is not possible as overlapping areas, like *transport research*, appear for both fields. However, based on those observations, the conjecture might be stated, that within CTP, there are two weakly connected research streams that can be divided into "Quantitative/Engineering (Engin)" vs. "Qualitative/Economics (Econ)."

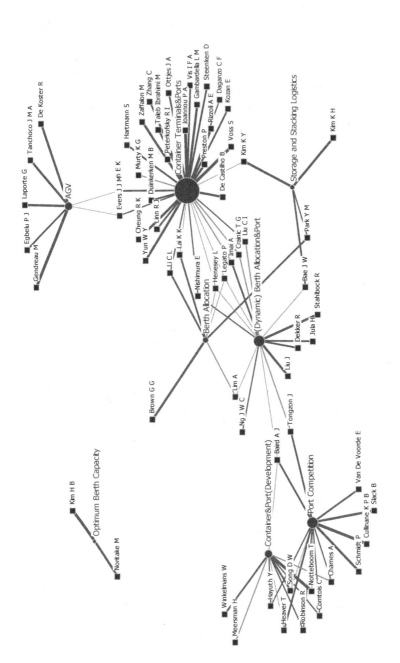

Fig. 2. Visualization of pure first-author co-citation analysis

5   Interaction by Co-word and Co-citation Analysis

To study the interaction between the areas SCMD and CTP, we carry out joint top-keyword and co-citation analysis. To investigate keywords of both fields, we extract 92 top-keywords with frequencies $f_{SCMD} \geq 13$ and $f_{CTP} \geq 13$. This includes 22 joint keywords, 30 expressions from SCMD and 40 from CTP. A 92×92 co-citation matrix is generated using Bibexcel (http://www8.umu.se/inforsk/Bibexcel/), an analytic tool for bibliographic data, and transformed to a Pearson correlation matrix. The result is visualized using *Netdraw* (http://www.analytictech.com/Netdraw/netdraw.htm) and *Ucinet*, a tool for social network analysis (http://www.analytictech.com/), using a Pearson correlation coefficient ≥ 0.6. Applying indegree-centrality as defined by social network analysis, we derive Figure 4. Keywords are given by squares. In particular, joint keywords are colored yellow, keywords from SCMD in blue and keywords from CTP in red. The line thickness illustrates the value of the Pearson correlation coefficient. The square sizes give the strength of the corresponding indegree-centrality.

Figure 4 illustrates that 13 joint top-keywords are located between SCMD and CTP. The joint keyword "Decision Making" has many direct connections to other keywords which results in a degree of centrality. Furthermore, the SCMD keyword *distribution of goods* and the CTP keywords *automation*, *cranes*, and *cargo handling* report a high degree of centrality. Moreover, it can be observed that two SCMD keywords, namely *computational methods* and *computer software* show a strong connection to CTP keywords. Finally, six keywords have no significant connection to other keywords and are provided isolatedly in Figure 4.

Finally, we study top-authors from SCMD and CTP by a joint co-author co-citation analysis. This investigation is based on 60 SCMD top-authors [13] and 71 top-authors from CTP; see Table 4. Authors having a self-cited rate $\geq 45\%$ are already excluded. Due to five joint authors (one joint author was already excluded because of high self-cited rate), we obtain a 126×126 co-citation matrix which is transformed into a Pearson correlation matrix. Analogous to the single-CTP study (see Section 4) we apply factor analysis (|factor value|≥ 0.3) to obtain a two-dimensional network representation; see Figure 5. Blue squares describe top-authors from SCMD whereas red squares give CTP top-authors. Joint authors are pictured in green. The subjects are indicated by yellow dots. The study delivers 16 subjects:

(1)   Container terminals & ports
(2)   Supply chain (design) & production distribution system (PDS) & distribution system design (DSS)
(3)   Port competition & global shipping
(4)   SCM & production distribution system (PDS)
(5)   Supply chain & demand uncertainty
(6)   Storage stocking logistics (SSL) & container terminals
(7)   Berth allocation
(8)   Genetic algorithm (GA) & distribution & location problem (LP)
(9)   Vehicle routing problem
(10)   SCM

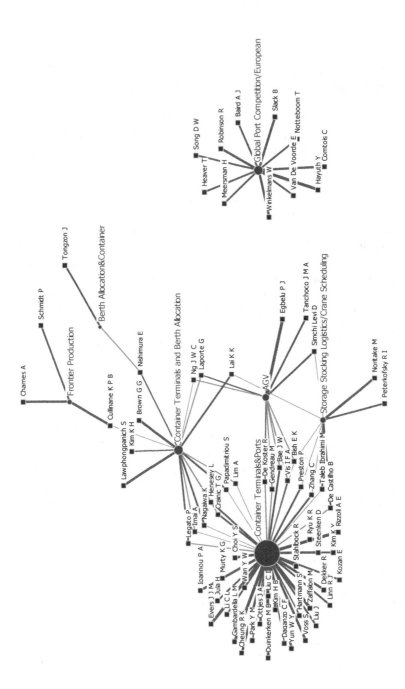

Fig. 3. Visualization of co-author co-citation analysis

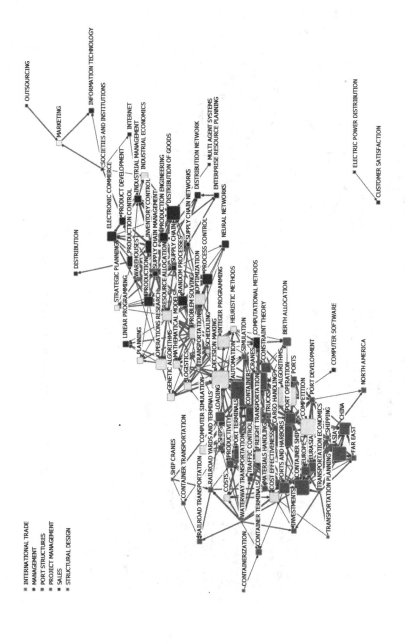

Fig. 4. Interaction of top-keywords in SCMD and CTP (by indegree-centrality)

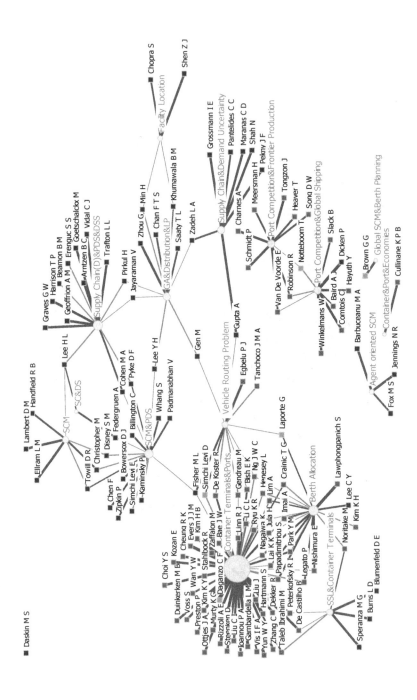

Fig. 5. Interaction of top-authors in SCMD and CTP

(11) Agent oriented SCM
(12) Port competition & frontier production
(13) Facility location
(14) Supply chain (SC) & decision support (DS)
(15) Container & port & economies
(16) Global SCM & berth planning

It can be observed that subjects (1) and (7) are connected to CTP whereas subjects (2), (4), (5), (8), (10), (11), (13), (14) are associated to SCMD. Considering shared subjects, Dicken and Notteboom are the only SCMD authors associated to subject (3). In addition, subject (12) belongs almost completely to CTP, except for one author who obtains citations in SCMD, too (Notteboom). Subject (9) attracts researchers from both areas, among them two joint authors, Simchi-Levi and Laporte.

6   Conclusion

The research areas *container terminals and ports* and *supply chain management in distribution networks* are both highly active and fast developing fields. Moreover, both subjects are overlapping in terms of thematic matters as ports are crucial elements of supply chains and distribution networks. Moreover, considering commonly used journals, joint articles, and important authors, those fields show connections. Thus, a study of research streams and collaborations is a consequent step to understand better the interaction among the subjects.

In this study, we have focused on a scientometric analysis of CTP and in particular, on describing the interplay with SCMD under scientometric aspects. Both areas share many top-keywords, some top-authors, but no top-articles. Moreover, among top-journals, there are 17 joint entries. Collaboration maps of top-authors show the interplay between CTP and SCMD not only in thematically overlapping areas.

References

1. Böse, J.W. (ed.): Handbook on Terminal Planning. Springer, New York (2011)
2. Child, D.: The Essentials of Factor Analysis, 3rd edn. Continuum International Publishing Group Ltd., London (2006)
3. Faria, J.R., Goel, R.K.: Returns to networking in academia. Netnomics 11(2), 103–117 (2010)
4. Garfield, E.: Citation analysis as a tool in journal evaluation. Science 178(4060), 471–479 (1972)
5. Garfield, E.: Citation Indexing: Its Theory and Application in Science, Technology, and Humanities. John Wiley & Sons, Inc., New York (1979)
6. Hirsch, J.E.: An index to quantify an individual's scientific research output. Proceedings of the National Academy of Sciences of the United States of America 102(46), 16569–16572 (2005)
7. Hood, W., Wilson, C.: The literature of bibliometrics, scientometrics, and informetrics. Scientometrics 52(2), 291–314 (2001)

8. Lawani, S.M.: On the heterogeneity and classification of author self – citations. Journal of the American Society for Information Science 33(5), 281–284 (1982)

9. Lotka, A.J.: The frequency distribution of scientific productivity. Journal of the Washington Academy of Sciences 16, 317–323 (1926)

10. Nalimov, V.V., Mulchenko, Z.M.: Scientometrics. Study of the Science Development as an Informational Process. Nauka, Moscow (1969)

11. Pearson, K.: On lines and planes of closest fits of systems of points in space. Philosophical Magazine 2, 559–572 (1901)

12. Rousseau, R., Zuccala, A.: A classification of author co-citations: Definitions and search strategies. Journal of the American Society for Information Science and Technology 55(6), 513–529 (2004)

13. Schwarze, S., Voß, S., Zhou, G., Zhou, G.: Supply chain management in distribution networks from a scientometric perspective. University of Hamburg, Institute of Information Systems. Working paper (2010)

14. Sciomachen, A., Acciaro, M., Liu, M.: Operations research methods in maritime transport and freight logistics. Maritime Economics & Logistics 11(1), 1–6 (2009)

15. de Solla Price, D.J.: Networks of scientific papers. Science 149(3683), 510–515 (1965)

16. de Solla Price, D.J.: Citation measures of hard science, soft science, technology, and non-science. In: Nelson, C.E., Pollock, D. (eds.) Communication among Scientists and Engineers, pp. 3–22. D.C. Heath and Company, Lexington (1970)

17. Stahlbock, R., Voß, S.: Operations research at container terminals: a literature update. OR Spectrum 30(1), 1–52 (2008)

18. Steenken, D., Voß, S., Stahlbock, R.: Container terminal operation and operations research - a classification and literature review. OR Spectrum 26(1), 3–49 (2004)

19. Stewens, M.: Supply Chain Management: Gestaltung und Steuerung unternehmensübergreifender Wertschöpfungsnetze. Josef Eul Verlag, Lohmar (2005)

20. White, H.D., Griffith, B.C.: Author Cocitation: A Literature Measure of Intellectual Structure. Journal of the American Society for Information Science 32(3), 163–171 (1981)

21. Zhao, D., Strotmann, A.: Comparing all-author and first-author co-citation analyses of Information Science. Journal of Informetrics 2(3), 229–239 (2008)

A Novel Predictive Control Based Framework for Optimizing Intermodal Container Terminal Operations

João Lemos Nabais[1], Rudy R. Negenborn[2], and Miguel Ayala Botto[3]

[1] IDMEC, Department of Informatics and Systems Engineering
Setúbal School of Technology, Polytechnical Institute of Setúbal
Setúbal, Portugal
joao.nabais@estsetubal.ips.pt
[2] Delft University of Technology, Marine and Transport Technology
Transport Engineering and Logistics,
Delft, The Netherlands
r.r.negenborn@tudelft.nl
[3] IDMEC, Instituto Superior Técnico, Technical University of Lisbon
Department of Mechanical Engineering
Lisboa, Portugal
ayalabotto@ist.utl.pt

Abstract. Due to the increase in world-wide containerized cargo transport port authorities are facing considerable pressure to increase efficiency of existing facilities. Container vessels with $18,000$ TEUs (twenty-foot equivalent units) are expected soon to create high flow peaks at container terminals. In this paper we propose a new framework for managing intermodal container terminals, based on the model predictive control methodology. A model based on queues and container categorization is used by a model predictive controller to solve the handling resource allocation problem in a container terminal in an optimal way, while respecting constraints on resource availability. The optimization of the operations is performed in an integrated way for the whole terminal rather than only for an individual subprocess. Containers are categorized into empty and full containers, and divided in classes according to their final destination. With more detailed information available, like container final destination, it is possible to establish priorities for the container flows inside the terminal. The order in which the container classes should be loaded into a carrier can now be addressed taking into account the carrier future route. The model ability to track the number of containers per class makes this framework suitable for describing terminals integrated in an intermodal transport network and a valuable tool for coordinating the transport modal shift towards a more sustainable and reliable transport. The potential of the proposed framework is illustrated with simulation studies based on a high-peak flow scenario and for a long-term scheduled scenario.

Keywords: intermodal transport, container terminals, flow networks, model predictive control.

H. Hu et al. (Eds.): ICCL 2012, LNCS 7555, pp. 53–71, 2012.
© Springer-Verlag Berlin Heidelberg 2012

1 Introduction

Despite the current economic situation, on the mid to long-term the transportation of goods over water and tracks will keep increasing [3]. Sea port Rotterdam in the Netherlands (the tenth largest container port in the world and the largest container port of Europe in TEU transhipped in 2011) expects in 2030 a doubling of the number of full and empty containers, and in addition aims at an increase of the modal split in favor of inland shipping from 25% to 45% in 2030. Already now major deep sea terminals (also outside The Netherlands) are reaching their maximum capacity. The expected increase in transported container volume will cause more terminals to reach their limits. In addition, the capacity of deep sea vessels has grown from $1,500$ TEU in 1980 to about $14,500$ TEU in 2006 [4]. This increase in vessel sizes leads to an increase in peak call sizes at terminals. Handling these larger volumes of instantaneously arriving load takes a significant amount of time and moreover delays other terminal operations. As a consequence, transit times of containers become more delayed. This on its turn affects the connecting transportation means (truck, barge and train), which therefore have to face long waiting times at terminals: in Rotterdam trucks may have to wait up to 6 hours and barges have been reported to wait between 24 and up to 72 hours [11].

The container transportation network is composed by nodes (describing terminals, depots or warehouses) and links (describing available connections). According to [12] inland transportation accounts for a considerable part of the total cost for container shipping between 40% to 80%. A container terminal is a complex system where solutions to different problems have to be integrated, like berth scheduling and resource allocation. Different scientific communities, such as operations research and more recently control systems, have devoted attention to the optimization of operations inside the container terminal, in particular those container terminals located at the sea [1, 13, 16]. One of the main approach for optimizing container terminal operations is based on finding an optimal handling resource allocation that can increase the freight flow through the terminal [5]. However, in some works only part of the terminal operations are considered: serving vessels, transfer between the quay and the yard [14]. All these approaches are common in the sense that they consider containers as undistinguished units and therefore they lack a basis to support strategic planning in a transportation network. Distinguishing containers can be extremely useful for developing measures at a strategic level to increase network performance.

The model and control strategy proposed in this paper is able to solve the handling resource allocation problem while at the same time tracking the containers final destination inside the network. The contribution of the model is the ability to deal with different container types, in particular it distinguishes empty and full containers and this last type is further categorized based on final destination. This feature allows further insight into the operations management of an intermodal terminal. More information regarding the container's final destination has to be shared in the transport network, while for trust reasons the privacy of the final customer should be respected. The information exchange required is likely to happen if benefits are shown to all actors in the transport network. With this framework it is possible to use a forecast of scheduled requests for unloading/loading of containers for each carrier. The container flow will be measured by the volume of TEUs in a time period. The container flows inside the intermodal terminal are determined in an optimal way by a so-called model predictive controller according to a defined performance index over a prediction horizon. Through the performance index it is possible to assign time varying priorities to container flows.

In this paper a new framework for intermodal container terminal operations management is proposed. In Section 2 the model used for describing the flows existing inside the intermodal container terminal is given. The resource allocation problem is formulated in Section 3 and addressed using a model predictive control strategy that solves an optimization problem at each discrete sample time. The performance of the proposed framework is tested through numerical simulations in Section 4 for a hinterland intermodal terminal taking into account the terminal layout and the available transport network connections. In Section 5 final conclusions are drawn and future research topics are addressed.

2   Modeling Intermodal Container Terminals

The intermodal container terminal is a key element in the transport network. A transport network can be represented by a graph $\mathcal{G} = (\mathcal{V}, \mathcal{E})$ where the nodes $\mathcal{V}$ represent terminals or hubs and the links $\mathcal{E}$ represent the available transport mode connections. The challenge when looking at the container transport problem from a network perspective is to assure the cooperation between the different transport network actors (merchants, forwarders, terminal managers, shippers, infrastructure owners...) towards a more sustainable and reliable transport system. A terminal model should capture the necessary information to support the transport network analysis that is aimed at a more sustainable transport system.

The basic goal of a transport network is to deliver the cargo at the agreed time and at the agreed location (customer request) while minimizing the cost of transport (service provider request). The transport network actors have a challenge of satisfying the customer request while reducing the transport costs to remain competitive in a competitive sector. Reducing transport costs is related to an optimal route choice inside the transport network. For example, the shortest route in time may be the best option when time comes as a priority for respecting the agreed due time or if there is sufficient time left the option may be using a longer route but with less transport costs. For this objective it is required to distinguish containers inside the transport network according to their final destination. In this work the final destination of a container means the last terminal the container should visit before being transported by truck to the final customer. In this way the privacy of a client is still assured.

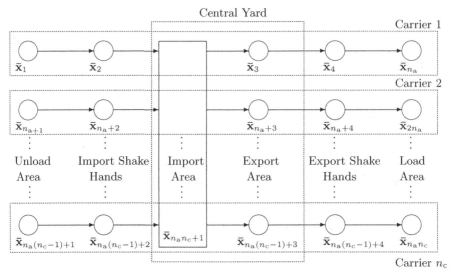

Fig. 1. Terminal-related network where the flow corresponding to a single carrier crosses 5 terminal areas plus a common area. The state-space vector $\bar{\mathbf{x}}_i$ description is given in equation (1).

2.1 Proposed Model

A transport network is composed of a group of terminals or depots where cargo is redirected to the final destination and may undergo a transport mode switch. The proposed intermodal terminal model for describing the terminal dynamics is based on a flow perspective. The terminal model is basically a network of stowage areas described as queues that are connected by container handling capacity represented by links. The model describing the terminal dynamics is based on two main features:

- queues, to model the stowage capacity related to well-defined areas inside the terminal. From a network perspective these terminal areas are also referred to as nodes of the terminal-related network.
- categorization of containers: if a container is empty or a full container, and for a full container a division is made according to its destination.

Combining the information of stowage volume and container category the intermodal terminal model can track the flow of containers of a particular class inside the terminal. The assumptions made in this work are intended to produce a general framework able to describe different terminal layouts.

The complexity of the terminal model is determined by the following parameters:

- n_t: number of container types considered in the transport network. A distinction is made between empty and full containers; full containers are further divided according to their final destination;

- n_c: number of different carriers served at the same time at the terminal. It is possible that a transport mode (deep sea, barge and trains) serves several carriers at the same time; for example more than one feeder or barge may be at the quay;
- n_a: number of terminal areas related specifically to one single carrier.

The terminal is considered divided in two main areas, see Fig. 1:

Import Operations: when a carrier arrives it brings containers that should be unloaded (unload demand – pushes containers to the terminal). The import flow starts at the *Unload Area* and goes until the *Import Area* at the *Central Yard* in Fig. 1;

Export Operations: when a load request for containers is assigned to a carrier (load demand – pulls containers from the terminal). In Fig. 1 starts from the *Export Area* and finishes at *Load Area*.

These two operations are the requested service the terminal should provide and are referred as a carrier service or demand. For each individual carrier a standard container flow is established consisting of the following operations:

1. unload the containers from the carrier according to the demand;
2. transport the containers from the *Unload Area* into the terminal *Import Area*;
3. rehandle the containers in the *Central Yard* from the *Import Area* to the *Export Area* according to the load demand;
4. take the containers from the *Export Area* to the *Load Area*;
5. load the containers into a carrier.

For the sake of simplicity and without loss of generality, according to this flow pattern the number of exclusive terminal areas per carrier $n_a = 5$ is assumed to be a fixed parameter in the model. This parameter can be made varying for each carrier to model different terminal layouts. The control action is the number of containers per container type to move between different terminal areas per unit time; that is the container flow. The unloading/loading of a container from/to a ship is done with the same resource (quay crane) while the transfer to/from the *Central Yard* is made by another resource (automated guided vehicle or other); this transport mode switch is realized at the *Import/Export Shake Hands* areas. The *Import Area* located at the *Central Yard* is a special area inside the terminal as it is the only area common to all carriers where containers are stacked and wait to be picked up by some shipper.

For each node in the terminal-related network a state-space vector $\bar{x}_i(k)$ is defined, and these are merged to form the state-space vector $x(k)$ of the complete terminal,

$$
\bar{x}_i(k) = \begin{bmatrix} x_i^1(k) \\ x_i^2(k) \\ \vdots \\ x_i^{n_t}(k) \end{bmatrix}, i = 1, \ldots, n_a n_c + 1, \quad x(k) = \begin{bmatrix} \bar{x}_1(k) \\ \bar{x}_2(k) \\ \vdots \\ \bar{x}_{n_a n_c + 1}(k) \end{bmatrix}, \quad (1)
$$

where $x_i^j(k)$ is the volume of containers of type j at node i at time instant k. The total number of nodes within a terminal network is associated with the number of carriers served and is given by $n_a n_c + 1$. The state-space $\mathbf{x}(k)$ dimension is given by $n_t(n_a n_c + 1)$ corresponding to the number of available destinations from the terminal and carriers served simultaneously. The model for the terminal dynamics can now be represented in a compact form as,

$$\mathbf{x}(k+1) = \mathbf{A}\mathbf{x}(k) + \mathbf{B}_u\mathbf{u}(k) + \mathbf{B}_w\mathbf{w}(k) \tag{2}$$
$$\mathbf{y}(k) = \mathbf{C}\mathbf{x}(k) \tag{3}$$
$$\mathbf{x}(k) \geq \mathbf{0}, \tag{4}$$
$$\mathbf{u}(k) \geq \mathbf{0}, \tag{5}$$
$$\mathbf{y}(k) \leq \mathbf{y}_{\max}, \tag{6}$$
$$\mathbf{P}_{uu}\mathbf{u}(k) \leq \mathbf{u}_{\max}, \tag{7}$$
$$\mathbf{x}(k) \geq \mathbf{P}_{xu}\mathbf{u}(k) \tag{8}$$
$$\mathbf{x}(k) \in \mathcal{X} \tag{9}$$
$$\mathbf{u}(k) \in \mathcal{U} \tag{10}$$

where $\mathbf{u}(k)$ is the control action vector with length $n_u \times 1$ with $n_u = n_t n_a n_c$, $\mathbf{w}(k)$ is a disturbance vector related to the arrival/departure schedule over time with dimension $2n_t n_c$, $\mathbf{y}(k)$ is the current ·container volume at all nodes with dimension $n_y = n_a n_c + 1$, $\mathbf{y}_{\max}$ are the maximum storage capacities of the terminal areas, $\mathbf{u}_{\max}$ the maximum handling capacities according to the terminal design, $\mathbf{A}, \mathbf{B}_u, \mathbf{B}_w$ and $\mathbf{C}$ are the state-space matrices, $\mathbf{P}_{xu}$ is the projection from the control action set $\mathcal{U}$ into the state-space set $\mathcal{X}$ and $\mathbf{P}_{uu}$ is the projection matrix from the control action set $\mathcal{U}$ into the maximum handling capacity set $\mathcal{U}_{\max}$.

The terminal state of $\mathbf{x}$ at the next time step, $k+1$, is determined using (2) as a function of the current terminal state $\mathbf{x}(k)$ plus the contribution due to the control action $\mathbf{u}(k)$ decided upon by the terminal manager and the corresponding disturbances $\mathbf{w}(k)$ capturing the arrival and departure of carriers. The model output $\mathbf{y}(k)$ can be chosen as a combination of the terminal areas state $\bar{\mathbf{x}}_i(k)$ through the use of matrix $\mathbf{C}$. The control action $\mathbf{u}(k)$ is the flow of containers between nodes and is imposed through a corresponding resource allocation. Disturbances are impulses happening in time instants related to the arrival and departure of carriers and with an intensity corresponding to the load/unload request for that carrier. Inequalities (4)–(8) are necessary in this framework for imposing the terminal structural layout and assumptions made:

Nonnegativity of States and Control Actions: negative storage is not physically possible, imposed by (4), and all decision variables are assumed to be nonnegative, this is guaranteed by (5);

Storage Capacity: each terminal area has to respect its own stowage capacity and this is represented by (6). Considering the terminal-related network in Fig. 1 it is important to note that different nodes may be associated to the same physical location. For example, the different state-space variables concerning *Import/Export Shake Hands* areas should be considered together as they are describing the same physical location, and naturally share the same constraints;

Maximum Handling Decisions: the terminal structural layout in terms of handling capacity and handling resource type used for the different container transfer inside the yard is represented by (7). Different terminal layouts can be easily translated into the model. For example, if the same handling resource is used for all terminal transfer operations [16] this will affect the projection matrix $\mathbf{P_{uu}}$;

Consistent Handling Decisions: not all handling decisions that satisfy (4) and (5) are allowed. The control action has to respect the existence of container type in the related terminal area and therefore equation (8) imposes this relation.

3 Model Predictive Control

Over the last decades Model Predictive Control (MPC) [9] has become an important strategy for finding control policies for complex, dynamic systems. MPC has shown successful applications in the process industry [9], and is now gaining increasing attention in fields like container terminals [2], power networks [6], water distribution networks [10] and road traffic networks [7].

MPC is an online optimization-based control approach that minimizes an objective function subject to constraints. The motivation for using such an approach arises from the following. In transport systems, costs can be associated to actions and states. Models can be constructed that describe how particular transport systems behave. By making predictions over a certain prediction horizon using these models, an MPC controller can determine which actions have to be chosen in order to obtain the best performance. An MPC controller determines which action to take at discrete control steps. At each control step the controller first obtains the current state of the system it controls using sensors, Fig. 2. It then formulates an optimization problem, using the desired goals existing constraints, disturbances and forecast information if available. The solution to the optimization problem determines the actions over the prediction horizon that give the best predicted performance. The controller implements these actions, using the existing actuators, until the beginning of the next control step, at which time the MPC controller repeats these steps in a receding horizon fashion, i.e., by obtaining new information about the current state and by reformulating the optimization problem starting from the next control step.

Cost Function: Terminal performance can be evaluated in different ways depending on the chosen perspective; the throughput of the terminal [1] or the customer satisfaction in terms of cost, time and service quality [15] are common choices. In this work we consider the throughput of the terminal as a performance index. With higher flows more competitive prices can be offered by the terminal managers in order to expand the market share and

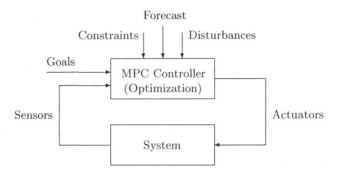

Fig. 2. Model predictive control structure

with that increase profit. The throughput can be increased by reducing the lay time of carriers, which increases the capacity available for receiving carriers. In our case, this performance index is translated into a mathematical representation using a weighted sum of the queues at the terminal areas while respecting the scheduled departure times. A weight $\mathbf{q}_i$ is associated at each sample time to the existing queues at each node,

$$\sum_{i=1}^{n_a n_c+1} \mathbf{q}_i^{\mathrm{T}}(k)\bar{\mathbf{x}}_i(k) = \left[\mathbf{q}_1^{\mathrm{T}}(k)\ \mathbf{q}_2^{\mathrm{T}}(k) \ldots \mathbf{q}_{n_a n_c+1}^{\mathrm{T}}(k)\right] \mathbf{x}(k) = \mathbf{q}_p^{\mathrm{T}}(k)\mathbf{x}(k)$$

(11)

where $\mathbf{q}_p$ can be time varying to allow changing the flow priorities according to the different terminal operation requests. Using this objective function it is possible to put different weights on different terminal areas, container types and carriers according to their role in the terminal dynamics and the desired strategic behavior. In this paper, we show that it is possible to act directly on the container flows inside the terminal. Flow priorities can be easily introduced in the optimization problem with a careful choice of weights, translating terminal operational requests into the optimization problem, namely:

- carriers can receive a higher priority according to the size of the requested operation;
- for the unloading and loading operations it is possible to define the desired order for handling each container type. This is particularly useful for letting the loading of empty containers be the last operation such that in case of a delay or anticipated departure the impact on transported cargo is bounded;
- any combination of priorities is possible. For example, in case of transshipment of one container type between two carriers simultaneously at the quay, maximum priority may be given for the pair container/carrier in the import area and minimum priority in the export area for the pair container/carrier such that the transhipment is fulfilled in the time window available.

The cost function is defined over the prediction horizon,

$$J(k) = \sum_{i=0}^{N-1} \mathbf{q}_p^T(k+1+i)\mathbf{x}(k+1+i), \tag{12}$$

where N is the length of the prediction horizon.

Constraints: constraints are necessary to incorporate into the optimization problem the terminal system dynamics (2)–(10). The loading request imposed by clients is introduced in the optimization problem through,

$$\mathbf{P}_{dx}\mathbf{x}(k) \leq \mathbf{w}_d(k) \tag{13}$$

where the forecast load request vector $\mathbf{w}_d(k+i)$ has to be updated at each sample time and $\mathbf{P}_{dx}$ is the projection matrix from the state-space set into the load request set.

MPC Problem Formulation: the MPC optimization problem can be formulated as:

$$\min_{\mathbf{u}(k)} \sum_{i=0}^{N-1} \mathbf{q}_p^T(k+1+i)\mathbf{x}(k+1+i) \tag{14}$$

$$\text{subject to} \quad \mathbf{x}(k+1+i) = \mathbf{A}\mathbf{x}(k) + \mathbf{B}_u\mathbf{u}(k) + \mathbf{B}_w\mathbf{w}(k), \tag{15}$$

$$\mathbf{y}(k+i) = \mathbf{C}\mathbf{x}(k), \quad i = 0,\dots,N-1, \tag{16}$$

$$\mathbf{x}(k+1+i) \geq \mathbf{0}, \tag{17}$$

$$\mathbf{u}(k+i) \geq \mathbf{0}, \tag{18}$$

$$\mathbf{y}(k+i) \leq \mathbf{y}_{max}, \tag{19}$$

$$\mathbf{P}_{uu}\mathbf{u}(k+i) \leq \mathbf{u}_{max}, \tag{20}$$

$$\mathbf{x}(k+i) \geq \mathbf{P}_{xu}\mathbf{u}(k+i), \tag{21}$$

$$\mathbf{P}_{dx}\mathbf{x}(k+1+i) \leq \mathbf{w}_d(k+1+i). \tag{22}$$

The problem is a constrained linear programming problem, due to the linear cost function and the existence of linear constraints.

4 Numerical Results

The presented framework is applied for a hinterland intermodal container terminal. Such a terminal is the basis of the hinterland transport network. Our focus is on considering the intermodal container transport problem as a network flow problem. We first define the throughput desired for the terminal in terms of import/export container flows, then the transport mode capacities available at the terminal and finally a fixed schedule for the hinterland transport mode connections is assumed to be imposed by shippers. The performance will be evaluated for two numerical experiments: a high-peak scenario and a long-term scenario.

Table 1. Hinterland terminal handling resources

Handling Resource	Maximum Flow	Handling Resource	Maximum Flow
Quay Cranes	90 TEUs/h	Quay - Yard	135 TEUs/h
Berth A	90 TEUs/h	Rehandling	190 TEUs/h
Berth B	45 TEUs/h	Train Gates - Yard	40 TEUs/h
Train Gate A	40 TEUs/h	Truck Gates - Yard	30 TEUs/h
Train Gate B	40 TEUs/h	Truck Gate	30 TEUs/h

4.1   Computational Scenario Design

Every intermodal container terminal faces two different types of flows:

Import Flow: all containers that are brought into the terminal by the available connections and that will be unloaded and stacked at the central yard waiting to be picked up by some other transport mode;

Export Flow: all containers that are waiting in the terminal and are redirected to an available connection proceeding towards the final destination.

It is assumed that the terminal will face an average week flow around 16,800 TEUs, divided smoothly into import and export flows. On a yearly basis the hinterland terminal will face a flow of 890×10^3 TEUs. Consider this terminal layout to face the desired yearly throughput:

- a quay area able to berth simultaneously two barges at maximum. Containers will be unloaded/loaded from/to barges by quay cranes. The maximum terminal capacity is of 90 TEUs/hour. In berth area A the maximum quay crane capacity of the terminal can be used while for berth area B only a handling capacity of 45 TEUs/hour is available;
- there are two rail tracks in the area reserved for the train transport mode. Containers will be unloaded/loaded from/to wagons using straddle carriers and a maximum capacity of 40 TEUs/hour is available;
- an area reserved for the truck transport mode is also included with a maximum capacity of serving 30 TEUs/hour in single mode.

The transport transfer between the quay and the *Central Yard* is implemented by the same handling resource. The rehandling of containers at the *Central Yard* from the *Import Area* to the *Export Area* (or in other words reshuffling containers to prepare the loading operation) is performed by a different handling resource. Trucks and trains have their own handling resources for unload/load operations and for transfer to/from the *Central Yard*. The terminal handling resources are given in Table 1. The available handling resources inside the terminal are expressed as flows (TEUs/unit time) in accordance with the flow perspective used for modeling the terminal. Concerning the storage capacities the *Central Yard* total capacity is considered sufficiently large to never restrict terminal operations. The *Import/Export Shake Hands* storage capacities are limited to the respective unload/load maximum capacity for each carrier: 90 TEUs for barge A,

Table 2. Hinterland transport mode split

Transport Mode	TEUs / week	TEUs / year	share
Barge	7, 200	382×10^3	42.9%
Train	3, 840	203×10^3	22.8%
Truck	5, 760	305×10^3	34.3%
Total	16, 800	890×10^3	100.0%

45 TEUs for barge B, 20 TEUs for train A, 20 TEUs for train B and 30 TEUs in single mode for trucks. These terminal areas can not be used for stowage purpose but only for internal transport transfer.

In order to respond to the desired hinterland container flows a network of connections and weekly schedules is created. We assume that the schedule is a result of agreements between the terminal and other actors in the transport network, and therefore the terminal has no permission to change it without consent. The following assumptions are made per transport mode:

Barges: this transport mode is characterized with uncertainty in its schedule and therefore we assume that three connections per day will be available in a 6 days week. An average handling of 280 TEUs/demand and 120 TEUs/demand for berth A and berth B, respectively, will be considered for numerical design;

Trains: two rail tracks are available that serve exclusively one train at the same time, the schedule for trains is assumed fixed and four canals for each rail track are available for a 6 days week. The maximum capacity per train is 40 TEUs;

Trucks: truck gates are only open for a 16 hour period on a 6 days week. The maximum served capacity during the day time is 500 TEUs.

According to the available connections and schedule the hinterland transport modal split is shown in Table 2 assuming maximum transport capacity for each transport mode.

For this terminal we assume that all carriers have an equal number of terminal areas, $n_a = 5$. Considering that the terminal is integrated in a transport network composed by 4 terminals the number of container classes is $n_t = 5$, including empty containers. Finally, the terminal is composed of 26 terminal areas and the terminal state-space vector is described by 130 states.

4.2 Simulation Configuration

The MPC controller is set to use a prediction horizon of 3 steps; the weights for the objective function are indicated in Table 3. The weight related to the *Import Area* at the *Central Yard* is kept neutral as it acts as a warehouse for containers between deliver and pick up times. The weights in the *Load Area* are taken negative, such that containers are pulled from the *Central Yard*. The minimum allowable prediction horizon is N = 3 as this is the number of time

Table 3. Weights used in the cost function (**1** stands for the column vector of length n_t with all entries with value 1)

Carrier	Unload Area	Import Shake Hands	Export Area	Export Shake Hands	Load Area
Barge A	[105 100 95 90 85]	$\mathbf{1}^T 5$	$\mathbf{1}^T 2$	$\mathbf{1}^T 2$	-[80 75 70 65 60]
Barge B	[55 55 45 45 45]	$\mathbf{1}^T 5$	$\mathbf{1}^T 2$	$\mathbf{1}^T 2$	-[40 35 35 35 20]
Train A	[50 30 30 30 30]	$\mathbf{1}^T 5$	$\mathbf{1}^T 2$	$\mathbf{1}^T 2$	-[15 15 15 15 10]
Train B	[25 25 25 25 25]	$\mathbf{1}^T 5$	$\mathbf{1}^T 2$	$\mathbf{1}^T 2$	-[15 15 15 15 5]
Trucks	[20 20 20 20 20]	$\mathbf{1}^T 5$	$\mathbf{1}^T 2$	$\mathbf{1}^T 2$	-[10 10 10 10 5]

steps needed to move containers from the *Import Area* to the *Load Area*. To assure the containers will be attracted towards the *Load Area* fulfilling the load request it is important to assure the following relation for each carrier,

$$- (\mathbf{q}_{3+i} + \mathbf{q}_{4+i}) > \sum_{j=1}^{N-2} \mathbf{q}_{5+i} \quad i = 0, \ldots, n_c - 1. \tag{23}$$

This means that the benefit of staying at the *Load Area*, during the prediction horizon, has to be greater than the penalty the container faces while moving from the *Import Area* at the *Central Yard* to the *Load area*.

According to Section 3 the weights are assigned to the cost function in order to impose container flow priorities related to the terminal strategic goals. We assume for this terminal that the goal is to serve the bigger calls first. The carriers served at the terminal in a decreasing order are: Barge A, Barge B, Train A, Train B and Trucks. The unload operation is always the first operation to do for each carrier and only after the conclusion of this operation the loading operation will begin. After defining the hierarchical relation between carriers further priorities are included in respect to the container type. Only the weights related to the unload and load areas are considered element wise to impose the desired order in which the containers should be unloaded and loaded.

The MPC optimization problem is solved at each time step of the simulation using the MPT v2.6.3 toolbox [8] with the CDD Criss–Cross solver for linear programming problems. The simulations are performed using MatLab R2009b on a personal computer with a processor Intel(R) Core(TM) i7 at 1.60GHz with 8GB RAM memory in a 64-bit Operating System.

Two scenarios are considered for the simulations: a high-peak flow scenario and a long-term scenario.

4.3 High-Peak Flow Scenario

In this scenario a challenging situation is created: all requests for one day start precisely at the same time. Although this is not a realistic scenario, it is appropriate for illustrating the framework ability to implement the desired priorities while respecting the constraints. The *Import Area* at the *Central Yard* is initialized with sufficient containers to fulfill all requests for loading containers. The

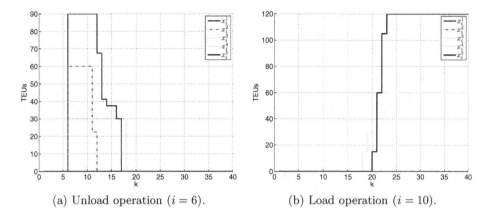

(a) Unload operation ($i = 6$).   (b) Load operation ($i = 10$).

Fig. 3. Evolution of container type unloaded/loaded to/into barge B for the high-peak scenario

departure of containers will not be executed to help visualize the terminal behavior. As a consequence the containers will be accumulated at the *Load Area*. In this congested situation the terminal operations management is put under severe pressure. All handling resources should be used to overcome this situation while respecting the carrier and container type priorities.

In Fig. 3 we see that the unloading and loading operation for barge B is done taking into account the container type priority. For the barge transport mode, depending on the size of the request, the time difference between unloading a given container type at the beginning or at the end of the scheduled time window may be important and have a significant impact on the *Central Yard* container flow management. The option to leave the empty containers as the last container type to load can reduce terminal costs in case of delays or anticipated departure.

Fig. 4 shows that the order by which the carriers are served is in agreement with the size of the unload/load operation request (Table 3). The transport modes by land – trains and trucks – are not affected by the quay congestion because they use different handling resources at the terminal regarding the connection to the *Central Yard*. This terminal is decomposed in three main areas associated to flows: quay–yard flows, train gates–yard and truck gates–yard . This decomposition is due to the terminal structural layout concerning the handling resources used to connect the different terminal areas.

With Fig. 5 we can track the evolution of container types at the *Central Yard*. In this scenario the total amount stacked at the *Import Area* faces a maximum increase around 900 TEUs. When looking in detail at the container type evolution only one container type – related to the location of the analyzed terminal – has a similar evolution. This is an improvement regarding the current situation that considers undistinguishable containers. In particular, it is possible for the strategic level to recognize the transport network routes that are facing more pressure and need a schedule enhancement.

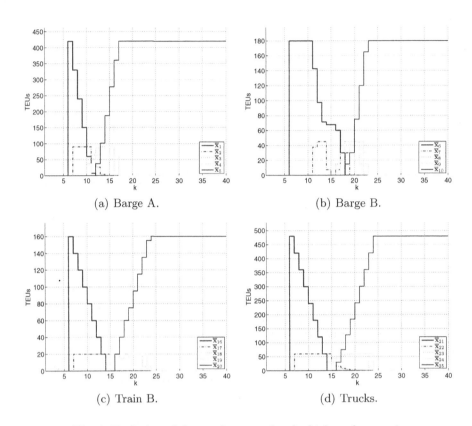

(a) Barge A.

(b) Barge B.

(c) Train B.

(d) Trucks.

Fig. 4. Evolution of the total storage for the high-peak scenario

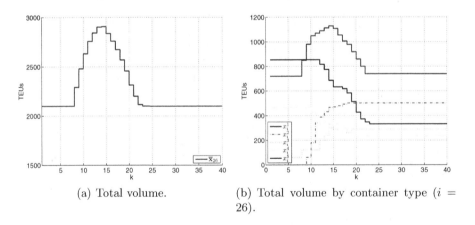

(a) Total volume.

(b) Total volume by container type ($i = 26$).

Fig. 5. Evolution of containers in the *Import Area* at the *Central Yard* for the high-peak scenario

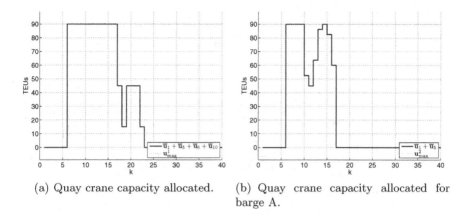

(a) Quay crane capacity allocated.   (b) Quay crane capacity allocated for barge A.

Fig. 6. Handling resources allocated for the high-peak scenario

In Fig. 6 we observe that all quay crane resources are firstly allocated to barge A. The transfer handling capacity between the quay and the *Central Yard* is at maximum capacity. So in this configuration introducing more quay crane capacity will not be translated in any terminal performance increase if a similar investment is not made for the transfer capacity between quay and *Central Yard*.

In this scenario the average computation time was 64.0 s with a standard deviation of 42.01 s. The maximum computation time occurred for $k = 14$ and took 244.09 s. This time step is close to the transition from unloading to loading operation for the majority of carriers at the terminal. The computation time is dependent on the problem complexity and also on the current terminal state.

4.4 Long-Term Scenario

This scenario represents one week. In this scenario it is assumed, in a sustainable environmental attitude, that all trains arriving and departing are at maximum capacity. This just requires more coordination from the terminal management and no loss of generality is produced. Trucks also deliver and pick up cargo simultaneously; there are no empty travels starting or ending at the terminal. Concerning barges, the call size is fixed according to the scenario presented in Section 4.1. The distribution between load and unload volumes is assumed random.

In Fig. 7 the containers evolution in the terminal are plotted for barges, train B and trucks. For the sake of clarity only the first 40 time iterations k are plotted, corresponding to almost two days of terminal operations management. Services concerning trains and trucks are periodic in volume as the load/unload volume is assumed constant and equal to the maximum transport mode capacity. For barges the scenario is not periodic due to the different distribution between load and unload demand for each service. For the time window shown in Fig. 7(a), barge A loading operation is finished two time step ahead of the departure time.

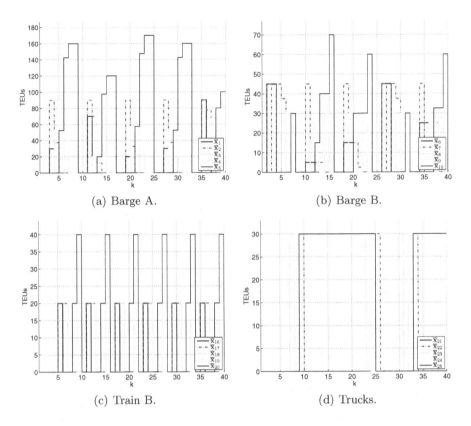

(a) Barge A.   (b) Barge B.

(c) Train B.   (d) Trucks.

Fig. 7. Evolution of the total storage for the long-term scenario

This means that the terminal can decrease the lay time of this carrier at the quay. The option to allow another carrier in berth A depends on the availability of handling resources at the terminal.

In Fig. 8(a) the current information about the *Import Area* state at the *Central Yard* is given in terms of undistinguishable containers, as is common in literature, while in Fig. 8(b) we have access to the current information about the container type. This is a new contribution regarding the current state and more information is available for the strategic level on a real time basis.

In Fig. 9 we see the allocated resources for quay–yard flows. The maximum resource availability at the quay is critical when a barge of type A is using full resource capacity at berth A. No resources are left to be used for berth B, which is assumed as a second priority regarding the terminal operations due to the call size. In Fig. 9(d) we see that the resource for transferring containers from the quay to the *Import Area* and from the *Export Area* to the quay is completely used. However, increasing the capacity of this resource has to be studied carefully as the quay crane capacity is also being used at full capacity during some time windows. Increasing the transfer capacity between the quay

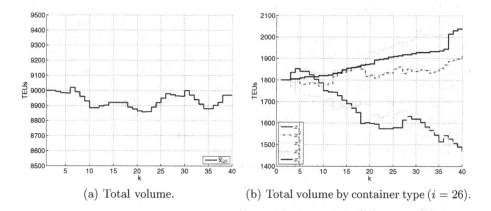

(a) Total volume.

(b) Total volume by container type ($i = 26$).

Fig. 8. Evolution of containers at the *Central Yard* for the long-term scenario

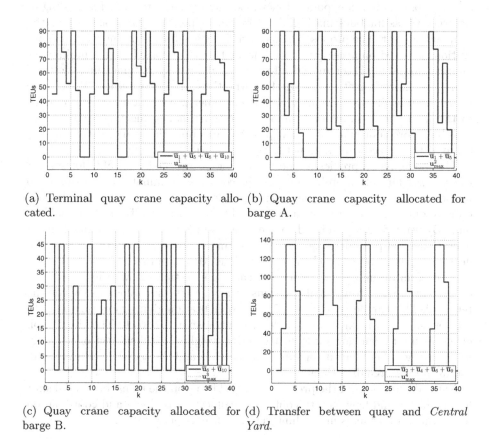

(a) Terminal quay crane capacity allocated.

(b) Quay crane capacity allocated for barge A.

(c) Quay crane capacity allocated for barge B.

(d) Transfer between quay and *Central Yard*.

Fig. 9. Handling capacities allocation for the long-term scenario

and the *Central Yard* may not be translated in a terminal throughput increase if similar increases are not made for different handling transfer resources. The fact that quay crane capacity allocated is zero during some time intervals gives the hint that the terminal is working bellow its maximum capacity. It will be possible with a different schedule of connections to be closer to the terminal maximum operating capacity. While doing so it is important to keep in mind the ability to react to some uncertainties in load and unload requests.

In this scenario the average computation time was 124.2 s with a standard deviation of 68.9 s. The maximum computation time was 382.9 s and the minimum computation time was 39.3 s. The computation time is dependent on the current terminal state and the load and unload demands.

5   Conclusions and Future Research

In this work we present a new perspective for looking at container terminal operations, based on a flow point of view. Containers are categorized according to criteria such as final destination, due time and type of cargo, depending on the terminal interest. The proposed framework for controlling container terminal operations is based on accessing more information than considering containers as undistinguishable. The required information about the container final destination is an improvement regarding the currently shared information. With more information available, without violating customer privacy, a different approach to the intermodal container terminal operations management is shown to be possible. More coordination is now possible regarding the goal of delivering the cargo at the agreed time and at the agreed location.

The model-based predictive control strategy is especially suitable for solving the resource allocation problem inside the container terminal. The possibility to include constraints in the optimization problem allows using all available handling resources at the terminal and the ability to consider different terminal layouts. By using forecasts related to client requests in terms of unloading/loading operations it is possible to accept updates in real-time and obtain the tactical decisions that respect the client request. The MPC approach through the resolution of an optimization problem in each sample time allows the translation of strategic goals into tactical decisions regarding resource allocation inside the terminal. This can be done in a real time configuration giving more flexibility to the terminal management as a node of the transport network. The translation of terminal strategic goals into cost function weights is still subject of research. Filling the gap between the operational decisions and the tactical goals is one of the future research directions.

Natural extensions of the present work will focus on the transport modal shift for the hinterland flow, empty container reallocation problem and coordination of intermodal terminals in the hinterland transport network.

Acknowledgements. This research is supported by the VENI project "Intelligent multi-agent control for flexible coordination of transport hubs" (project

11210) of the Dutch Technology Foundation STW, a subdivision of the Netherlands Organisation for Scientific Research (NWO) and by the Portuguese Government, through Fundação para a Ciência e a Tecnologia, under the project PTDC/EEACRO/102 102/2008 - AQUANET, through IDMEC under LAETA.

References

1. Alessandri, A., Cervella, C., Cuneo, M., Gaggero, M., Soncin, G.: Management of logistics operations in intermodal terminals by using dynamic modelling and nonlinear programming. Maritime Economics & Logistics 11, 58–76 (2009)
2. Alessandri, A., Sacone, S., Siri, S.: Modelling and optimal receding-horizon control of maritime container terminals. Journal of Mathematical Modelling and Algorithms 6, 109–133 (2007)
3. Baird, A.J.: Optimising the container transhipment hub location in northern Europe. Journal of Transport Geography 14(3), 195–214 (2006)
4. ESPO, Annual report 2006-2007. European Sea Ports Organisation, Technical report (2007)
5. Gambardella, L.M., Mastrolli, M., Rizzoli, A.E., Zaffalon, M.: An optimization methodology for intermodal terminal management. Journal of Intelligent Manufacturing 12, 521–534 (2004)
6. Geyer, T., Larsson, M., Morari, M.: Hybrid emergency voltage control in power systems. In: Proceedings of the European Control Conference, Cambridge, UK, paper 322 (2003)
7. Hegyi, A., De Schutter, B., Hellendoorn, J.: Optimal coordination of variable speed limits to supress schock waves. IEEE Transactions on Intelligent Transportation Systems 11(1), 102–112 (2005)
8. Kvasnica, M., Grieder, P., Baotić, M.: Multi-parametric toolbox, MPT (2004), http://control.ee.ethz.ch/~mpt/
9. Maciejowski, J.M.: Predictive control with constraints. Prentice Hall, Harlow (2002)
10. Negenborn, R.R., Van Overloop, P.J., Keviczky, T., De Schutter, B.: Distributed model predictive control of irrigation canals. Networks and Heterogeneous Media 4, 359–380 (2009)
11. Nieuwsblad Transport: Contargo voert congestietoslag (July 16, 2007)
12. Notteboom, T., Winkelmans, W.: Factual report on the European port sector. Report commissioned by European Sea Ports Organisation, ESPO (2004)
13. Stahlbock, R., Voß, S.: Operations research at container terminals - a literature update. OR Spectrum 30, 1–52 (2008)
14. Vis, I.F., de Koster, R., Savelsbergh, M.W.P.: Minimum vehicle fleet size under time-window constraints at container terminal. Transportation Science 39, 249–260 (2005)
15. Wang, T.-F., Cullinane, K.: The efficiency of European container terminals and implications for supply chain management. Maritime Economics and Logistics 8, 82–99 (2006)
16. Zehendner, E., Absi, N., Dauzère-Pérès, S., Feillet, D.: Solving the Resource Allocation Problem in a Multimodal Container Terminal as a Network Flow Problem. In: Böse, J.W., Hu, H., Jahn, C., Shi, X., Stahlbock, R., Voß, S. (eds.) ICCL 2011. LNCS, vol. 6971, pp. 341–353. Springer, Heidelberg (2011)

Impact of Port Disruption on Supply Chains: A Petri Net Approach

Jasmine Siu Lee Lam[1] and Tsz Leung Yip[2,*]

[1] Division of Infrastructure Systems and Maritime Studies, School of Civil and Environmental Engineering, Nanyang Technological University, 50 Nanyang Avenue, Singapore 639798
`sllam@ntu.edu.sg`
[2] C.Y. Tung International Centre for Maritime Studies, Department of Logistics and Maritime Studies, Faculty of Business, The Hong Kong Polytechnic University, Hung Hom, Hong Kong
`lgttly@polyu.edu.hk`

Abstract. Seaports play the roles as nodes for maritime and multimodal transport in both inbound and outbound logistics processes and as logistical platforms where logistics-related activities occur. These logistical platforms are important and indispensable for the effective and efficient management of flows of materials, products and information in the supply chain management. However, any disruptions at a port can have direct impact on the port's ability to continue operations, therefore affect the supply chains and the parties served by the port. The research devotes to the study of the impact of port disruption on supply chains. It aims to illustrate the application of the Petri Net approach in analysing the impact of port disruption on supply chains and the parties involved. The paper shows that a Petri Net model can provide stepwise processes and an efficient environment for conducting simulation and other analyses on the study topic.

Keywords: port disruption, supply chain, logistics, Petri Net, simulation.

1 Introduction

Seaports play the key role of global transport facilitators in both inbound and outbound supply chains, and are thus important to global and regional economic activities. A port that is able to meet the evolving requirements of supply chain management can ensure that its value chain system remains competitive and enables the comparative and competitive advantages of the system's hinterlands to be attained. The role of the port is therefore essential since port systems and operations are important and indispensable for the effective and efficient management of flows of cargo in the supply chain. However, any disruptions affecting one port anywhere along the supply chain can have a direct effect on the supply chain ability to continue operations, get the goods to market and provide services to customers.

Since about 90% of the world trade volume is carried by maritime transport, the majority of the supply chains involve seaports in the trade flows. For maritime trade,

H. Hu et al. (Eds.): ICCL 2012, LNCS 7555, pp. 72–85, 2012.

there is hardly any supply chain involving overseas sourcing or markets that will function without a port. Ports' functions vary and their impacts on supply chains are different. The most interesting issue is to develop a concept for a general port disruption in the supply chain system. A major port disruption may lead to a collapse of the whole supply chain system. This paper discusses port disruption and aims to better understand the impact of such disruption on supply chains.

In this paper, the definition of disruption is an event that causes a sudden interruption on material or product flow in a supply chain, leading to a halt in movement of cargoes (Wilson, 2007). Such a port disruption is possible in many events, for example, a port accident (e.g. ship collision), terrorist or political acts, natural hazards (e.g. earthquake, hurricanes) and breakdown of port equipment. A port disruption may result in long delays of material flow at ports and then enormous adverse impacts on multiple elements of a supply chain simultaneously.

Petri Nets (Petri, 1962), as a graphical and mathematical tool, have been successfully used in risk management. Petri Nets offer the flexibility to simulate a complex system, like supply chain network. Therefore, we attempt to use Petri Nets as the modelling tool of a supply chain system of multiple ports. The study aims to illustrate the application of the Petri Net approach in analysing the impact of port disruption on supply chain and the parties involved. By extending the Petri Net model to the supply chain system, one will be able to assess the impact due to port disruption.

This paper is divided into four main sections. This section has given the background to port disruption and introduced the research problem. Section 2 reviews previous studies on port disruption, their relationship with supply chain management and the Petri Nets. Section 3 presents the methodology used, case study and modelling. Section 4 concludes the paper.

2   Literature Review

2.1   Port Disruption and Supply Chains

The world economy has become more interconnected since the era of globalization. In recent years, the maritime industry is also progressing towards higher degree of supply chain integration (Lam, 2012a). However, in a more interconnected global supply chain, a disruption at any stage of the chain leads to a domino effect on the rest of the parties and the impact can span several continents. Ports and shipping as vital trade facilitators and components of supply chains are among the most significant causes for uncertainty (Sanchez-Rodrigues et al., 2010). Ports and shipping, when compared to other transportation contexts, are more international and have more interfaces with other stages and members in the supply chains which represent potential weak points. But the related risk issues have only been researched on a limited scale.

We found a few research studies on port disruption in the literature. Chang (2000) analysed Kobe's earthquake in Japan occurred in 1995 and found that the disaster was detrimental to the port's traffic including losing a substantial share of transhipment traffic. Focusing on man-made risk, the economic impact of the shutdown of Los Angeles and Long Beach ports due to terrorist attack was studied by Rosoff and von Winterfeldt (2007) and Park (2008). They showed that such port disruption generated major economic losses and widespread State-to-State trade interruptions. Focusing on major accidents in port area, Ronza et al. (2009) developed a procedure to estimate the cost of damages suffered by people, equipment and environment. The study by Paul and Maloni (2010) simulated the effects of port disasters through case studies of the North American container port network. To the authors' knowledge, only one port related study is related to supply chains. Gurning and Cahoon (2011) analysed multiple mitigation strategies for managing maritime disruptions in the wheat supply chain. Nevertheless, they did not specifically study port and how disruption affects the various stages and parties in a supply chain. Furthermore, due to the increasing level of sophistication in global supply chain networks nowadays and the dynamic behaviour in association with risks, we propose the Petri Nets method which can better accommodate complex systems compared to Markov chain used by Gurning and Cahoon (2011). As a whole, it is observed that port disruption and risk study is relatively new which started from the last decade. More research with greater depth should be undertaken to better understand this emerging and important topic. After discussing the state of the literature in the research topic, the following section reviews the Petri Nets method that will be applied in this study.

2.2   Petri Nets and Its Applications

The concept of Petri Nets (PN) is originally developed by Carl Adam Petri (1962) as a general purpose mathematical tool for the study of communication with automata. Petri Nets method is characterized by its ability to model and visualize the properties of complex systems such as process synchronization, asynchronous events, concurrent operations and conflicts or resource sharing (Zurawski and Zhou, 1994). This feature effectively enables the modeling of almost any kind of discrete event systems. The concept and application of discrete event systems are relevant in many aspects of various industries, including communication protocols, manufacturing systems, supply chains and transportation. The modeling and analysis of communication protocols (Diaz, 1982; Berthomieu and Diaz, 1991) and manufacturing systems (Zhou and di Cesare, 1993) are among the most successful application areas of PN.

Applications of PN in transportation and supply chains, on the other hand, are relatively new and underdeveloped. Nevertheless, the limited amount of study on transportation and supply chains has shown the potential of PN and its various extensions for describing the complex and dynamic behaviors of such network systems. For example, Febbraro and Sacco (2004) employed a hybrid Petri Nets comprised of a discrete and a continuous component to model the traffic flow of road intersections in urban transportation networks, which exhibits good model efficacy. Dotoli and Fanti (2006) proposed an alternative method using colored timed PN to model the traffic networks problem with a proved improvement on the description power of PN. Another study on traffic flow performance can be found in

Tolba et al. (2005), where the analogy between continuous and discrete behavior of traffic networks and PN with extensions is discovered and exploited. In air transport, PN is shown to be an effective tool for modeling and analyzing air cargo terminal operations (Lee et al., 2006), as well as optimization of air traffic (Davidrajuh and Lin, 2011). An interesting study was conducted by Dotoli et al. (2010), in which the authors presented a modeling technique for intermodal transportation systems (ITS) containing timed PN framework. The study showed that an integrated ITS with modern Information and Communication Technologies can significantly improve utilization of system resources with lower cost.

The application of Petri Nets on risk management in transportation and supply chains is an even more immature area, since most studies do not take disruptive factors into consideration (Tuncel and Alpan, 2010). As such, it is of great interest, to the academia and industry alike, to explore the applications of Petri Nets in stochastic systems. In particular, uncertainty and stochastic behaviors can be effectively captured by an extension called stochastic timed Petri Nets. The existing literature on this extension is rather limited. Blackhurst et al. (2006) developed a hierarchical Petri Net extension for conflict detection of integrated supply chain systems. The method permits a high-level customizable interface for the supply chain management process, which is one of the major advantages of incorporating Petri Nets method. Wu et al. (2007) and Zegordi and Davarzani (2012) applied Petri Nets concept with different extensions in supply chain disruption analysis. Both methods demonstrate the capability of tracing the propagation of disruptions, which can shed some light on the actual risk assessment process of disruptions. Cheng and Yang (2009) adopted a fuzzy Petri Net approach to model and complement the decision rules of train dispatchers to assure the service quality of the railway system against abnormal conditions. Rossi et al. (2005) and Tuncel and Alpan (2010) incorporated PN in formal risk analysis, assessment and management process for supply chain networks. Time is an important factor in risk management related to transportation. However, only one of the studies (Tuncel and Alpan, 2010) mentioned above has taken the time factor into consideration by employing a timed PN framework. Moreover, none of the studies attempts to capture the complexity and dynamics of transportation networks. We also do not find any analysis on port and maritime transport disruption in respect of supply chain risk. The major advantages of PN are its graphic interface which allows tracking of material and information flows, and its strong mathematical foundation which provides the opportunity for software development. Such a tool, once developed, can significantly benefit the risk management process for intermodal transportation systems and have a wide range of other industrial implications.

3   Timed Petri Nets Modelling of Port Disruption

Considering the merits of the PN method, this study takes the first step among research studies in applying the PN approach in analysing the impact of port disruption on supply chains and the parties involved. The role of seaports as key logistical platforms is important and indispensable for the effective and efficient management of flows of materials, products and information in the supply chain. However, any disruptions at a port can have direct impact on the port's ability to continue operations, therefore affect the supply chains and the parties served by the port (Lam, 2012b). To include the time factor, this study has chosen stochastic timed PN as a modelling and analyzing tool. The graphic and mathematical modelling can provide the system designer a uniform environment for analyzing each individual process in the supply chain. A case will be explained in detail to illustrate the stochastic timed PN modelling of port disruption below.

3.1   Case Study

The selected focal seaport in this study is Shenzhen (SZ), which is located in the south of the Pearl River Delta in China. Shenzhen was designated as a Special Economic Zone started in 1979 to promote foreign investment in mainland China. With China acting as the *'factory of the world'*, the manufacturing industry has created a huge demand on maritime trade. The Pearl River Delta is a key manufacturing base which is also home to fast growing seaports and river ports serving the region. The port of Shenzhen is the world's 4th busiest port in terms of container throughput handled in 2011 (WSC, 2011). The port comprises of 176 berths and a part of 230 international container routes. Shenzhen serves numerous global and regional supply chains and is considered an interesting case for studying the impact of port disruption on supply chain.

In addition to its significant role and cargo volume handled, the study of Shenzhen Port is also motivated by its exposure to both human risks and non-human risks with reference to historical records. The port employees of Shenzhen called for more safety protection at workplace and an extended insurance coverage because of the potential danger of working in the port area (OCI, 2007). Port workers also expressed concerns on their salary and welfare along the years. In 2007, strikes occurred in the three major terminals, namely Shekou, Yantian and Chiwan, involving 300 cranes operators and truck drivers and thus causing the delay of at least 10,000 containers (Tan, 2007). Strikes were on the rising trend in Shenzhen (CLB, 2009). The vice-chairman of the Shenzhen Federation of Trade Unions remarked that strikes were *"as natural as arguments between a husband and wife"* (SMD, 2008). Hence, it is evidential that labour strikes would be a kind of disruptive risk in Shenzhen Port.

Regarding non-human risks, natural catastrophes are seen as events having low probability of occurrence. However, the impact of such catastrophes is usually very high (Knemeyer et al., 2009). Furthermore, the occurrence and severity of catastrophes has intensified over the years in light of anthropogenic climate change and global warming (Ermoliev et al., 2000). There is an increase in economic losses from weather- and climate-related disasters and the estimates of world annual losses have been around US$200 billion during 1980s-2010 (IPCC 2011). Munich Re (2012) reported that the overall earthquakes and weather-related catastrophes in 2011 are the costliest year ever, recorded a total natural catastrophe losses at about US$380 billion and total insured losses of US$105 billion (Munich Re, 2012). The Tohoku earthquake in March 2011 damaged not only Japanese seaports but also long distance seaports in California. As for Shenzhen, it is in a typhoon-prone area especially in the summer season (EM-DAT, 2012). Therefore, various kinds of natural hazards present certain risk in Shenzhen Port.

There are many other kinds of risk such as equipment breakdown, electrical outages and industrial accidents which can lead to port disruption. The factors causing port disruption can be identified as stimulators (Merrick et al., 2002). Identifying risks is usually the first step in developing a risk management process (Manuj and Mentzer, 2008). Wagner and Bode (2006) illustrated disruption as an unintended, untoward situation that contributes to risks in supply chain management and it is an exceptional and irregular situation compared to daily business. Disruption is a function of probability and consequences involving estimation (Sheffi and Rice, 2005). While the above discussion has shed light on the casual factors that may lead to port disruption in Shenzhen, there is uncertainty in risk exposure with regards to the precise likelihood of occurrence, timing and consequences since risk is considered to be unanticipated. Due to the inherent nature of uncertainty in risk studies, it is not our focus to predict port disruption, but to present a versatile modeling tool so that any risk level can be taken into consideration and any port can be studied. PN based simulation analysis will be able to fulfill such requirement effectively.

3.2   Modeling

In the first step, we translate a multi-modal and multi-port supply chain system into a PN model given by Figure 1. The entire process from the material supplier to the end product customer can be traced. Raw materials are imported from the port of Kaohsiung as an example, i.e., a supplier is located in Kaohsiung and it is also the export port. International shipping carries the cargoes (raw materials) to Shenzhen which is the focal port representing the import port for raw materials. Inland transport carries these cargoes to the manufacturer in SZ. After the manufacturing process, the finished products are carried by inland transport to SZ Port for export. In other words, SZ also serves as the export port for finished products. Then international shipping carries the cargoes (finished products) to a customer in Long Beach which is the import port for finished products.

In the second step, for analyzing the effects generated from port disruptive events, we involve the risk factors into the PN model by specifying events in the port characterized by a probability of occurrence. Timed PN based simulation can observe the cause and effect relationships among port disruptive events and the supply chain process using performance measurement regarding different scenarios. Plenty of outputs can be generated according to the needs of decision makers for risk management purpose.

In a PN model, events that may occur are known as transitions (signified by bars) and conditions are represented as places (signified by circles). The directed arcs link up the transitions and places to show the process (signified by arrows). In stochastic timed PN, transitions have probabilistic firing conditions or stochastic firing times. The expression for places and transitions can be constructed using standard programming language such as C and C++. Tables 1 to 4 are used to summarize the general execution process and give the detailed interpretation of each place and transition in each stage of the supply chain system.

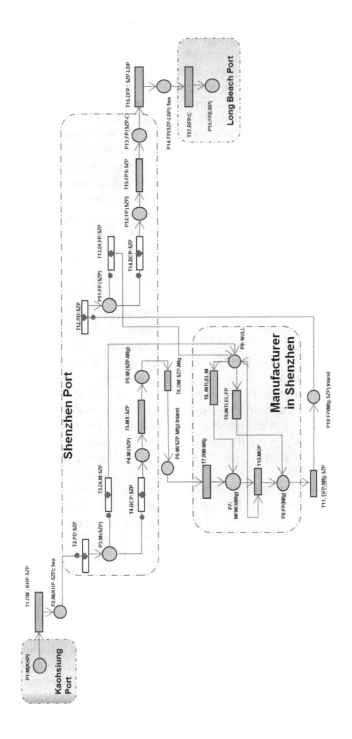

Note: circle = place; rectangle = transition; ◆ = disruption

Fig. 1. Petri Nets model of the multimodal and multi-port supply chain system

Figure 1 may look like a fault tree at the first sight. Different from the fault tree, Figure 1 includes the logical functions and time factor of basic disruption events in the port network, which is very useful for the analysis of sequences and timing of events due to a disruption.

As a major gateway port, Shenzhen serves the inbound and outbound logistics of numerous supply chains. As shown in Figure 2 and Table 1, we model that the occurrence of port disruption happening in SZ Port (transition 2 PD:SZP) after the raw materials are transported by sea, represented by P2:M(KHP-SZP):Sea in Table 2. The flexibility of the method enables any types of risk to be modelled. Here we take typhoon as an example of natural hazard. The potential impacts of port disruption on various parties in the supply chain are considered. The major parties include manufacturers, shipping companies, inland transport providers and customers importing finished products. Safety is the most important concern in shipping companies' operations and a key determinant whether they continue to call at a port (Lam, 2012b). For serious port disruption, carriers would bypass intended ports-of-call that are disrupted and a chain of effects on carriers and shipping operations such as lower schedule reliability, higher fuel costs, longer transit time may occur. Hence, transition 2 can model that cargoes do not arrive at the port if the ship carrying the cargoes is re-routed.

If the cargoes arrive safely, there can be two possibilities. First, the materials may be damaged or lost if the disruption such as typhoon hits the cargo directly. Hence after P3:M(SZP), one directed arc leads to transition 3 (DLM:SZP) in Figure 2. Then the impact of such port disruption on the manufacturer's inbound logistics in the supply chain is: manufacturer has to use existing inventory to continue with the production. But if there is insufficient inventory, the production schedule would be delayed. No matter if there is adequate inventory, the manufacturer will have to replenish inventory since the material is damaged/lost. Thus, after transition 3 in port (DLM:SZP), transition 8 in manufacturer (INTEL:M) happens which is setting up inventory level of material. All the possible actions required with regards to material inventory held by manufacturer can be modeled in transition 8.

The second possibility after port disruption by typhoon is no cargo damage but a halt in port operations and cargo flow. Thus the other directed arc leads to transition 4 (BCP:SZP) which is the time when the port tries to resume port operations. Then material will be staying in port which is represented by transition 5 (MS:SZP). Various effects on supply chains can be simulated with different number of days of port disruption. After the port backup time, the material can be delivered by inland transport to manufacturer for production. The inland transport is shown by transition 6 and place 6. For example, if there is significant delay in production schedule due to a major port disruption, manufacturer can still fulfil customer demand on finished product if there is sufficient inventory. Otherwise, overseas customer in Long Beach cannot receive the product on time. All the possible actions required with regards to finished product's inventory held by manufacturer can be modeled in transition 9 (INTEL:FP). Inland transport operators are also inevitably affected and the impacts would include longer waiting time, re-routing, longer transit time and missed connections among others.

Considering outbound logistics for finished products after the manufacturing process, cargoes are sent by inland transport operators to SZ Port as can be seen from transition 11 (DFP:Mfg-SZP) and place 10 (FP(Mfg-SZP):Inland). Transition 12 (PD:SZP) models port disruption that occurs in outbound logistics of the supply chain. Similar to the inbound logistics portion, cargoes may be damaged/ lost (transition 13 DLFP:SZP) or there can be a halt in the product flow (transition 15 FPS:SZP). After the cargoes are damaged/ lost, the manufacturer has to manufacture the products again so the directed arc goes back to place 9 and then the inventory will be set up. The chain of events can be modeled like the illustrations as given above in inbound logistics. We would like to highlight that port disruption occurred in inbound logistics may affect outbound logistics and vice versa.

Table 1. Interpretation of transitions connected to and from Shenzhen Port and operations in the port

Coding Number	Transition Name	Description
1	T1:DM:KHP-SZP	Deliver material: from Supplier in Kaohsiung to Manufacturer in Shenzhen
2	T2:PD:SZP	Port disruption in Shenzhen Port
3	T3:DLM:SZP	Damage or loss of material in Shenzhen Port
4	T4:BCP:SZP	Back up the port disruption (attempt to resume port operations)
5	T5:MS:SZP	Material staying at Shenzhen Port during the backup time of Shenzhen port disruption
6	T6:DM:SZP-Mfg	Deliver material: from Shenzhen Port to Manufacturer
12	T12:PD:SZP	Port disruption in Shenzhen Port
13	T13:DLFP:SZP	Damage or loss of finished product in Shenzhen Port
14	T14:BCP:SZP	Back up the port disruption (attempt to resume port operations)
15	T15:FPS:SZP	Finished product staying at Shenzhen Port during the backup time of Shenzhen port disruption
16	T16:DFP:SZP-LBP	Deliver finished product: from Shenzhen Port to customer in Long Beach
17	T17:RFP:C	Receiving finished product at customer in Long Beach

Table 2. Interpretation of places connected to and from Shenzhen Port and operations in the port

Coding Number	Place Name	Description
1	P1:M(KHP)	Material at Supplier's port (Kaohsiung)
2	P2:M(KHP-SZP):Sea	Material on the way from Kaohsiung Port to Shenzhen Port (Sea transportation)
3	P3:M(SZP)	Material staying in Shenzhen Port
4	P4:M(SZP)	Material waiting for backup in Shenzhen Port
5	P5:M(SZP-Mfg)	Material ready to be delivered from Shenzhen Port to Manufacturer
6	P6:M(SZP-Mfg):Inland	Material on the way from Shenzhen Port to Manufacturer (Inland transportation)
11	P11:FP (SZP)	Finished product staying in Shenzhen Port
12	P12:FP (SZP)	Finished product waiting for backup in Shenzhen Port
13	P13:FP (SZP-C)	Finished product ready to be delivered from Shenzhen Port to Customer
14	P14:FP(SZP-LBP):Sea	Finished product on the way from Shenzhen Port to Long Beach Port (Sea transportation)
15	P15:FP(LBP)	Finished product at Customer's port (Long Beach)

Table 3. Interpretation of transitions in Manufacturer

Coding Number	Transition Name	Description
7	T7:RM:Mfg	Receiving material at Manufacturer
8	T8:INTLEL:M	Setting up inventory level of material
9	T9:INTLEL:FP	Setting up inventory level of finished product

Table 3. (*continued*)

| 10 | T10:MOP | Manufacturing operation for product |
| 11 | T11:DFP:Mfg-SZP | Deliver finished product: from Manufacturer to Shenzhen Port |

Table 4. Interpretation of places in Manufacturer

Coding Number	Place Name	Description
7	P7:MFMO(Mfg)	Material for manufacturing operation in Manufacturer
8	P8:FP(Mfg)	Finished product in Manufacturer
9	P9:NULL	NULL
10	P10:FP(Mfg-SZP):Inland	Finished product on the way from Manufacturer to Shenzhen Port (Inland transportation)

4   Conclusions

This conceptual paper is our first attempt to develop a Petri Nets model for studying the dynamic behaviour of the supply chain system due to port disruption. The investigation uses the Petri Nets model to combine two elements (a) the framework structure of supply chain, and (2) the cause-and-effect structure for analysis. Since the Petri Nets are more sophisticated than the standard risk assessment techniques (e.g. fault tree, event tree), they enable a new and richer insight in supply chain system behaviour. The study shows that Petri Nets model can provide stepwise processes and an efficient environment for conducting simulation and other analyses on the study topic. It can be seen that the impact of port disruption propagates in the supply chain which can be very extensive and complicated. Thus a detailed study in analysing the impact would be highly valuable to various supply chain parties for risk management purposes. The paper has illustrated a scientific and replicable research process on assessing and managing port disruptions. The approach undertaken by this study is widely applicable to any ports. The flexibility of the method also enables any types of risk to be modelled.

Future work of this research will study various supply chain systems with dynamic and more complex port disruptions. To avoid any alternative ports being hit by the same incident, a possible option for ports is to partner up with a neighbour port. When a disruption occurs at the regional level (e.g. earthquake, nuclear crisis), the transport and supply chain network may be reconfigured. Another line of future research is to conduct computational experiments and to develop migration strategies at the port and regional levels for different scenarios. Computational experiments can be further conducted to evaluate the overall mitigation strategies applied to a combination of disruptions at all levels.

Acknowledgements. This research is partially funded by Singapore MOE AcRF project, NTU ref: RF20/10 and The Hong Kong Polytechnic University under Grant Number: A-PL05.

References

1. Berthomieu, B., Diaz, M.: Modeling and verification of time dependent systems using time Petri nets. IEEE Transactions on Software Engineering 17(3), 259–273 (1991)
2. Blackhurst, J., Wu, T., Craighead, C.W.: A systematic approach for supply chain conflict detection with a hierarchical Petri net extension. Omega 36(5), 680–696 (2006)
3. Chang, S.E.: Disasters and transport systems: loss, recovery and competition at the Port of Kobe after the 1995 earthquake. Journal of Transport Geography 8(1), 53–65 (2000)
4. Cheng, Y., Yang, L.: A fuzzy Petri nets approach for railway traffic control in case of abnormality: evidence from Taiwan railway system. Expert Systems with Applications 36(4), 8040–8048 (2009)
5. China Labour Bulletin: Going It Alone, The Workers' Movement in China (2007-2008) (2009), http://www.clb.org.hk (accessed March 15, 2012)
6. Davidrajuh, R., Lin, B.: Exploring airport traffic capability using Petri net based model. Expert Systems with Applications 38(9), 10923–10931 (2011)
7. Diaz, M.: Modeling and analysis of communication and cooperation protocols using Petri net based models. Computer Networks 6(6), 419–441 (1982)
8. Dotoli, M., Fanti, M.P.: An urban traffic network model via colored timed Petri nets. Control Engineering Practice 14(10), 1213–1229 (2006)
9. Dotoli, M., Fanti, M.P., Mangini, A.M., Stecco, G., Ukovich, W.: The impact of ICT on intermodal transportation systems: a modeling approach by Petri nets. Control Engineering Practice 18(8), 893–903 (2010)
10. EM-DAT: Natural Disasters Trends (2012), http://www.emdat.be/natural-disasters-trends (accessed March 30, 2012)
11. Ermoliev, Y.M., Ermolieva, T.Y., MacDonald, G.J., Norkin, V.I., Amendola, A.: A system approach to management of catastrophic risks. European Journal of Operational Research 122(1), 452–460 (2000)
12. Febbraro, A.D., Sacco, N.: On modeling urban transportation networks via hybrid Petri nets. Control Engineering Practice 12(10), 1225–1239 (2004)
13. Gurning, S., Cahoon, S.: Analysis of multi-mitigation scenarios on maritime disruptions. Maritime Policy and Management 38(3), 251–268 (2011)
14. IPCC: Summary for Policymakers: Intergovernmental Panel on Climate Change Special Report on Managing the Risks of Extreme Events and Disasters to Advance Climate Change Adaptation. Cambridge University Press, Cambridge (2011)
15. Knemeyer, A.M., Zinn, W., Eroglu, C.: Proactive planning for catastrophic events in supply chains. Journal of Operations Management 27(2), 141–153 (2009)

16. Lam, J.S.L.: Benefits and barriers of supply chain integration: Empirical analysis of liner shipping. International Journal of Shipping and Transport Logistics (in press, 2012a)

17. Lam, J.S.L.: Risk management in maritime logistics and supply chains. In: Song, D.W., Panayides, P.M. (eds.) Maritime Logistics: Contemporary Issues, Emerald, pp. 117–132 (2012b)

18. Lee, C., Huang, H.C., Liu, B., Xu, Z.: Development of timed Colour Petri net simulation models for air cargo terminal operations. Computers and Industrial Engineering 51(1), 102–110 (2006)

19. Manuj, I., Mentzer, J.T.: Global supply chain risk management. Journal of Business Logistics 29(1), 133–156 (2008)

20. Merrick, J.R.W., Van-Dorp, J.R., Mazzuchi, T., Har, J.R.: The Prince William Sound risk assessment. Interfaces 32(6), 25–40 (2002)

21. Munich Re: (2012), http://www.munichre.com (accessed March 16, 2012)

22. OCI (Office of the Commissioner of Insurance): Extended insurance coverage to the Shenzhen Bay Port Hong Kong Port Area (June 25, 2007), http://www.oci.gov.hk/download/pr_20070625.pdf (accessed February 15, 2012)

23. Park, J.: The economic impacts of dirty bomb attacks on the Los Angeles and Long Beach Ports: Applying the supply-driven NIEMO (National Interstate Economic Model). Journal of Homeland Security and Emergency Management 5(1), 1–20 (2008)

24. Petri, C.: Kommunikation mit Autimaten. PhD dissertation, University of Bonn (1962)

25. Rosoff, H., von Winterfeldt, D.: A risk and economic analysis of dirty bomb attacks on the ports of Los Angeles and Long Beach. Risk Analysis 27(3), 533–546 (2007)

26. Rossi, T., Noe, C., Dallari, F.: A formal method for analyzing and assessing operational risk in supply chains. In: Proceedings of the 23rd International Conference of the System Dynamics Society, Boston (2005)

27. Sanchez-Rodrigues, V., Potter, A., Naim, M.M.: Evaluating the causes of uncertainty in logistics operations. International Journal of Logistics Management 21(1), 45–64 (2010)

28. Sheffi, Y., Rice, J.B.: A supply chain view of the resilient enterprise. MIT Sloan Management Review 47(1), 41–48 (2005)

29. SMD (Southern Metropolis Daily): Shenzhen trade union sees strikes as a natural phenomenon, Southern Metropolis Daily (April 15, 2008)

30. Tan, X.: Port salary dispute resolved (April 9, 2007), http://www.newsgd.com/citiesandtowns/shenzhen/news/200704090 026.html (accessed February 15, 2012)

31. Tolba, C., Lefebvre, D., Thomas, P., Moudni, A.E.: Continuous and timed Petri nets for the macroscopic and microscopic traffic flow modeling. Simulation Modelling Practice and Theory 13(5), 407–436 (2005)

32. Tuncel, G., Alpan, G.: Risk assessment and management for supply chain networks: A case study. Computers in Industry 61(3), 250–259 (2010)

33. Wagner, S.M., Bode, C.: An empirical investigation into supply chain vulnerability. Journal of Purchasing and Supply Management 12(6), 301–312 (2006)

34. Wilson, M.C.: The impact of transportation disruptions on supply chain performance. Transportation Research Part E 43(4), 295–320 (2007)

35. WSC (World Shipping Council): Top 50 World Container Ports (2011), http://www.worldshipping.org/about-the-industry/global-trade/top-50-world-container-ports (accessed March 16, 2012)

36. Wu, T., Blackhurst, J., O'Grady, P.: Methodology for supply chain disruption analysis. International Journal of Production Research 45(7), 1665–1682 (2007)
37. Zegordi, S.H., Davarzani, H.: Developing a supply chain disruption analysis model: Application of colored Petri-nets. Expert Systems with Applications 39(2), 2102–2111 (2012)
38. Zhou, M.C., DiCesare, F.: Petri Net Synthesis for Discrete Event Control of Manufacturing Systems. Kluwer, Boston (1993)
39. Zurawski, R., Zhou, M.: Petri nets and industrial applications: A tutorial. IEEE Transaction on Industrial Electronics 41(6), 567–583 (1994)

Extended Mis-overlay Calculation
for Pre-marshalling Containers

Stefan Voß

Institute of Information Systems (Wirtschaftsinformatik), University of Hamburg,
Von-Melle-Park 5, 20146 Hamburg, Germany
stefan.voss@uni-hamburg.de

Abstract. Pre-marshalling at container terminals refers to re-organizing
container stacks so that they are ready to be retrieved without further
relocations. In a recent paper Lee and Chao considered this problem and
provided some ideas to deal with it. Here we comment on some issues
and provide an extended lower bound calculation for the problem.

1 Introduction

Most of the long-distance transportation of goods today is carried out through
the use of containers at container terminals/seaports. The berthing time of ships
at ports is perhaps the most important measure of port container terminal performance. Moreover, the ability to efficiently handle containers is paramount in
enhancing the service level of ports [6,5].

It is common practice to store outbound containers in a yard before loading
them onto a vessel. Often containers are given priorities which may refer to
several indicators such as destination, time of sail, weight class, etc. For instance,
a container that is planned to leave the port some days before another container
should have a higher priority. One simple way of reducing the time of loading
operations (during berthing time) is to pile up containers taking into account
their priorities. That is, a container with higher priority is avoided to be placed
below a container with lower priority. While such operation is carefully planned
with this goal in mind, the final layout of a bay is strongly influenced by the
arrival order of, e.g., unloading trucks to the yard. For this reason, in the final
bay configuration, high priority containers can still be found below low priority
ones. Similar issues arise in the inbound operations.

The problem of arranging containers within a yard to maximize efficiency is
extensively discussed; see [6,5] for a general review on container terminals as well
as related references. To ease the situation and to ensure a high performance of
ship, train and truck operations at container terminals, containers sometimes are
pre-stowed near to the loading place in a way that their order fits the loading
sequence. This is done after the stowage plan is finished and before ship loading
starts. A related problem, known as *pre-marshalling* problem, is focused on determining the final layout of a bay at a port yard such that no relocation moves
are necessary to load the containers into a vessel.

H. Hu et al. (Eds.): ICCL 2012, LNCS 7555, pp. 86–91, 2012.

The pre-marshalling problem can, therefore, be seen as the problem of reshuffling the initial configuration of the bay in order to obtain a bay in which the retrieval operation can be carried out without further relocations, while minimizing the total number of moves required to reshuffle. Recently, this problem has been studied, e.g., by [3]. A specific survey on the topic as well as related references can be found in [1].

In line with the literature we make use of some basic assumptions:

1. Pre-marshalling is considered only within the same bay (consisting of a certain number of stacks and tiers). No intra-bay movement is considered.
2. Containers (also addressed as *blocks*) are assumed to be of the same size.
3. The loading preferences of blocks are known, *i.e.*, precedences among blocks are assumed to be given in advance. Precedences or priorities are given as integer numbers with a smaller number representing a higher priority than a larger number.

The aim of this short communication is to comment on some issues raised in [3] and to provide and discuss an extended lower bound calculation for the pre-marshalling problem. First, we extend the problem description and illustrate the lower bound calculation. Section 3 provides an example for the 'hardest' benchmark instance treated in [3]. In passing we provide an optimal solution for that instance improving the best value provided in that reference by more than 50 %. Finally, Section 4 offers some concluding remarks.

2 Mis-overlay Calculation

The goal of the pre-marshalling problem is to reshuffle blocks with the minimum number of movements such that the final configuration of the bay has zero forced relocations. A simple and obvious lower bound known from the literature (see, e.g., [3]) calculates the number of forced relocations.

Let us first define the concept of *mis-overlay* or *forced relocations*.[1] Let h and s denote the number of tiers (i.e., the height limit of the stacks) and the number of stacks of a given bay, respectively. Given a current bay configuration, the number of forced relocations $m(i)$ of stack i is given by the number of blocks in that stack currently on top of a block with higher priority. Such blocks will necessarily be relocated, in order to retrieve the block with higher priority located below. The mis-overlay is the number of all forced relocations of a bay, i.e., $\sum_{i=1}^{s} m(i)$. For example, consider the situation in Figure 1 for a bay with at most $h = 4$ tiers and $s = 3$ stacks. The number of forced relocations over all stacks, i.e. the mis-overlay, is equal to 4, as indicated by the shaded blocks. The mis-overlay or number of forced relocations in a bay constitutes a valid lower bound of the minimum number of relocations required to complete the retrieval operation.

A first idea to improve this bound is based on the fact that there might be a number of stacks that need to be freed for replacement. Consider again the

---

[1] In the industry occasionally one can also find the term *overstowage*.

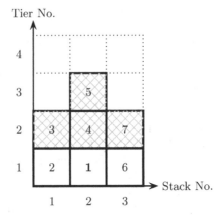

Fig. 1. An example of forced relocations within a bay. Blocks 3, 4, 5, and 7 will necessarily be relocated to retrieve blocks with higher priority.

situation in Figure 1. Obviously, block 7 will always cause a relocation unless there is a stack where it can be placed on the first tier. In such a situation, the lower bound may be increased by one.

Let us distinguish between a *direct* (forced) relocation and an *indirect* (forced) relocation. A direct relocation simply refers to a relocation of a block which does not imply another relocation. If relocating a block in a way that an additional relocation is necessary, the latter will be called indirect relocation.

Let us define a *zero mis-overlay number* $zm(i)$ for each stack i as the priority of the highest block in stack i such that, if all blocks on top are relocated, there remains no forced relocation or mis-overlay in that stack. For the example in Figure 1 we have $zm(1) = 2$, $zm(2) = 1$, and $zm(3) = 6$. Based on this observation we have a second mechanism for increasing the lower bound based on the number of mis-overlays. On one hand, we check whether we need to free at least one stack for replacement (Rule 1). On the other hand, if we need to relocate a block with priority, say p, with $p > max_i zm(i)$ and we cannot do so without causing an indirect relocation, then we need to increase the lower bound by one (Rule 2).

Note that each of our mechanisms for increasing the lower bound need not work consecutively, i.e., even if it looks so at first glance we do not claim that consecutive application of these ideas necessarily imply further increases of the lower bound. However, there are some ideas that go a little further than Rules 1 and 2. Assume that we have not only one of those blocks p with a highest priority that need to be relocated but a number q of them. Then we might need to free more than one stack (we say that a stack is freed if no more containers with a priority smaller than p are within such a stack) and the lower bound may be increased by j with $j = |q/h|$, where the notation $|x|$ represents the smallest integer greater or equal to x (Rule 1a).

For the small instance of Figure 1 we need to free one stack. If it is the first one we imply at least one indirect relocation and we still have the necessity to free block 7 as it now has a block on top which needs to be relocated before handling it. Moreover, block 7 cannot be put onto any stack but a freed one as $7 > max_{i=1,2} zm(i) = 2$. (Note that $i \neq 3$ because block 7 is moved out of stack 3.) Based on this the initial mis-overlay needs to be increased by 2. Starting from the layout provided in Figure 1 the following relocations can be performed to actually obtain an optimal sequence of length 6:[2]

(7,3,2), (3,1,3), (2,1,3), (7,2,1), (5,2,1), (4,2,1).

3   A Benchmark Example

Let us consider the benchmark instance provided by Lee and Chao [3]. It is a bay with 10 stacks and maximum height of 5 tiers. Stacks are numbered from 1 to 10, from left to right. There are 35 blocks in the bay, with a utilization factor of 70%. Blocks are divided into 10 classes, numbered from 0 to 9. Therefore, blocks with the same priority belong to the same class. The initial layout is shown in Figure 2.

1								4	
3		7			0	6		6	5
3	0	6		5	5	7		9	5
3	6	5	2	8	0	5		6	1
5	8	1	5	8	2	8	2	1	4

Fig. 2. Benchmark instance from [3]: Initial layout

1		5		2			5		
3	0	5		4			6		
3	0	6	1	5		5	6		
3	6	7	2	8	0	5	6		1
5	8	9	5	8	2	8	7	1	4

Fig. 3. Benchmark instance from Figure 2: Final layout obtained after a sequence of 15 relocations

The feasible solution for this instance (with a final mis-overlay of 0) provided by [3] consists of a sequence of 31 relocations. In [2] this solution was

---

[2] Regarding notation we assume that (b, s_o, s_i) indicates moving the topmost block b out of stack s_o into stack s_i.

considerably improved to a value of 19 relocations. The lower bound calculation proposed above provides a mis-overlay of the initial configuration of 13 with $m = (0,0,3,0,0,2,2,0,4,2)$, a vector of values $zm = (1,0,1,2,5,0,5,2,1,1)$ and an extended lower bound of 15 for the minimal number of relocations.

Starting from the layout provided in Figure 2 the following relocations can be performed to actually obtain an optimal sequence of length 15:

(4,9,5), (2,8,5), (7,3,8), (6,3,8), (6,7,8), (6,9,8), (5,3,8), (1,3,4), (9,9,3), (7,7,3), (6,9,3), (5,10,3), (5,10,3), (0,6,2), and (5,6,7).

The respective final layout is presented in Figure 3.

4   Some Final Comments

In this paper we have discussed the concept of mis-overlays or forced relocations within the pre-marshalling problem related to maritime shipping. Besides other results, the best known solution of a benchmark instance from the literature has been considerably improved and proven to be optimal.

Originally, Lee and Chao "define the quality of a movement sequence as the weighted sum of the number of the mis-overlay index of its corresponding final bay layout and the length of the sequence," and they specify the weights as 0.1 and 1, respectively ([3], p. 470). Basically, this raises the issue of a bi-objective problem. Such a problem, however, has not yet been comprehensively treated in the literature. Also [3] treated it as a single objective problem by fixing the values as mentioned before. For those practical settings mentioned by [3] and a proportion of the two objectives of 1 to 10 the objective would most probably go for a mis-overlay of 0 anyway while solely minimizing the length of the corresponding sequence. Consider as an example the situation from Figure 2. Any stack could be completely removed and put back in a modified sequence according to their priorities with at most ten moves as the size of the bay already follows that proportion. That is, the proposed weights of [3] seem superficial and need some more thought before actually being used.

The idea to remove a whole stack and reorder it in an appropriate way, however, does not necessarily work in all cases. Consider an example situation with $h = 6$ tiers and $s = 3$ stacks with six containers with priorities (0,1,0,0,1,0) from bottom to top in the first stack and three containers in the second and third stack with priorities (0,1,0) in both cases. Of course in such a situation even the algorithm of [3] would not find an initial feasible solution even if one exists (specifically, "Minor subroutine 1" presented in Section 3.3 of [3] could not find a "conflict-free" sequence).

Future work could formalize and extend the situation described here. As an example consider Rule 1a indicated above and a large benchmark instance provided in Figure 4 with 12 stacks and up to 5 tiers taken from [4]. The mis-overlay is 25. Based on the initial configuration we can see that any removal while freeing a first stack (which means two relocations) causes that at least two additional indirect relocations need to be considered. (Note that freeing stack 4 has no block that could be relocated without causing any indirect relocation. From any

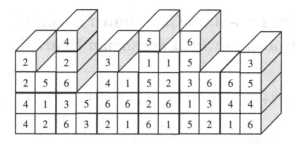

Fig. 4. Benchmark instance from [4], p. 3312

other stack with at least three blocks we can relocate at most one block – on top of tier 1 – without causing an additional indirect relocation.) Based on this, the mis-overlay of that example needs to be increased by 4, two for freeing the first stack and two due to the indirect relocations. Moreover, the lowest priority within the bay is 6 and there are $q = 7$ blocks with that priority that need to be relocated. That is, we need to free a second stack causing an increase of the mis-overlay by at least 1. That is, overall the lower bound for this example is 30 (and it is easy to see that there is a sequence that achieves this bound; starting from the layout provided in Figure 4 the following relocations can be performed to actually obtain an optimal sequence of length 30:

(1,6,1), (6,6,2), (1,6,8), (6,2,6), (6,9,6), (6,10,6), (6,11,6), (5,4,6), (3,5,4), (3,12,4), (3,10,4), (2,10,4), (5,2,10), (5,7,10), (5,9,10), (5,12,10), (4,3,12), (4,5,12), (4,11,12), (1,8,2), (1,8,2), (1,11,2), (6,5,11), (2,3,5), (6,3,11), (2,8,5), (6,8,11), (3,9,3), (1,7,9), and (5,7,11)

Finally, our ideas might be included in an efficient branch and bound or a hybrid metaheuristic/matheuristic approach.

References

1. Caserta, M., Schwarze, S., Voß, S.: Container rehandling at maritime container terminals. In: Böse, J.W. (ed.) Handbook of Terminal Planning, pp. 247–269. Springer, New York (2011)
2. Caserta, M., Voß, S.: A Corridor Method-Based Algorithm for the Pre-marshalling Problem. In: Giacobini, M., Brabazon, A., Cagnoni, S., Di Caro, G.A., Ekárt, A., Esparcia-Alcázar, A.I., Farooq, M., Fink, A., Machado, P. (eds.) EvoWorkshops 2009. LNCS, vol. 5484, pp. 788–797. Springer, Heidelberg (2009)
3. Lee, Y., Chao, S.-L.: A neighborhood search heuristic for pre-marshalling export containers. European Journal of Operational Research 196, 468–475 (2009)
4. Lee, Y., Hsu, N.Y.: An optimization model for the container pre-marshalling problem. Computers & Operations Research 34, 3295–3313 (2007)
5. Stahlbock, R., Voß, S.: Operations research at container terminals: a literature update. OR Spectrum 30, 1–52 (2008)
6. Steenken, D., Voß, S., Stahlbock, R.: Container terminal operations and operations research – a classification and literature review. OR Spectrum 26, 3–49 (2004)

Solving the Two-Stage Capacitated Facility Location Problem by the Lagrangian Heuristic

Igor Litvinchev[1] and Edith Lucero Ozuna Espinosa[2]

[1] Complex Systems Department
Computing Centre of Russian Academy of Sciences
Moscow, Russia
litvin@ccas.ru
[2] Faculty of Mechanical and Electrical Engineering
Nuevo Leon State University
Monterrey, Mexico
lucero@yalma.fime.uanl.mx

Abstract. In the two-stage capacitated facility location problem a single product is produced at some plants in order to satisfy customer demands. The product is transported from these plants to some depots and then to the customers. The capacities of the plants and depots are limited. The aim is to select cost minimizing locations from a set of potential plants and depots. This cost includes fixed cost associated with opening plants and depots, and variable cost associated with both transportation stages. In this work a Lagrangian relaxation is analyzed and a Lagrangian heuristic producing feasible solutions is presented. The results of a computational study are reported.

1 Introduction

The two-stage capacitated facility location problem can be defined as follows: a single product is produced at plants and then transported to depots, both having limited capacities. From the depots the product is transported to customers to satisfy their demands. The use of the plants/depots incurs a fixed cost, while transportation from the plants to the customers through the depots results in a variable cost. We need to identify what plants and depots to use, as well as the product flows from the plants to the depots and then to the customers such that the demands are met at a minimal cost.

The literature on facility location problem and its applications is quite extensive. We refer here only for a few recent review papers [8, 14, 24, and 26]. In what follows we focus more on approximate techniques to solve facility location problems. For exact approaches see, e.g., [1, 15] and the references therein.

Approximate approaches can be roughly divided into two large groups: metaheuristics and Lagrangian based techniques [30]. Metaheuristic approaches to the problem like tabu search, GRASP, are discussed in [9, 28]. A cross entropy-based metaheuristic algorithm for the capacitated facility location problem was studied in [5]. An algorithm for large instances is presented in [2], they used a heuristic procedure that produces a feasible integer solution and used a Lagrangian relaxation to obtain a lower bound on the optimal value.

H. Hu et al. (Eds.): ICCL 2012, LNCS 7555, pp. 92–103, 2012.

A Lagrangian based heuristic for solving the capacitated plant location problem with side constraints was presented in [27]. Approaches and relaxations proposed in the literature for the capacitated facility location problem are compared in [7]. Fenchel cutting planes methodology was applied in [25] to capacitated facility location problems and compared the results obtained by a Lagrangian relaxation.

A linear programming based heuristic is considered in [12] for a two-stage capacitated problem with single source constraints. A hybrid algorithm was presented in [19], integrating the approximation approach, neural network and a simulated annealing to solve a capacitated fuzzy two-stage location-allocation problem. In [31] a greedy construction heuristic was proposed and combined with a Variable Neighborhood Descent and a Variable Neighborhood Search for the multi-stage facility location problem with staircase costs and splitting of commodities. In [16] the asymmetry inherent to the problem in plants and depots is taking into account to enforce the formulation. Two formulations for the problem are presented in [10], the linear relaxations are compared with the binary relaxation of the model.

Several Lagrangian relaxation approaches have been proposed for the two stage facility location problem. For the uncapacitated case in [6] they studied the effectiveness of the formulation for the two level simple plant location problem incorporating polyhedral cuts and of an approach combining a Lagrangian relaxation method and simulated annealing algorithm. In [20] an algorithm was proposed based on Lagrangian heuristics for a 0-1 mixed integer model of a two level location problem with three types of facility to be located. In [22] a mixed integer formulation and several Lagrangian relaxations to determine lower bounds for the two stage uncapacitated facility location problem are presented.

The Lagrangian relaxation for the capacitated case was studied and numerically tested in [3]. Alternative model formulations of the capacitated problem were studied in [4] obtaining lower bounds by Lagrangian relaxations of the flow-balancing constraints. They developed also heuristic procedures to obtain feasible solutions. Several Lagrangian relaxations for two different formulations of the two-stage problem are computationally compared in [21]. A Lagrangian relaxation-based branch and bound algorithm for the two-echelon, single source, capacitated problem was proposed in [29]. A Lagrangian heuristic is proposed in [13] using relaxation of the capacity constraints for the problem with a fixed number of plants. Feasible solutions are constructed from those of the Lagrangian subproblems by applying simple reassignment procedures.

In many techniques Lagrangian relaxation is used in twofold: the optimal value of the Lagrangian (dual) problem is used as a dual bound, while the Lagrangian solution is used as a starting or reference point to produce a feasible solution and a corresponding primal bound. Frequently a relaxation is considered as *good* if it produces a tight dual bound. Meanwhile, the quality of the feasible Lagrangian based solution has also to be taken into account in evaluating the relaxation. There are often different ways in which a given problem can be relaxed in a Lagrangian fashion. It is unlikely to highlight a single relaxation producing high quality bounds of both types, primal and dual. Moreover, if the quality of the dual bound is basically defined by the constraints relaxed, the quality of the primal bound depends also on the algorithm used to restore the feasibility of the Lagrangian solution.

In this paper we consider a simple decomposable relaxation and an algorithm to re-store the feasibility of the corresponding Lagrangian solution. This relaxation produces a poor dual bound and never been considered before as a promising relaxation. Meanwhile, the relaxation results in a very tight feasible solution typically within 0.5-1.0% of the relative suboptimality.

The rest of the paper is organized as follows. The next section presents a mathematical formulation for the two-stage facility location problem and the Lagrangian bound. A heuristic procedure to get feasible solutions is presented in Section 3. Computational results are reported in Section 4, while Section 5 concludes.

2   Problem Formulation and Lagrangian Bound

You To formally describe the problem, let $I = 1,...,n$ be the index set of potential plants, $J = 1,...,m$ the index set of potential depots and $K=1,...,k$ the index set of clients. Then, the problem can be formulated as the following mixed integer linear program:

$$w = min \sum_{i \in I} f_i y_i + \sum_{j \in J} g_j z_j + \sum_{i \in I, j \in J} c_{ij} x_{ij} + \sum_{j \in J, k \in K} d_{jk} s_{jk} \tag{1}$$

$$\sum_{j \in J} s_{jk} \geq q_k, k \in K, \tag{2}$$

$$\sum_{i \in I} x_{ij} \geq \sum_{k \in K} s_{jk}, j \in J, \tag{3}$$

$$\sum_{j \in J} x_{ij} \leq b_i y_i, i \in I, \tag{4}$$

$$\sum_{i \in I} x_{ij} \leq p_j z_j, j \in J, \tag{5}$$

$$x_{ij}, s_{jk} \geq 0, y_i, z_j \in \{0,1\}; i \in I, j \in J, k \in K \tag{6}$$

Here f_i and g_j are the fixed costs associated with the installation of plant i and depot j; c_{ij} and d_{jk} are the costs of transportation from plant i to depot j and from depot j to client k, respectively; q_k is the demand of client k; while b_i and p_j are the capacities of the corresponding plant and depot. The variables in this formulation are $y_i = 1$ if plant i is installed and $y_i = 0$ otherwise, $z_j = 1$ if depot j is installed and $z_j = 0$ otherwise, x_{ij}, s_{jk} are the transportation flows between the corresponding units.

Constraint (2) is the demand constraint (for each customer, at least the demand must be met); (3) is the relaxed flow conservation constraint (the product transported from the depot must at least be transported to it from the plants); constraints (4) and (5) represent capacity limits for plants and depots and assure the flow only from plants and depots opened. Note that by minimizing the objective (1), constraints (2) and (3) are fulfilled as equalities for an optimal solution of (1)-(6).

Lagrangian bounds are widely used as a core of many numerical techniques, e.g. in branch and bound schemes for integer and combinatorial problems, see [11] and the references therein. Most Lagrangian relaxation approaches for the capacitated facility location problem are based either on dualizing the demand constraints or the depot capacity constraints [12]. In this paper we consider the relaxation of the demand and the plant capacity constraints (2) and (4), respectively. For fixed multipliers $u, v \geq 0$ the corresponding Lagrangian problem is stated as follows:

$$L(u,v) = min \sum_{i \in I} f_i y_i + \sum_{j \in J} g_j z_j + \sum_{i \in I, j \in J} c_{ij} x_{ij} + \sum_{j \in J, k \in K} d_{jk} s_{jk} + \sum_{k \in K} u_k (q_k - \sum_{j \in J} s_{jk}) + \sum_{i \in I} v_i (\sum_{j \in J} x_{ij} - b_i y_i)$$

$$\sum_{i \in I} x_{ij} \geq \sum_{k \in K} s_{jk}, j \in J,$$

$$\sum_{i \in I} x_{ij} \leq p_j z_j, \ j \in J,$$

$$x_{ij}, s_{jk} \geq 0, \ y_i, z_j \in \{0,1\},$$

providing the lower bound $L(u,v) \leq w$. Rearranging the terms in the objective function yields:

$$L(u,v) = \sum_{k \in K} q_k u_k + min \left\{ \sum_{i \in I} (f_i - b_i v_i) y_i + \sum_{j \in J} [g_j z_j + \sum_{i \in I} (c_{ij} + v_i) x_{ij} + \sum_{k \in K} (d_{jk} - u_k) s_{jk}] \right\}$$

Thus the Lagrangian problem decomposes into I independent subproblems in y_i, $L_i(v_i) = min_{y_i \in \{0,1\}} (f_i - v_i b_i) y_i$, that are solved analyzing the sign of the coefficients $(f_i - v_i b_i)$, and J independent subproblems each having only one binary variable z_j:

$$L_j(u,v) = min \left\{ g_j z_j + \sum_{i \in I} (c_{ij} + v_i) x_{ij} + \sum_{k \in K} (d_{jk} - u_k) s_{jk} \right\}$$

$$\sum_{i \in I} x_{ij} \geq \sum_{k \in K} s_{jk},$$

$$\sum_{i \in I} x_{ij} \leq p_j z_j,$$

$$x_{ij}, s_{jk} \geq 0, \ z_j \in \{0,1\}.$$

The latter problem is analyzed by inspection, fixing z_j to 0 or 1 and then solving the remaining (network flow) problem in continuous variables (x, s).

Thus we may conclude that the computational cost to solve the Lagrangian problem corresponding to the relaxation of the demand and the plant capacity constraints is very low, in fact no integer problem is involved. In [18] another equivalent formulation for the problem (1)-(6) was considered and 10 different Lagrangian relaxations were compared numerically for both formulations. We refer the reader to [18] for details of this numerical study. The problem of finding the best, *i.e.* bound maximizing Lagrange multipliers, is called the Lagrangian dual. To solve the Lagrangian dual problem one can apply a subgradient technique. Another popular approach is the constraint generation scheme (Benders method) transforming the dual problem into a large-scale linear programming problem. The advantage of using Benders technique is that it generates two-sided estimations for the dual bound in each iteration thus producing a near-optimal dual bound with guaranteed quality. Meanwhile, the computational cost of this scheme is typically high. In contrast to the Benders method, the subgradient technique does not provide the value of the bounds with the prescribed accuracy. That is, terminating iterations of the subgradient method using some stopping criteria we can expect only approximate values of the bound. We do not consider here these two well known approaches in details, referring the reader to [17, 23] for the constraint generation (Benders) technique, and to [23, 32] for the subgradient scheme. Note also that in [18] the bounds were calculated by both techniques and the results obtained by the subgradient technique were very close to those obtained by Benders technique.

3   Getting Feasible Solutions

To get a feasible solution from the Lagrangian one we use a simple algorithm to recover feasibility. In fact, this approach can be applied to any non-feasible solution.

Algorithm

Let $\bar{x}_{ij}, \bar{s}_{jk}$ be a non-feasible solution

Do $y_i = 0, \forall i, I_1 = \varnothing, I_0 = I$; $z_j = 0, \forall j, J_1 = \varnothing, J_0 = J$.

Step 0: Do $y_i \leftarrow (\sum_{j \in J} \bar{x}_{ij}) / b_i, z_j \leftarrow (\sum_{k \in K} \bar{s}_{jk}) / p_j$.

Step 1: $i^* = \arg max \{ y_i | i \in I_0 \}$

Step 2: $y_{i^*} \leftarrow 1, I_1 \leftarrow I_1 \cup \{ i^* \}, I_0 \leftarrow I_0 - \{ i^* \}$.

Step 3: If $\sum_{i \in I_1} b_i \geq \sum_{k \in K} q_k$ go to Step 4 and do $y_i = 0, \forall i \in I_0$, otherwise, return to step 1.

Step 4: $j^* = \arg max \{ z_j | j \in J_0 \}$.

Step 5: $z_{j^*} \leftarrow 1, J_1 \leftarrow J_1 \cup \{ j^* \}, J_0 \leftarrow J_0 - \{ j^* \}$.

Step 6: If $\sum_{j \in J_1} p_j \geq \sum_{k \in K} q_k$ go to step 7 and do $z_j = 0, \forall j \in J_0$, otherwise, return to step 4.

Step 7: Fix y_i and z_j in the original problem and solve corresponding linear problem to obtain the flows.

In this algorithm we calculate for each plant a "saturation" indicator representing the relative usage of its capacity (step 0). Then the plant having the highest saturation is opened (step 1). If the capacity is sufficient to satisfy the total customers' demand, the rest of the plants are closed, otherwise the plant having the next highest indicator is opened, too (steps 2 and 3). The depots are opened in a similar way (steps 3, 5 and 6). Fixing the binary variables obtained by this procedure, the flows are determined from the corresponding linear problem.

4   Computational Results

A numerical study for the two-stage capacitated facility location problem was conducted to compare the bounds. The following sets of instances were generated according to the values $(I; J; K)$: A(3; 5; 9); B(5; 7; 30); C(7; 10; 50); D(10; 10; 100); E(10;16;30); F(30;30;30); G (30;36;120); H(30;30;100); I (50;50;200). Every set contains 20 problem instances. The data were random integers generated as follows:

$$c_{ij}, d_{jk} \in U[10,20], \; q_k \in U[1,10],$$

$$b_i \in \left\lceil 10\frac{J+K}{I} \right\rceil + U[0,10], \; p_j \in \left\lceil 10\frac{K}{J} \right\rceil + U[0,10].$$

Two different ways to generate the fixed costs were implemented. For the first ten instances in each class the fixed costs f_i, g_j were random integers generated independently on the number clients, plants and depots: $f_i, g_j \in U[100,200]$. For the remaining ten instances the fixed costs f_i for plants were proportional to the number of depots and clients, while the fixed costs g_j for depots were proportional to the number of clients:

$$f_i \in \left\lceil 100\frac{K+J}{I} \right\rceil + U[0,100]; g_j \in \left\lceil 100\frac{K}{J} \right\rceil + U[0,100]$$

The dual bound corresponding to the Lagrangian relaxation was calculated by the subgradient technique. In each iteration of this method the feasible solution was obtained by the algorithm.

The best (over all iterations) feasible solution was stored. The current best feasible solution was used to update the step size. If after 5 consecutive iterations of the subgradient technique the dual bound was not improved, the half of the step size scaling parameter was used. The process stops if the step size scaling parameter is less than 0.0001, or if the maximum number (300) of iterations is reached.

The procedure was implemented in GAMS/CPLEX 11.2 using a Sun Fire V440 terminal, connected to 4 processors Ultra SPARC III with 1602 Mhz, 1 MB of CACHE, and 8 GB of memory. For all the instances we have calculated: z_{IP} - the value of the optimal objective of the two stage location problem; z_L - the value of the best Lagrangian bound; z_{BF} - the objective value corresponding to the best feasible solution. The relative quality of the Lagrangian bound and of the best feasible solution was measured by the corresponding

$$\varepsilon_L = 100\%(z_{IP} - z_L)/z_{IP}, \; \varepsilon_{BF} = 100\%(z_{BF} - z_{IP})/z_{BF}.$$

Tables 1-3 present the results obtained for the first way to generate data, while Tables 4-6 give the results for the second.

The results are shown for 5 different instances for each problem size. The first two columns present the proximity indicators for the corresponding dual bound (ε_L) and for the best (over all iterations) feasible solution (ε_{BF}) obtained by the algorithm. The last two columns give the proximity indicator for the feasible solution corresponding to the last (ε_{LF}) and the first (ε_{FF}) iteration of the subgradient technique. The number in parenthesis indicates the number of the iteration corresponding to the bound value.

Table 1. Instances A-C, first type

Size	ε_L (%)	ε_{BF} (%)	ε_{LF} (%)	ε_{FF} (%)
A1	12.30	1.81 (14)	5.07 (135)	12.51
A2	2.31	0.00 (31)	0.00 (89)	14.95
A3	7.74	0.57 (5)	4.21 (138)	4.21
A4	6.39	0.00 (9)	0.00 (128)	11.63
A5	11.03	0.00 (4)	3.79 (130)	3.79
B1	6.04	0.00 (27)	0.99 (124)	3.47
B2	4.03	0.00 (17)	0.00 (135)	2.35
B3	5.93	1.26 (16)	4.73 (132)	2.66
B4	4.97	0.00 (15)	4.91 (147)	4.18
B5	4.15	0.18 (28)	0.18 (102)	8.37
C1	4.89	0.00 (36)	1.78 (118)	3.39
C2	4.43	0.35 (9)	2.81 (116)	8.22
C3	2.88	0.03 (8)	2.28 (151)	7.59
C4	4.59	0.00 (28)	6.57 (116)	8.49
C5	3.03	0.00 (28)	2.43 (118)	6.91

Table 2. Instances D-F, first type

Size	ε_L (%)	ε_{BF} (%)	ε_{LF} (%)	ε_{FF} (%)
D1	2.89	0.00 (16)	4.26(113)	5.30
D2	2.43	0.00 (24)	3.14(129)	7.44
D3	3.75	0.00 (96)	5.55(131)	9.71
D4	3.70	0.49 (1)	2.16(130)	4.19
D5	2.07	0.00 (105)	1.75(153)	3.79
E1	4.56	0.00 (59)	0.10(225)	11.65
E2	5.03	0.53 (92)	0.75(217)	7.79
E3	3.94	1.37 (49)	5.67(231)	12.86
E4	3.47	0.52 (134)	2.05(256)	9.14
E5	4.25	0.46 (191)	6.07(256)	9.10
F1	2.21	0.75 (109)	1.44(300)	13.92
F2	1.89	0.00 (53)	0.89(235)	13.67
F3	1.88	0.037 (58)	1.17(198)	15.48
F4	1.61	1.55 (264)	3.67(300)	19.74
F5	1.91	0.55 (60)	1.66(266)	13.71

Table 3. Instances G-I, first type

Size	ε_L (%)	ε_{BF} (%)	ε_{LF} (%)	ε_{FF} (%)
G1	1.10	0.37(240)	1.91(300)	8.11
G2	0.99	1.18 (88)	1.58(300)	7.63
G3	1.13	0.21(249)	1.24(300)	8.69
G4	0.94	0.56(100)	1.81(300)	7.42
G5	0.67	0.23(194)	0.87(300)	9.92
H1	1.04	0.46(284)	2.02(300)	10.28
H2	1.29	0.47(168)	1.04(300)	5.84
H3	1.49	0.38(191)	1.57(300)	8.18
H4	1.39	0.77(284)	2.57(300)	7.16
H5	1.73	0.73(147)	3.93(300)	8.83
I1	0.96	0.52(199)	1.27(300)	5.98
I2	0.93	0.81(130)	2.52(300)	6.44
I3	0.78	1.09(196)	1.49(300)	7.01
I4	0.73	0.92(202)	1.57(300)	5.94
I5	0.64	1.04(94)	1.90(300)	6.44

Table 4. Instances A-C, second type

Size	ε_L (%)	ε_{BF} (%)	ε_{LF} (%)	ε_{FF} (%)
A1	13.64	0.51 (9)	4.72 (214)	10.31
A2	4.79	0.00 (29)	0.00 (166)	14.48
A3	5.33	0.43 (2)	13.46(158)	18.41
A4	6.89	0.00 (28)	10.17(188)	11.98
A5	19.09	0.00 (1)	0.00 (157)	0.00
B1	13.18	0.00(137)	0.79 (212)	2.09
B2	9.09	0.00 (58)	1.62 (250)	1.44
B3	8.29	1.57 (22)	9.79 (250)	8.63
B4	5.49	0.00 (61)	6.01 (243)	6.01
B5	9.32	0.11 (21)	0.11 (252)	14.79
C1	6.68	0.00 (62)	8.28 (223)	9.95
C2	10.83	0.25(181)	2.11 (270)	5.06
C3	6.84	0.56 (76)	2.28 (258)	4.64
C4	8.55	0.00 (27)	4.80 (237)	5.28
C5	6.47	0.00 (47)	1.49 (250)	4.34

Table 5. Instances D-F, second type

Size	ε_L (%)	ε_{BF} (%)	ε_{LF} (%)	ε_{FF} (%)
D1	6.32	0.20 (62)	2.12(284)	6.79
D2	6.08	0.40(237)	4.34(256)	4.48
D3	8.48	0.00 (67)	1.62(277)	5.64
D4	7.29	1.91 (18)	8.18(250)	8.45
D5	5.57	0.19(153)	3.58(276)	2.19
E1	4.04	2.54 (44)	9.06(227)	13.75
E2	9.56	0.79 (71)	0.79(205)	4.93
E3	3.71	5.76 (51)	6.83(293)	14.73
E4	6.25	0.00(108)	1.69(233)	7.35

Table 5. (*continued*)

E5	7.40	0.32 (56)	8.03(277)	8.79
F1	3.15	0.67(133)	1.31(257)	13.41
F2	2.94	0.00 (60)	1.14(261)	15.65
F3	2.28	0.95 (56)	2.93(250)	14.24
F4	2.90	0.93 (51)	2.06(261)	13.58
F5	2.96	0.64 (32)	5.42(277)	20.07

Table 6. Instances G-I, second type

Size	ε_L (%)	ε_{BF} (%)	ε_{LF} (%)	ε_{FF} (%)
G1	3.33	0.61(194)	1.12(300)	6.94
G2	1.98	0.82(128)	1.56(300)	8.22
G3	1.27	0.46(120)	2.60(300)	8.29
G4	0.87	0.16(260)	1.11(300)	7.15
G5	1.51	0.70(87)	1.87(300)	9.14
H1	1.64	1.16(206)	2.52(300)	8.33
H2	2.23	0.58(214)	2.88(300)	8.28
H3	1.54	0.23(240)	2.25(300)	7.26
H4	1.47	0.58(127)	3.49(300)	5.37
H5	1.14	0.43(78)	2.64(300)	8.81
I1	1.09	0.79(211)	1.09(300)	6.61
I2	1.95	0.81(207)	2.27(300)	5.62
I3	1.59	1.41(221)	1.81(300)	5.28
I4	1.29	1.01(168)	2.89(300)	6.59
I5	1.48	0.94(146)	1.78(300)	5.67

As we can see from the tables for both ways to generate the data the approach provides very tights feasible solutions, typically within 0.5-1.0% of the relative proximity.

Figure 1 shows the proximity of the Lagrangian bounds in the course of the subgradient iterations for an instance of size A.

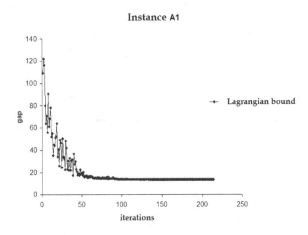

Fig. 1. Proximity of the Lagrangian bounds

So we may expect that the population of the Lagrangian solutions generated by the subgradient technique in the course of solving the Lagrangian dual is "sufficient" for the algorithm to generate high quality feasible solutions. The quality of the dual bound is poor, improving for larger instances.

The feasible solution derived from the solution of the Lagrangian dual and corresponding to the last iteration of the subgradient technique not necessarily is the best feasible solution, as we can see from Figure 2 which shows the proximity of the feasible solution in the course of the subgradient iterations for an instance of size A. Moreover, typically $\varepsilon_{LF} > \varepsilon_{BF}$ and the best feasible solution is obtained on the early iterations of the subgradient method. Thus we may conclude that it is important to generate feasible solutions in all iterations of the subgradient technique.

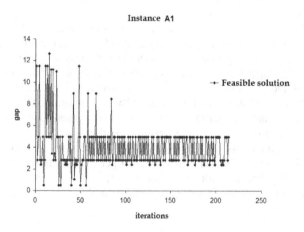

Fig. 2. Proximity of the feasible solution

5   Conclusions

In many Lagrangian heuristics the optimal value of the Lagrangian (dual) problem is used as a dual (lower) bound for the optimal objective, while the Lagrangian solution is used as a starting or reference point for a heuristic to produce a feasible solution (upper primal bound). This way the proximity of the feasible solution to the optimal one is estimated. It is assumed implicitly that the best dual bound and the corresponding Lagrangian solution produces the best primal bound by a heuristic approach. Thus, the feasible solution is constructed using heuristics (e.g., greedy approaches) based on the Lagrangian solution obtained for the optimal Lagrange multipliers corresponding to the best dual bound.

One of the core ideas of the metaheuristic approaches is recognizing the role of "near optimal" solutions. That is, instead of using for the next iteration the locally optimal solution obtained for the current iteration, near optimal solutions are also taken into account to define the next iteration. Metaheuristic approaches using this idea were successfully applied for many hard combinatorial and integer problems.

We propose to combine the use of near optimal solutions with the Lagrangian approach. We demonstrate that the best primal solution typically is generated by the Lagrangian solution which is far from optimal. That is, if we apply an iterative approach (e.g., subgradient technique) to solve the Lagrangian dual, the Lagrangian solutions corresponding to current (non optimal) multipliers result in better feasible solutions. Lagrangian bound was presented for the two stage capacitated facility location problem. Two indicators were considered: the quality of the dual bound and the proximity of the Lagrangian based feasible solution. It turned out that relaxing the demand and the capacity plant constraints provides a rather poor dual bound, but the Lagrangian based feasible solutions are good, typically within 0.5-1.0% of the relative suboptimality. Relaxing the demand and the capacity plant constraints result in a decomposable Lagrangian problem with all subproblems analyzed by inspection. Thus this low cost relaxation seems to be promising to form the core of the Lagrangian based heuristics.

Solving the dual problem by the subgradient technique we compared two approaches to generate a feasible Lagrangian based solution. One is to get a feasible one by the solution of the dual problem, i.e. at the last iteration of the subgradient technique. Another approach is to generate feasible solutions in all iterations of the subgradient method and then choose the tightest. It turned out that the best (over all iterations) feasible solution never was obtained at the last iteration. That is, simply solving the Lagrangian dual and getting a corresponding Lagrangian based feasible solution is not sufficient to produce a tight feasible solution. On the contrary, the population of the Lagrangian solutions generated by the subgradient technique in the course of solving the Lagrangian dual is "sufficient" to generate high quality feasible solutions. An interesting direction for the future research is improving the heuristic used to derive the feasible solutions. Some complements in this direction are in course.

References

1. Avella, P., Boccia, M.: A cutting plane algorithm for the capacitated facility location problem. Computational Optimization and Applications 43, 39–65 (2009)
2. Barahona, F., Chudak, F.: Near-optimal solutions to large-scale facility location problems. Discrete Optimization 2, 35–50 (2005)
3. Barros, A., Labbé, M.: A general model for the uncapacitated facility and depot location problem. Location Science 2, 173–191 (1994)
4. Bloemhof-Ruwaard, J.M., Salomon, M., Van Wassenhove, L.N.: The capacitated distribution and waste disposal problem. European Journal of Operational Research 88, 490–503 (1996)
5. Caserta, M., Quiñonez, E.: A cross entropy-based metaheuristic algorithm for large-scale capacitated facility location problems. Journal of the Operational Research Society 60, 1439–1448 (2009)
6. Chardaire, P., Lutton, J.L., Sutter, A.: Upper and lower bounds for the two-level simple plant location problem. Annals of Operations Research 86, 117–140 (1999)
7. Cornuejols, G., Sridharan, R., Thizy, J.M.: A comparison of heuristics and relaxations for the capacitated plant location problem. European Journal of Operational Research 50, 280–297 (1980)
8. Daskin, M., Snyder, L., Berger, R.: Logistics Systems: Design and Optimization. Springer, New York (2003)

9. Filho, V.J., Galvão, R.D.: A tabu search heuristic for the concentrator location problem. Location Science 6, 189–209 (1998)
10. Gendron, B., Semet, F.: Formulations and relaxations for a multi-echelon capacitated location-distribution problem. Computers & Operations Research 36, 1335–1355 (2009)
11. Guignard, M.: Lagrangian relaxation. TOP 11, 151–228 (2003)
12. Klose, A.: An LP-based heuristic for two-stage capacitated facility location problems. Journal of the Operational Research Society 50, 157–166 (1999)
13. Klose, A.: A Lagrangian relax and cut approach for the two-stage capacitated facility location problem. European Journal of Operational Research 126, 408–421 (2000)
14. Klose, A., Drexl, A.: Facility location models for distribution system design. European Journal of Operational Research 162, 4–29 (2004)
15. Klose, A., Drexl, A.: Lower bounds for the capacitated facility location problem based on column generation. Management Science 51, 1689–1705 (2005)
16. Landete, M., Marín, A.: New facets for the two-stage uncapacitated facility location polytope. Computational Optimization and Applications 44, 487–519 (2009)
17. Lasdon, L.S.: Optimization Theory for Large Systems, Boston, Dover (2002)
18. Litvinchev, I., Ozuna, E.L.: Lagrangian bounds and a heuristic for the two-stage capacitated facility location problem. International Journal of Energy Optimization and Engineering 1, 60–72 (2012)
19. Liu, Y., Zhu, X.: Capacitated fuzzy two-stage location-allocation problem. International Journal of Innovative Computing, Information and Control 3, 987–999 (2007)
20. Lu, Z., Bostel, N.: A facility location model for logistics systems including reverse flows: The case of remanufacturing activities. Computers & Operations Research 34, 299–323 (2005)
21. Marín, A., Pelegrín, B.: Applying Lagrangian relaxation to the solution of two-stage location problems. Annals of Operation Research 86, 179–198 (1999)
22. Marín, A.: Lower bounds for the two-stage uncapacitated facility location problem. European Journal of Operational Research 179, 1126–1142 (2007)
23. Martin, R.: Large Scale Linear and Integer Optimization: A Unified Approach. Kluwer, Boston (1999)
24. Melo, M.T., Nickel, S., Saldanha-da-Gama, F.: Facility location and supply chain management – A review. European Journal of Operational Research 196, 401–412 (2009)
25. Ramos, M.T., Sáenz, S.: Solving capacitated facility location problems by Fenchel cutting planes. Journal of the Operational Research Society 56, 297–306 (2005)
26. Sahin, J., Süral, H.: A review of hierarchical facility location models. Computers & Operations Research 34, 2310–2331 (2007)
27. Sridharan, R.: A Lagrangian heuristic for the capacitated plant location problem with side constraints. Journal of the Operational Research Society 42, 579–585 (1991)
28. Sun, M.: A tabu search heuristic procedure for the capacitated facility location problem. Journal of Heuristics 17, 1–28 (2011)
29. Tragantalerngsak, S., Holt, J., Ronnqvist, M.: An exact method for the two-echelon, single-source, capacitated facility location problem. European Journal of Operational Research 123, 473–489 (2000)
30. Uysal, M.: Using heuristic search algorithms for predicting the effort of software projects. Applied and Computational Mathematics 8, 251–262 (2009)
31. Wollenweber, J.: A multi-stage facility location problem with staircase and splitting of commodities: model, heuristic approach and application. OR Spectrum 30, 655–673 (2008)
32. Wolsey, L.A.: Integer Programming. Wiley, New York (1999)

Applying Radio Frequency Identification Technology in Retail Trade from a Logistics Point of View – An Overview over Opportunities and Limitations

Joachim R. Daduna

Berlin School of Economics and Law
Badensche Straße 52, 10825 Berlin, Germany
daduna@hwr-berlin.de

Abstract. The requirements for logistics processes in retail trade have increased significantly over the recent years due to the growing complexity and the globalization of the economic structures. In order to achieve an efficient planning, monitoring and control, a powerful and reliable information management become necessary which is mostly based on real-time data. In this case it is essential to apply Radio Frequency Identification (RFID) technology. In this contribution at first the underlying technical frameworks will be explained. Then some economic aspects of RFID applications will be discussed in terms of costs and benefits. After that, three different areas of RFID applications will be presented: the support of logistical processes along the supply chain and in connection with efficient in-store logistics as well as for the traceability of the origin of products. Based on this, some critical aspects of the application of RFID technology will be analyzed and evaluated. Finally an outlook and trends of possible developments in the coming years will be provided.

1   Information Management Requirements in Retail Trade

The ever increasing complexity of industry and retail trade caused by globalization and changing market structures require structural adjustments of internal and cross-company information management. Thus, process-related data has to be available in real-time to be able to process and to provide the required information as needed. Besides the appropriate software tools for data handling and a mediabreak free information provision, this calls for tailor-made and efficient collection of arising data. Only if it can be guaranteed that these requirements can be met, an efficient and demand-driven monitoring control of logistical processes is possible.

An essential basis is the application of appropriate technical systems for mostly automated data detection. For several years the use of the *barcode technology* with its diverse technical approaches (see e.g. Lenk 2008; Martin 2009: 486pp) was in the foreground. Currently, barcode technology is still of major importance. Despite its worldwide prevalence, this approach exhibits a variety of technical disadvantages, which lead to limitations and hence also to inefficiencies in the organization of (logistical) processes as well as for the information management. It is for this reason that the use of *Radio Frequency Identification* (RFID) technology (see e.g. Ranasinghe / Cole 2008)

H. Hu et al. (Eds.): ICCL 2012, LNCS 7555, pp. 104–119, 2012.
© Springer-Verlag Berlin Heidelberg 2012

has gained increasing importance. Based on simplified and improved data detection, primarily an integrated monitoring and control of logistical processes, the security control as well as the application of systems for access control, working time recording and accounting play a predominant role. A detailed data basis together with the *quantitative* and *qualitative* improved level of information involved lead to positive effects on the monitoring of the operational processes, and hence also on the controlling.

In the foreground of the following considerations are the (potential) applications for retail trade as there are a variety of possibilities for using RFID in logistics. Before explicitly discussing the various application possibilities, the essential technical framework conditions will be defined. Based on this, several economic aspects will be looked at, also with a view to the discussion of cost and benefits of the RFID application (see e.g. Günther et al. 2008: 126pp). Following that, more detail is provided about these three areas: the fields of application of RFID systems for the *support* of *logistical processes* along supply chains and for the *organization* of efficient *in-store logistics* as well as for the traceability of the origin of products. Based on this, the critical aspects of the RFID application which arise frequently in the public debate will be examined. Besides drawing some conclusions with respect to the use of this technology, it will be finally looked at possible developments for the coming years.

2   Technical Framework

The basic structure of a RFID system comprises two components: the tag (or *transponder*) (see Figure 1) which is attached to the object being traced, as well as the *detection* or *reading device*. Depending on the technical design, with this device it is possible to perform solely reading operations or reading and write operations together. Here no direct contact between the tag and the reader is needed. For a comprehensive overview of the technical procedures used for data collection and data transmission see e.g. Finkenzeller (2010: 283pp).

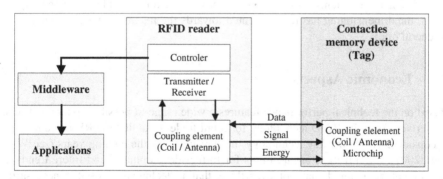

Fig. 1. Basic structure of RFID systems

The reading device is connected to different applications via *middleware* components (see e.g. Melski et al. 2008; Mitton et a. 2010), e.g. on the basis of the *Electronic Product Code* (EPC) standard in conjunction with the *EPCglobal Network* (see e.g. Ranasinghe et al. 2008; Finkenzeller 2010: 274pp). The objective is to ensure an *open* and *cooperative collaboration* within the supply chain structures.

From a logistics point of view, the following characteristics of RFID systems are essential (see e.g. Finkenzeller 2010: 11pp): the *storage capacity*, the *writing properties*, the *transmission rate* as well as the *maximum distance* between the object (or the tag) and the reading device. Those characteristics affect the performance and hence the applicability of the systems. In detail, the following aspects arise:

- *Amount of storable data*: The range of data capacity varies from (passive) 1-bit-tags up to (active) data media with an amount of many kilobytes.

- *Writing properties*: Here, a differentiation is made between *read-only memory devices* (ROM) which are recorded during production, as well as *write-once* and *re-writable* (read/write) *storage devices*.

- *Transmission rate*: It has to be ensured that the speed of movements of objects (also at high speed, like it is the case in sorting facilities) and the data transmission are synchronized with sufficient accuracy to guarantee an error-free data transmission.

- *(Maximum) distance*: Essentially, the maximum distance depends on the operating frequency (see e.g. Finkenzeller 2010: 155pp). It is functionally differentiated into *close coupling* ($\leq$ 1 cm), *remote-coupling* ($\leq$ 1 m) and *long-range coupling* (> 1 m) systems (see e.g. Finkenzeller 2010: 21p).

Another important aspect from a logistical point of view is the *bulk reading* in connection with *anti-collision procedures* (see e.g. Melski et al. 2007; Ranasinghe / Cole 2008) making it possible to handle sequentially several tags which have been recognized simultaneously. In addition, the *multi-tag handling* (see e.g. Gillert / Hansen 2007: 156p) allows for a targeted access of an object within a bulk.

The *technical dimension* of tags is based on the functional requirements and data needs, meaning that they are mostly designed as needed (see e.g. Ranasinghe / Cole 2008). However, the cost aspects have to be taken into consideration as well. In case of different requirements within logistical processes, for example along the supply chain, the dimensioning has to be oriented towards the maximum required values (as a general rule).

3   Economic Aspects

Based on the technical performance features a wide range of possible applications can be derived from the RFID technology for retail trade. Like that the RFID technology is considered to be the key technology in retail trade for the coming years (see Wolfram 2007). Even if there are no limits for further developments and future trends, it should not be ignored that not everything that is technically possible necessarily makes (commercial) sense. Therefore, it has to be questioned repeatedly how the relation between the incurring *investments cost* and the ongoing *operational costs* in comparison to the achievable *cost advantage* and *increase in efficiency* looks like.

Since not all effects to be included are clearly quantifiable, it is appropriate to do a *cost-benefit analysis* to investigate and evaluate the planned (or existing) applications (for a calculation scheme of costs and benefits see, e.g., Günther et al. 2008: 126pp).

The crucial factor results from the relationship of article-related unit cost and the price of the needed tag. Owing to the current price structure it can be said that application at present still refers to higher value goods, whereas labeling in other cases is limited to the package unit and carrier level. However, cost considerations can become less important if the RFID technology is crucial for the implementation of *legal requirements* (see Section 4) or if there are binding *client requirements* (see e.g. Gaukler et al. 2007; Gille 2009: 81 p) which leave no room of manoeuvre in decision making (see Section 4).

Cost advantages also result from a more *efficient monitoring* and *control* of the *(logistical) service provision processes* by collecting data immediately and less faulty on a RFID basis. This also involves a better evaluation and recording of the operational processes which affect the performance of the (internal and external) *information management* respectively. Finally, another issue is the increase of the reliability of the data provided which could lead to positive effects concerning *informational value* for *decision making processes* as well as for *controlling*.

4   Capabilities of Radio Frequency Identification in Retail Trade

Over the past years RFID applications have experienced widespread use in the field of retail trade. The improvement of monitoring and control of the logistical operations along the supply chain as well as in (stationary) shopping venues is in the foreground, especially by means of an intra and inter-organizational information management (see e.g. Bhattacharya et al. 2010; Wamba / Chatfield 2011). The objective is to coordinate all movement of goods with the related information flow across companies. Like that the information that is needed is available in due time and in the required quality (see e.g. Melski et al. 2007).

In the following the use of RFID systems in three core areas of retail trade will be presented: support with the monitoring and control of distribution logistics processes, the application in (stationary) shopping venues and the use for product traceability. Even though the objectives and the measures under consideration do in fact differ, those are aligned to improve the performance of trade, also in view of the structures that are necessary to serve the clients.

4.1   Use in Distribution Logistics Processes

The use of RFID technology along the *supply chain* on the way from the producer to the shopping venues of stationary (over-the-counter) retail trade (or to the warehouses of mail-order retail trade) has significantly gained importance over the past years. On the one hand this results from the extreme developments in the field of *information and communication technology* (ICT) and on the other hand from the ever increasing requirements on the performance of logistical systems. Therefore, the following considerations concentrate on a cooperative approach which keeps in mind the interests of all parties involved. One of the main aspects is the linkage of material and information flows (see e.g. Wamba / Chatfield 2011) which aims at ensuring the efficient control of arising processes. Figure 2 provides an insight into the basic structures.

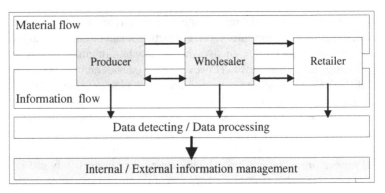

Fig. 2. Basic structures in distribution logistics

The following four tasks are in the foreground (see Melski et al. 2007):

° *Identification* of the logistical objects involved in the supply chain by means of the information stored.

° *Storage* of object-related (and changeable) data on re-writable tags which are attached on each logistical object.

° *Monitoring and control* of logistical objects taking real-time data relating to the current surrounding as well as to the (technical) condition into account.

° *Decentralized control* of logistical objects on the basis of suitable software systems, including tags as well.

Besides the availability of powerful technology, the crucial prerequisite for the functioning is a sufficient labeling of the objects to ensure the necessary accuracy when detecting those objects. At this point, a cost problem which could not yet be solved arises from the current price structure of RFID tags (see above). Only for products with a sufficiently high value or which are characterized by high safety requirements individual labeling is profitable which means that a significant part of the assortment in retail trade is not explicitly included. In these cases labeling is limited to the level of packaging units and load carriers (pallets, etc.). The following three issues are in the foreground of the considerations:

■ *Transportation tracking*:

This is about RFID-based tracking of defined objects over the whole transportation process, from the manufacturer to the (stationary) shopping venues of retail trade (or to the warehouses of mail-order retail trade). Three cases can be distinguished with respect to the basic structure:

° *Detection of objects at each loading and unloading point*: In these cases the detection process takes place via RFID exclusively at defined points which means that there is no *continuous* detection. Examples include processes in forwarding companies, parcel services and in principle also within multi-level distribution structures. For further information about the actual position (satellite-based) location systems (see e.g. Dodel / Häupler 2010: 177pp) are necessary, for instance in combination with the use of *fleet management systems* or *load unit tracking systems* (see e.g. Daduna 2005; Daduna 2011). Based on the position of the vehicle or the load unit (container, swap body, semitrailer, etc.) which is detected with the help of a satellite-based procedure the object can be identified. A precondition is, however, that the loading process has been carried out correctly.

° *Continuous detection* of objects in *logistics facilities* (warehouses, sorting facilities, production plants, etc.): In that case a sufficient antenna density is required as well as the use of electronic gates at defined points (for example in the incoming and outgoing goods sections). Like that every movement of the object is recorded in *real-time* so that immediate measures can be taken in case of non-authorized events, which is important also in view of an improved theft protection (see below).

° *Continuous detection* of *objects outside logistics facilities*: This type of detection within transport operations cannot be carried out within the scopes of RFID systems as the necessary wayside infrastructure is not available. In such cases, satellite-based location systems are normally used as it is the case in vehicle and load unit tracking (see e.g. Daduna 2011).

However, it is useful for a number of applications to make a link between *fleet management systems* and the RFID technology. This is in the case, for example, in monitoring and control of transportation processes of *perishable products* (s. e.g. Krüger / Böckle 2007; Edmond 2008; Amador et al. 2009; Cartasegna et al. 2010; Zöller et al. 2010) and *hazardous material* (see e.g. Planas et al. 2008). Here the emphasis is on the collection and recording of measured data and a (overall) continuous documentation of all processes (*tracing*), which are stipulated by legislative regulation in these areas.

Besides the *tracking* and (often mandatory) *tracing* as a basis for an efficient *supply chain event management* (SCEM) an improved *customer information* is possible, for example by providing actual *status information* (e.g. the position of the vehicle or load unit, the predicted delivery date, etc.).

■ *Inventory management* on *storage stages*:

Inventory management in warehouses as well as related processes (storage, stock relocation, stock removal, order picking, etc.) can be completely covered by RFID systems. On this level, the objects in question are usually packaging units or load carriers. Furthermore, the use of RFID technology is often the basis for *fully automated* storage, sorting, and order picking systems.

■ *Management of empty load carrier and container* :

The use of RFID systems showed substantial deficits in the field of load carrier and container management. It turned out that in many cases high levels of stock were outstanding due to the fact that the location of available units was often not known. Therefore, an efficient information management for *empties* is necessary to be able to attain a sustainable reduction in circulation. An improved level of information is also interesting in conjunction with a more efficient planning of *empties schedules*, also in view of avoiding or reducing empty runs (see e.g. Uckelmann et al. 2009). Keeping these points in mind when tracking transport processes, the aspect of returns and provision of load carriers and containers for further use has to be included in the areas of monitoring and control. Improvements in the organizational processes by applying RFID technology also lead to cost savings, particularly in container management (see e.g. Harder / Voß 2012). Moreover, with the help of RFID tags also it is also easier to identify the owner of empties, especially within the scope of lending systems as they are often used in this area.

By means of the preceding remarks it becomes clear that the use of RFID technology during the monitoring and control of distribution logistics processes allows for significant efficiency improvements and also for a higher transparency. However, the question about the profitability has to be kept constantly in mind to guarantee a positive cost-benefit ratio. Areas of application are, among others, the food industry (see e.g. Amador et al. 2009; Cartasegna et al. 2010; Hsueh / Chang 2010), the pharmaceutical industry (see e.g. Acierno et al. 2011; Maffia et al. 2012), and the textile industry (see e.g. Jacobs 2011; Garrido Azevedo / Carvalho 2012).

4.2   Applications within Shopping Venues

In-store logistics has not experienced a lot of attention within the field of retail trade (see e.g. Kotzab et al. 2007). Traditionally, the arising tasks were understood as being an integral part of the activities of the sales staff and hence were not considered to be a logistical problem. However, within that field of application cost pressure and information demand is constantly increasing so that the use of RFID systems is of growing importance. It is focused on the following applications:

■ *Incoming goods inspection*
   The *inspection* and *registration* of the goods delivered is usually considered very time consuming and hence is associated with personnel costs. Applying RFID in upstream stages (see above) it can be continued, for example when using automated systems in the incoming goods area. One example for the considerable advantages (in comparison with barcode systems) is the bulk detection (see e.g. Melski et al. 2007; Ranasinghe / Cole 2008). That allows for a virtually simultaneous detection of a large number of packaging units (for instance on a pallet) or for sales entities (for instance in packaging units) which significantly reduces the cost for the detection and provision of data.

■ *Product authentication*
   Product counterfeiting constitutes a serious *economic problem* for retail trade as approximately 5 to 7 % of the goods traded worldwide are forged (see e.g. Schuster et al. 2007: 105; Wu et al. 2011). This affects for example the clothing industry and in particular well-known brands. In addition, *security problems* arise in other industries, such as in the pharmaceutical industry (see e.g. Schuster et al. 2007: 86pp; Schapranow et al. 2011). By using RFID systems, the securing of authenticity can be improved and hence a protection against product counterfeiting can be established (see e.g. Staake et al. 2008; Lakafosis et al. 2011; D'Amato et al. 2012).

Here different technical solution approaches can be applied. One available application is based on rewritable tags which can be used to modify the stored data at defined points along the transportation route (see e.g. Ungurean et al. 2011). By encoding data, it can be guaranteed that only the recipient is able to read the modified data and consequently is able to clearly identify the goods. Like this it is prevented or at least it is made more difficult for forged products to enter the market, neither with copied tags. Another approach is the inclusion of forgery-proof "RF finger-prints" for the products (see e.g. Lakafosis et al. 2011), that allow verifying the authenticity of products with the help of scanning processes.

■ *Stock control*
This application deals with the most important field of RFID technology utilization in retail trade from a user´s perspective (see e.g. Bamfield 2011: 34). In the foreground are the *quantitative detection* and *management* of inventory and transaction data, e.g. based on *inventory management systems* (see e.g. ten Hompel / Schmidt 2008: 255pp; Hertel et al. 2011: 247pp), which represents an essential part of an *Enterprise Resource Planning* (ERP)-*system* (see e.g. Hansen / Neumann 2009: 675pp; Hertel et al. 2011: 241pp). However, at this point also *case-related qualitative aspects* are of importance, which must be included, for example to improve stock transparency. This qualitative information could include specifications about storage instructions, dates of expiry in the food industry or information about sales bonuses for the personnel in clothing stores if a particular object has not been sold for too long. In addition, this kind of data can be also used for more detailed customer information. Further relevant aspects are the facilitation of *inventory control measures* or the control of *restocking* within the scopes of *automated replenishments*.

■ *Theft protection*
Theft in shopping venues (and the attached warehouses) is a serious problem in many areas of retail trade. In 2011 theft-related costs (based on surveys in retail trade) amounted to US$ 99,736 billion (see Bamfield 2011: 25). However, thefts are not only committed by the customers (currently with a share of 51.6 %), but in many cases also by the own personnel (41.8 %) as well as by the employees of suppliers and external service staff (6.6 %). In 2011 US$ 8,746 billion were spend on technical measures for theft prevention (see Bamfield 2011: 29 p) which illustrated the market potential of powerful RFID technology. The basic structures comply with the structures of a continuous detection of objects in logistics facilities (see above), as long as there is a limitation (because of financial reasons) to a selective detection by means of electronic gates.

Besides the improvement of stock control, prevention is the most important aspect for the introduction of RFID systems from a retail trade perspective (see e.g. Bamfield 2011: 34). The reason for this is the performance which has improved significantly compared to the technology which has been used so far. In addition, there are different functional enhancements which allows for preventive measures. Schuster et al. (2007: 144pp) distinguish between three levels with respect to anti-theft devices:

° *Prediction*: This is about *preventive measures* to hinder (especially internal) theft by using appropriate technology. The focus here is on the deterrent effect and the increase of risk.

° *Detection*: The objective involves the identification of thefts that take place right in that moment (especially with external clients). Like that one is able to react in a targeted manner and in time. This classic type of theft protection is about the detection of (possibly not permitted) movements of goods within the shopping venues as well as the control of exits, if applicable video surveillance measures can be undertaken as well. In this context, it is possible to also include (ex-ante) the analysis of theft occurrences to be able to locate problematic areas.

° *Proof:* This is about the prevention of trick theft as well as the identification of stolen goods on (mostly) illegal markets.

The experiences made so far with theft protection in shopping venues on the basis of RFID systems show substantial benefits from a retail trade perspective. This is especially true with respect to efficiency of processes and of cost structures. However, like in many cases when customers are directly affected, a critical discussion about privacy aspects has to be taken into consideration as well (see below).

■ *Goods issue area and payment transactions*
The detection of the customers´ purchases takes place via automated systems in the goods issue area (similar to the receipt of goods). Given a suitable interconnection with an *inventory management system* (see e.g. ten Hompel / Schmidt 2008: 255pp; Hertel et al. 2011: 247pp) the stock can be adjusted in real-time. At the same time, the issuing of the invoice takes place. This form of processing can be integrated into an automated payment system (applying e.g. credit card transactions and automated bank transfers).

A much discussed application of a model in the field of application is the *Future Store* which belongs to the METRO Group in Rheinberg (Germany) (see e.g. Melski et al. 2008; Salditt 2008: 113pp; Kalyanam et al. 2010). Besides the support of logistical tasks and billing transactions with the help of RFID technology, also customer oriented measurements are included during the past few years, such as providing a *Personal Shopping Assistant* (PSA) to improve the convenience of shopping. But for cost reasons an extensive market penetration of this approach when designing structures for the stationary retail trade will probably not take place over the next few years.

4.3   Application in Product Traceability

Not only in the area of retail trade, the question about the *traceability* of a products´ origin is of major importance. This might be necessary if material defects or production errors are being noticed, or also if contamination or spoilage of the good occurs (for example in the food or pharmaceutical industry). To be able to prevent such cases and to limit the damage and the incurring costs, it is necessary searching for the upstream source of error in very little time. At the same time it has to be found out based on the detected source of error (downstream) if there are defective or not-marketable products along the different levels of retail trade or with the customer (back-tracking). In Figure 3 the basic process structure is sketched with the help of an example of the food industry, which makes this important (but unfortunately complex) problem relatively clear.

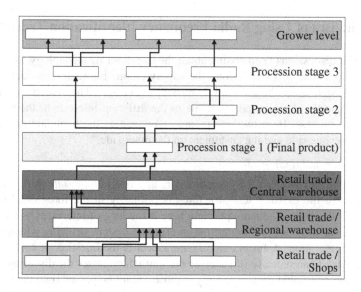

Fig. 3. Basic structure of traceability in food industries

Even though the required technical and administrative measures are quite costly, these might have to be contrasted to the occurring damage which arises if the traceability cannot or can only be partly carried out because of missing information. Under certain circumstance these results in significantly higher costs (possibly because of compensation and penalty payments) as well as in the damage of the reputation with severe financial consequences (see e.g. Fischer 2006).

The pharmaceutical industry is an area of again and again recurring drug counterfeiting also with respect to possible effects of personal injury and its effects on the public. A similar situation can be observed in the food industry. However, these problems are very specific, as for example the manufacturing of products out of living animals (see e.g. Doluschitz et al. 2010). In that area the *European Community* (EC) stipulates a far-reaching and strict general framework with the regulation EG/178/2002[1]. The compliance with that regulation has to be extensively documented. Here, the *administrative effort* can be reduced significantly, for example by linking these tasks to the data collecting processes of controlling and monitoring the logistical processes (see above).

The complexity of these tasks will continue to rise over the next few years due to an ever increasing internationalization of production processes as well as the rising division of work. A sufficiently exact and comprehensive data acquisition requires that a respective standardization of the RFID system across all production and distribution levels can be pushed through. Only that way a mediabreak free data exchange is possible.

---

[1] Regulation (EC) No 178/2002 of the European Parliament and of the Council of 28 January 2002.

5   Criticism of Using Radio Frequency Identification Technology

Controversial discussions keep arising about the use of RFID technology for the management of logistical processes along the supply chains between manufacturers and retail trade as well as for the application in shopping venues. The objections raised are complex and partly also contradictory due to the different interests of the parties involved in the process. Here two groups are of relevance: the manufacturers and the retailers on the one side and the customers on the other side.

■ *Manufacturer and retail trade*:

From the point of view of the manufacturers and retailers the *integration* of RFID technology in the existing ICT structures is primarily in the foreground (see e.g. Strücker et al. 2009). The main problem here is the lack of interfaces as well as the expected financial effort to implement an efficient system structure which shows a sufficient integration. A further significant aspect is the question of costs. The use of tags results in an increase of the costs per unit which raises the discussion of who will bear the additional cost, especially if those cannot be passed onto the customers through the price. The results of a survey among potential users to identify problems in connection with a RFID implementation within their company are shown in Figure 4 (see e.g. Strüker et al. 2009).

Costly integration in inter-company business processes	(68)
Costly integration into the existing IT infrastructure	(55)
Limited chances for prognosis and / or measurement of benefits	(50)
Costly integration in in-company business processes	(48)
Costs exceed the economic benefits	(46)
Too high costs for testing the technology	(41)
Insufficient quality and / or functionality of RFID systems	(39)
Missing default profiles	(37)
Strong resistance from suppliers and clients	(36)
Objections about data protection from customers and / or buyers	(32)
Unresolved legal aspects	(32)
Unclear security aspects	(29)
Too few employees with sufficient qualifications	(23)
Other obstacles	(21)
Management of volumes of data	(17)
Doubt of employees concerning a breach of their privacy	(16)

Fig. 4. Problems of the introduction of RFID from the user's perspective[2]

Also the problem of standardization has to be seen in conjunction with the before mentioned system oriented advantages which can actually only be realized given a broad market penetration. *Industry-specific solutions* could be a first step into that direction. However, with the further increasing interconnection of processes taking place in industry as well as in retail trade, the call for structures across sectors will also increase. In addition, safety aspects have to be taken into consideration as well,

---

[2] User of RFID technology (n = 102) / Answer: "Great importance" and "Rather great importance".

especially due to the increasing automation of (internal and external) information management and the ever increasing and thus less transparent amount of data. However, a differentiated approach is necessary here as safety requirements do differ with respect to their application (see e.g. Hwang et al. 2009).

■ *Customers*:

For the customers other aspects are of relevance. With respect to data security, the discussion about the "transparent society" is in the foreground here (see e.g. Renegar / Michael 2009). Even though the focus is put on electronic identification documents and smartcard systems, there are some similar problems in various fields of retail trade. The deterrent example that is often referred to is the use of tags in the clothing sector. It is criticized that there is the possibility of identifying a buyer also on a subsequent date. Therefore, it is also questionable whether other proposal for RFID-based applications (which are common in the commercial sector) can be applied on the *business-to-consumer* (B2C)-*level*. Interesting examples such as the "intelligent fridge" (see e.g. Gangadhar et al. 2011; Rouillard 2012) are being discussed but the acceptance by the customers seems to be very low.

Furthermore, there are at times clear tendencies for *organized rejection* on *the part of the customers* which is mostly an ideological matter. The reason for this situation is the general hostility towards technology which even reaches the political level and which can hardly be dealt with in a reasoned manner. In addition, there is a certain fear about changes that are often hard to understand, especially if possible risks are unknown and a risk aversion also exists (see e.g. Thiesse 2005). However, the discussion about *data protection* and *supervision* (by *national governments*) is in the foreground. In order to encourage the acceptance by citizens, a greater transparency with respect to data collection and use of data is essential. Moreover, it is necessary that public-law institutions and the companies involved actively seek for dialogue.

The aspects that are being criticized show that it is mandatory to solve the *organizational* and *technical problems* as well as the discussed *legal questions* which actually exist so that resistance can be reduced and hence acceptance can be increased. At the same time a more proactive discussion with the critics has to take place to emphasize the positive sides of RFID application, particularly in retail trade logistics.

6   Conclusion and Outlook

As the preceding remarks have shown, the use of RFID technology in logistics offers substantial possibilities to sustainably improve logistical structures and processes in retail trade (see e.g. Bhattacharya et al. 2010) and also in logistics services (see e.g. Pacciarelli et al. 2011). In the foreground here is the support of the (logistical) information management along the supply chain from the manufacturer to shopping venues of retail trade. The most important problems that have to be addressed (see e.g. Melski et al. 2007) are the *data collection*, the *data organization*, the *data transformation* (to usable information), and the *data security*. In addition, a worldwide standardization on the basis of *open* and *integrated systems* is necessary, as it is for example strived for with the *EPCglobal Network* (see e.g. Ranasinghe et al. 2008; Finkenzeller 2010: 274pp).

However, it is mandatory to push a consistent implementation of this technology. Only if a sufficiently broad market penetration is reached, sustainable improvements in the process flows can be achieved on a larger scale. Due to (among other things) the insufficient financial capacities as well as the existence of bottlenecks in the production of the technical components, a comprehensive introduction of the RFID technology requires a longer time. Therefore, it has to be ensured that suitable temporary solutions are being used to bridge the next years. Connected with this objective *hybrid solutions* that make use of the RFID *and* the barcode technology at the same time are often applied. Like that it can be guaranteed that there are no interruptions during the data detection and the processing which are the most reason for inefficiencies in information management. As mentioned above, the profitability of using RFID has to be always kept in mind (at least in the long run). That means it does not make sense to establish structures that are permanently subsidized.

References

[1] Acierno, R., Maffia, M., Mainetti, L., Patrono, L., Urso, E.: RFID-based tracing systems for drugs - Technological aspects and potential exposure risks. In: Proceedings of the IEEE Topical Conference on Biomedical Wireless Technologies, Networks, and Sensing Systems (BioWireleSS), pp. 87–90 (2011)

[2] Amador, C., Emond, J.-P., do Nascimento Nunes, M.C.: Application of RFID technologies in the temperature mapping of the pineapple supply chain. Sensing and Instrumentation for Food Quality and Safety 3, 26–33 (2009)

[3] Bamfield, J.: Das globale Diebstahlbarometer - Zu den Ursachen und Kosten von Warenschwund und Kriminalität im weltweiten Einzelhandel. Study Centre for Retail Research Newark, Nottinghamshire, UK (2011)

[4] Bhattacharya, M., Chu, C.-H., Hayya, C., Mullen, T.: An exploratory study of RFID adoption in the retail sector. Operations Management Research 3, 80–89 (2010)

[5] Cartasegna, D., Cito, A., Conso, F., Donida, A., Grassi, M., Malvasi, L., Rescio, G., Malcovati, P.: Smart RFID-label for monitoring the preservation conditions of food. In: Malcovati, P., D'Amico, A., Baschirotto, A., Di Natale, C. (eds.) Sensors and Microsystems - AISEM 2009 Proceedings, pp. 381–385. Springer, Dordrecht (2010)

[6] Daduna, J.R.: Einsatz von Flottenmanagementsystemen zur Überwachung und Steuerung logistischer Prozesse. Logistik Management 7(4), 45–63 (2005)

[7] Daduna, J.R.: Aspects of Information Management in Road Freight Transport. In: Böse, J.W., Hu, H., Jahn, C., Shi, X., Stahlbock, R., Voß, S. (eds.) ICCL 2011. LNCS, vol. 6971, pp. 29–43. Springer, Heidelberg (2011)

[8] D'Amato, I., Papadimitriou, T., Baglieri, E.: The anti-counterfeiting potential of RFID technologies in the fashion supply chain (2012), http://www.medifas.net/IGLS/Papers2012/Paper232.pdf (July 12, 2012)

[9] Dodel, H., Häupler, D.: Satellitennavigation, 2nd edn., Hüthig, Bonn (2010)

[10] Doluschitz, R., Engler, B., Hoffmann, C.: Quality assurance and traceability of foods of animal origin - Major findings from the research project IT FoodTrace. Journal für Verbraucherschutz und Lebensmittelsicherheit 5, 11–19 (2010)

[11] Emond, J.P.: The cold chain. In: Miles, S.B., Sarma, S.E., Williams, J.R. (eds.) RFID - Technology and Applications, pp. 144–156. Cambridge University Press, Cambridge (2008)

[12] Finkenzeller, K.: RFID handbook - Fundamentals and applications in contactless smart cards, radio frequency identification and near-field communication, 3rd edn. Wiley, Chichester (2010)

[13] Fischer, S.: Traceability Management - Wie Unternehmen die Risiken von Produktrückrufen begrenzen können. In: Engelhardt-Nowitzki, C., Lackner, E. (eds.) Chargenverfolgung - Möglichkeiten, Grenzen und Anwendungsbereiche, pp. 174–191. DUV, Wiesbaden (2006)

[14] Fosso Wamba, S., Chatfield, A.T.: The impact of RFID technology on warehouse process innovation - A pilot project in the TPL industry. Information Systems Frontiers 13, 693–706 (2011)

[15] Gangadhar, G., Subramanya, N., Puttamadappa, C.: Intelligent refrigerator with monitoring capability through Internet. International Journal on Computer Applications, Special Issue on Wireless Information Networks & Business Information Systems (2), 65–68 (2011)

[16] Garrido Azevedo, S., Carvalho, H.: Contribution of RFID technology to better management of fashion supply chains. International Journal of Retail & Distribution Management 40, 128–156 (2012)

[17] Gaukler, G.M., Seifert, R.W., Hausman, W.H.: Item-level RFID in the retail supply chain. Production and Operations Management 16, 65–76 (2007)

[18] Gille, J.: Technische Ausgestaltung und wirtschaftliche Beurteilung des überbetrieblichen RFID-Einsatzes. Eul, Lohmar/Köln (2009)

[19] Gillert, F., Hansen, W.-R.: RFID für die Optimierung von Geschäftsprozessen. Hanser, München (2007)

[20] Günther, O., Kletti, W., Kubach, U.: RFID in manufacturing. Springer, Berlin (2008)

[21] Hansen, H.R., Neumann, G.: Wirtschaftsinformatik 1 - Grundlagen und Anwendungen, 10th edn. Lucius & Lucius, Stuttgart (2009)

[22] Harder, F.-C., Voß, S.: A simple RFID cost model for the container shipping industry. International Journal of Shipping and Transport Logistics 4, 172–181 (2012)

[23] Hertel, J., Zentes, J., Schramm-Klein, H.: Supply-Chain-Management und Warenwirtschaftssysteme im Handel, 2nd edn. Springer, Heidelberg (2011)

[24] Hsueh, C.-F., Chang, M.-S.: A model for intelligent transportation of perishable goods. International Journal of Intelligent Transportation Systems Research 8, 36–41 (2010)

[25] Hwang, M.-S., Wie, C.-H., Lee, C.-Y.: Privacy and security requirements for RFID applications. Journal of Computers 20(3), 55–61 (2009)

[26] Jacobs, S.: Das Internet der Dinge - Wie die Bekleidungswirtschaft von der RFID-Technologie profitieren kann. In: Wagner, U., Wiedmann, K.-P., von der Oelsnitz, D. (eds.) Das Internet der Zukunft, pp. 363–368. Gabler, Wiesbaden (2011)

[27] Kalyanam, K., Lal, R., Wolfram, G.: Future store technologies and their impact on grocery retailing. In: Krafft, M., Mantrala, M.K. (eds.) Retailing in the 21st Century - Current and Future Trends, 2nd edn., pp. 141–158. Springer, Berlin (2010)

[28] Kotzab, H., Reiner, G., Teller, C.: Beschreibung, Analyse und Bewertung von Instore-Logistikprozessen. Zeitschrift für Betriebswirtschaft ZfB 77, 1135–1158 (2007)

[29] Krüger, M., Böckle, M.: Kühlketten lückenlos online überwachen - Intelligente Sendungsverfolgung schließt Lücke bei unternehmensübergreifenden Transportprozessen. In: Bullinger, H.-J., ten Hompel, M. (eds.) Internet der Dinge, pp. 273–280. Springer, Berlin (2007)

[30] Lakafosis, V., Traille, A., Lee, H., Gebara, E., Tentzeris, M.M., DeJean, G.R., Kirovski, D.: RF fingerprinting physical objects for anticounterfeiting applications. IEEE Transactions on Microwave Theory and Techniques 59, 504–514 (2011)

[31] Lehtonen, M., Staake, T., Michahelles, F., Fleisch, E.: From identification to authentication - A review of RFID product authentication techniques. In: Cole, P.H., Ranasinghe, D.C. (eds.) Networked RFID Systems and Lightweight Cryptography, pp. 168–187. Springer, Berlin (2008)

[32] Lenk, B.: Identifikationssysteme mit optischen Datenträgern. In: Arnold, D., Isermann, H., Kuhn, A., Tempelmeier, H., Furmans, K. (eds.) Handbuch Logistik, 3rd edn., pp. 816–825. Springer, Berlin (2008)

[33] Maffia, M., Mainetti, L., Patrono, L., Urso, E.: Evaluation of potential effects of RFID-based item-level tracing systems on the integrity of biological pharmaceutical products. International Journal of RF Technologies - Research and Applications 3, 101–118 (2012)

[34] Martin, H.: Transport-und Lagerlogistik, 7th edn. Vieweg, Wiesbaden (2009)

[35] Melski, A., Thoroe, L., Schumann, M.: Managing RFID data in supply chains. International Journal of Internet Protocol Technology 2, 176–189 (2007)

[36] Melski, A., Thoroe, L., Schumann, M.: RFID - Radio Frequency Identification. Informatik Spektrum 31, 469–473 (2008)

[37] Mitton, N., Schmidt, L., Simplot-Ryl, D.: RFID middleware - Concepts and architecture. In: Bolić, M., Simplot-Ryl, D., Stojmenović, I. (eds.) RFID Systems - Research, Trends, and Challenges, pp. 271–295. Wiley, Chichester (2010)

[38] Pacciarelli, D., D'Ariano, A., Scotto, M.: Applying RFID in warehouse operations of an Italian courier express company. Netnomics (2011), doi:10.1007/s11066-011-9059-4

[39] Planas, E., Pastor, E., Presutto, F., Tixier, J.: Results of the MITRA project - Monitoring and intervention for the transportation of dangerous goods. Journal of Hazardous Material 152, 516–526 (2008)

[40] Ranasinghe, D.C., Cole, P.H.: Networked RFID systems. In: Cole, P.H., Ranasinghe, D.C. (eds.) Networked RFID Systems and Lightweight Cryptography, pp. 45–58. Springer, Berlin (2008)

[41] Ranasinghe, D.C., Harrison, M., Cole, P.H.: EPC network architecture. In: Cole, P.H., Ranasinghe, D.C. (eds.) Networked RFID Systems and Lightweight Cryptography, pp. 59–78. Springer, Berlin (2008)

[42] Renegar, B.D., Michael, K.: The privacy-value-control harmonization for RFID adoption in retail. IBM Journal of Research and Development 53(2), 1–16 (2009)

[43] Rouillard, J.: The pervasive fridge - A smart computer system against uneaten food loss. In: Proceedings of The Seventh International Conference on Systems (ICONS 2012), pp. 135–140 (2012)

[44] Salditt, T.C.: Netzwerkmanagement im Handel - Prozessinnovationen im Handel am Beispiel der RFID-Technologie. Gabler, Wiesbaden (2008)

[45] Schapranow, M., Müller, J., Lorenz, M., Zeier, A., Plattner, H.: What are authentic pharmaceuticals worth? In: Turcu, C. (ed.) Designing and Deploying RFID Applications, pp. 203–220. InTech, Rijeka (2011)

[46] Schuster, E.W., Allen, S.J., Brock, D.L.: Global RFID. Springer, Berlin (2007)

[47] Staake, T., Michahelles, F., Fleisch, E.: The application of RFID as anti-counterfeiting technique - Issues and opportunities. In: Miles, S.B., Sarma, S.E., Williams, J.R. (eds.) RFID - Technology and Applications, pp. 157–168. Cambridge University Press, Cambridge (2008)

[48] Strüker, J., Gille, D., Faupel, T.: RFID-Report 2008 - Optimierung von Geschäftsprozessen in Deutschland (2009), http://www.telematik.uni-freiburg.de/opendownloads/rfid_report_2008_de.pdf (July 13, 2012)

[49] ten Hompel, M., Schmidt, T.: Warehouse Management - Organisation und Steuerung von Lager- und Kommissioniersystemen, 3rd edn. Springer, Berlin (2008)

[50] Thiesse, F.: Die Wahrnehmung von RFID als Risiko für die informationelle Selbstbestimmung. In: Fleisch, E., Mattern, F. (eds.) Das Internet der Dinge - Ubiquitous Computing und RFID in der Praxis, pp. 363–378. Springer, Berlin (2005)

[51] Uckelmann, D., Hamann, T., Zschintzsch, M.: Performance increase and benefit compensation in supply chains by partial information sharing and billing based on identification of returnable transport items. International Journal of RF Technologies - Research and Applications 1, 23–43 (2009)

[52] Ungurean, I., Turcu, C., Gaitan, V., Popa, V.: An RFID-based anti-counterfeiting track and trace solution. In: Turcu, C. (ed.) Designing and Deploying RFID Applications, pp. 251–266. InTech, Rijeka (2011)

[53] Wolfram, G.: RFID - Schlüsseltechnologie für die Zukunft des Handels. In: Bullinger, H.-J., ten Hompel, M. (Hrsg.) Internet der Dinge, pp. 305–313. Springer, Berlin (2007)

[54] Wu, Y., Ranasinghe, D.C., Sheng, Q.Z., Zeadally, S., Yu, J.: RFID enabled traceability networks - A survey. Distributed and Parallel Databases 29, 397–443 (2011)

[55] Zöller, S., Meyer, M., Steinmetz, R.: Drahtlose Sensornetze als Werkzeug zur Echtzeiterkennung und -verarbeitung von Events in der Supply Chain. In: Schönberger, R., Elbert, R. (eds.) Dimensionen der Logistik - Funktionen, Institutionen und Handlungsebenen, pp. 805–820. Gabler, Wiesbaden (2010)

Solving Vehicle Routing
with Full Container Load and Time Windows

Line Blander Reinhardt, Simon Spoorendonk, and David Pisinger

DTU Management Engineering, Technical University of Denmark
Produktionstorvet, Building 426, 2800 Kgs. Lyngby, Denmark
{lbre,pisinger}@man.dtu.dk, spoo@dtu.dk

Abstract. A service provided by the liner shipping companies is the transport of containers by truck between the terminal and customers. These transports consist of import orders and export orders. Even though these transports concern containers and, therefore, each order is a full load, an import and an export order can be combined in one trip where the container is emptied at an import customer and taken to an export customer to be filled. Finding a set of optimal vehicle routes allowing these combinations is NP-hard. However, exploring the fact that the number of possible routes is small in the problem presented, we in this report show a model which can within seconds solve the problem to optimality. The model is tested on real-life data sets and additional constraints to the problem are considered.

1 Introduction

The transport of containers between (inland) customers and ports is an additional service offered by shipping companies. This intermodal transportation problem contains opportunities for the shipping companies to perform optimizations to reduce cost. Even though there are good manual techniques for performing optimizations an automatized exact method exploring all possible combinations will be able to reduce the cost further and even a small reduction may be able to save a company large amounts of money as the yearly costs are often very large. The transportation investigated in the problem is most often done by truck, but rail and barges are used when available for large amounts of inland container transport.

The transportation concerns deliveries of goods (imports) and pickup of goods (exports). Even though the transport by truck mostly is served by subcontractors the transported containers are owned by the shipping company. Therefore, in an import a full container must be delivered from a location to the customer where the container is emptied and the empty container is either taken to an export customer where it is filled or to a terminal for stowage. A major cost in these transports is the entry at a port or inland terminal. Thus the aim is to follow an import service by an export service so that emptied containers are put to use immediately. To do an import followed by an export using the same container is also called triangulation of orders. Examples of triangulation can be seen

H. Hu et al. (Eds.): ICCL 2012, LNCS 7555, pp. 120–128, 2012.

in Figure 1. Triangulating the orders will reduce the cost by reducing the total distance driven by the trucks. A column enumeration method has been applied to the problem. Solving the problem for a transportation day using this method will find minimal cost by finding an optimal combination of triangulated and single order routes. Usually the container is transported to a single customer location. However, it may happen that a container stops at multiple customers to get filled for an export or to get emptied for an import. The order of the customers for these multiple customer visits are given by the customer and therefore cannot be changed. This can as an example be caused by requirements on the arrangement of the cargo in the container. Since the order of the customer visits is given for the orders with multiple customers then the journey between the first and the last customer is fixed and the triangulation can only occur after the last customer for imports or before the first customer for exports.

Another type of triangulation is the chassi-triangulation where the trucks can leave the trailer containing the container at the customer for the customer to fill or empty and a truck will be assigned to pick the container and trailer up when the task has been completed. This may give the truck time to do other deliveries while the container is being filled or emptied. However, the trucks are often not able to leave the trailer behind as the trucks do not always have this feature (see [2] for Japan). Moreover, for the interchange of trailer between two trucks the trucks need to be of the same type. In Japan [2] and Europe the chassi-triangulation is generally not possible. However, in the US and Mexico the possibility of leaving trailers behind exists.

We have received data for a day of operation from a shipping company. In this data the origin/destination of the full container and the stowage location of the empty container is given. Moreover, for each order there is provided a service time window. These times are set by the customers when they place an import or export order. However, these windows could possibly be placed better with regard to triangulation if the shipping company could influence the time window choice of the customer. The time window of orders may then be placed by using information about orders which are already placed or which will likely be arriving. All orders considered are with dry containers as refrigerated containers may not be triangulated due to the need for cleaning before being refilled. The dry containers can have four different sizes:

- 20 feet
- 40 feet
- 20 feet high
- 40 feet high

An import order can be triangulated with an export order if the container size is the same or if the container of the import order is high and the container for the export and import orders has the same size in feet.

Shipping companies may have requirements about where the empty containers are stowed and we will here look into how we can model such requirements. The stowage of the empty container is currently at the port the full container

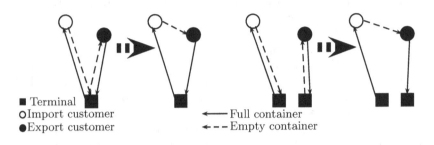

■ Terminal
○ Import customer   ←——— Full container
● Export customer   ←- - - Empty container

(a) Standard triangulation.   (b) Multi depot triangulation.

Fig. 1. Figure (a) shows how an import trip and an export trip both connected to the same depot are merged. Figure (b) shows how an import trip and an export trip belonging to two different depots can be merged (called triangulation).

arrived in. This, however, may result in more travel than needed as empty containers may have to be relocated to inland container yards near the location where they were first emptied. If we let the vehicle transport the empty container to and from the closest container yard always then the empty containers are not transported unnecessary distances. This, however, may result in some container yards overflowing with containers while others become empty. A way to solve this could be to use knowledge about the future to put restrictions on the imbalance of specific container yards and possibly by punishing any imbalances. However, such information was not available to us.

2   Literature

The problem of routing full container loads using linkage between delivery and pickup can be viewed as a simplified version of the vehicle routing problem with backhauls ([3],[4] and [7]). In the survey [5] many different vehicle routing problems are covered including the vehicle routing problem with backhauls. However, the full-truck-load problem is not covered in detail in the survey. In the second part of the survey [6] different pickup and delivery problems are covered. The vehicle routing problem with triangulation of full container loads has been studied by Imai et al. [2] where time windows are not included. They solve the problem using a heuristic method based on Lagrangian relaxation. In the case where there is only imports or only exports and a trip/route contains exactly one order then the problem can be seen as an assignment problem and be solved in polynomial time using the Hungarian method (also in the case where the trucks have different costs depending on speed). However, when the routes can contain more than one order the problem becomes a generalized assignment problem which is known to be NP-hard. This is described in more detail in [2].

Caris and Janssens in [1] expanded the problem to include time windows. Such a model is closer to the real-life routing problem of inland container haulage. In [1] this is solved with a local search heuristic. However, when including time windows the problem often becomes more restricted and easier to solve using a path representation of the problem as there are a limited number of feasible paths. In this paper we have used this property and solved the problem to optimality using an exact path model. Both Imai et al. [2] and Caris and Janssens [1] only considered one port and both have an objective of minimizing the number of trucks and distance traveled. In Imai et al. [2] the possibility of dropping off a container at a customer is mentioned but not considered as this is not applicable for their problem as the location is Japan where the trucks only seldom have this feature. In the problem considered in this paper multiple ports are considered. This results in multidepot triangulation such as presented in Figure 1(b) whereas the problems in [2] and [1] only apply the standard triangulation presented in Figure 1(a).

3   Mathematical Model

For this paper we assume a homogeneous fleet of vehicles and all containers to be identical. The capacity of a vehicle is one container.

- P is the set of all possible paths (trip patterns),
- K is the set of all orders,
- c_p is the cost of a path,
- α_{kp} is 1 if path p covers order k (move of full container),
- β_{kp} is 1 if path p covers the move of the empty container related to order k,
- O_k is the demand for order k,
- a_{kp} arrival time of vehicle p at the customer related to order k,
- d_{kp} departure time of vehicle p at the customer related to order k,
- s is the time it takes to stuff or strip a container,
- y_p is a binary variable which is one if path p is used.

Note that when generating the paths for the set P the time window requirement is insured to be satisfied. The a_{kp} and d_{kp} is only needed in the case of using chassi-triangulations where the empty and full container part of an order can be part of two different routes.

The problem can be formulated as the following linear integer program:

$$\text{IP1: min} \quad \sum_{p \in P} c_p y_p \tag{1}$$

$$\text{s.t.} \quad \sum_{p \in P} \alpha_{kp} y_p = O_k \qquad \forall k \in K \tag{2}$$

$$\sum_{p \in P} \beta_{kp} y_p = O_k \qquad \forall k \in K \tag{3}$$

$$\sum_{p \in P} a_{kp} y_p + s \leq \sum_{p \in P} d_{kp} y_p \qquad \forall k \in K \tag{4}$$

$$y_p \in \{0, 1\} \tag{5}$$

The objective (1) is to minimize overall path cost. The constraints (2) ensure that all orders are met during the planning horizon, constraints (3) ensure that all empty container pickup and deliveries related to the orders are done, and constraints (4) ensure, that for export orders an empty container has arrived before the departure of the full containers, and for imports that the full container has arrived before the empty is being picked up. Constraints (5) define the variable domain. If only box triangulation patterns are considers then constraints (4) are redundant. Moreover, constraints (3) is not needed when only considering box triangulations as delivery and return of the empty container would be completed in the same trip as the order (full container transport).

The solution approach is simply to enumerate all the feasible paths, the set P, and solve the model by a commercial mixed-integer solver. Path generation is done by full enumeration of all feasible patterns. The feasibility of these paths depends on the definition of the problem. In the case as described in IP1 where the number of vehicles is not minimized, the paths can be found by finding all single-location paths and all triangulated paths. A single-location path is for an export order to bring an empty container from a terminal to the customer, fill it and bring the full container back or for an import to bring the full container to a customer empty it bring the empty container back. To find all (non-chassi) triangulation paths we combine all import orders with all export orders and verify the feasibility of the path, i.e, bringing a full container to an import customer, empty it, then bring the empty container to an export customer, fill it, and then bring the full container to the destination terminal. Here we do not consider chassi-triangulation since we work with data from Europe and since optimizing a single day of operations as was desired then the chassi-triangulation will not be attractive. However, if looking at more days the chassi-triangulation may reduce cost as the containers can be left at customers over night. Moreover, the data we received for the problem is for a country in Europe where chassi-triangulation is not practiced due to various reasons where some are given in Section 1.

If minimizing the number of vehicles used then all feasible combinations of the paths generated must be enumerated as well. This means that the paths in the new set Q will contain the paths in the set P and all feasible combinations of the paths in P. Since the distances in the data provided are quite large and the time windows tight, then this does not result in an unreasonable amount of paths. However, if the time windows were relaxed and the distances were small this could result in an exponential amount of paths. When reducing the number of vehicles the objective must be changed to the following:

$$\text{IP2:} \quad \min \quad \sum_{q \in Q} (c_q + C) y_q \qquad (6)$$

where C is the cost of using a vehicle. Note that the constraints will be the same as the constraints from (2) to (5) where p and P are replaced by q and Q, respectively.

As mentioned earlier it may not be possible to pickup or to deposit empty containers at the nearest terminal. There may exist some requirement on how the balance is of empty containers at a terminal on a given day due to resource limitations. Please note that we do not include empty container repositioning in the problem. However, introducing the following requirements here will make it possible to take the desired locations of the empty containers into account. If such requirements are needed they can be introduced by letting:

- T is the set of all depots,
- B_t is the balance requirement for terminal t,
- ψ_{tp+} is the number of empty containers returned to terminal t on a path p,
- ψ_{tp-} is the number of empty containers taken from terminal t on a path p.

Note that the parameters ψ_{tp+} and ψ_{tp-} are determined when generating the route p just as the parameters α_{kp} and β_{kp}. The formulation of the linear integer model is as follows:

$$\text{IP3: min} \quad \sum_{p \in P} c_p y_p \tag{7}$$

$$\text{s.t.} \quad \sum_{p \in P} \alpha_{kp} y_p = O_k \qquad\qquad \forall k \in K \tag{8}$$

$$\sum_{p \in P} \beta_{kp} y_p = O_k \qquad\qquad \forall k \in K \tag{9}$$

$$\sum_{p \in P} (\psi_{tp+} y_p - \psi_{tp-} y_p) = B_t \qquad\qquad \forall t \in T \tag{10}$$

$$y_p \in \{0, 1\} \tag{11}$$

Note that in the requirement formulated in (10) we assume an exact difference. This might make the problem infeasible. However, a limit of the balance at the terminal can be introduced by removing constraints (10) and then introducing constraints:

$$\sum_{p \in P} (\psi_{tp+} y_p - \psi_{tp-} y_p) \leq B_t \qquad\qquad \forall t \in T \tag{12}$$

$$\sum_{p \in P} (\psi_{tp-} y_p - \psi_{tp+} y_p) \leq B_t \qquad\qquad \forall t \in T \tag{13}$$

This gives a lower and upper bound on the empty container difference in the terminals from the beginning of the day to the end of the day. If desired, B_t can also be split into two different values: B_{ta} for additional empty containers allowed for stowage and B_{td} for a decrease in the number of empty containers allowed at terminal t. Depending on how the B_{ta} and B_{td} are chosen the problem might be feasible Another option could be to instead introduce a penalty for violation of the balance constraints (10). The model could be formulated as:

$$\text{IP4: min} \quad \sum_{p \in P} c_p y_p + \sum_{t \in T} c_{et} e_t + c_{mt} m_t \tag{14}$$

$$\text{s.t.} \quad \sum_{p \in P} \alpha_{kp} y_p = O_k \qquad \qquad \forall k \in K \tag{15}$$

$$\sum_{p \in P} \beta_{kp} y_p = O_k \qquad \qquad \forall k \in K \tag{16}$$

$$\sum_{p \in P} (\psi_{tp^+} y_p - \psi_{tp^-} y_p + e_t) \geq B_t \qquad \forall t \in T \tag{17}$$

$$\sum_{p \in P} (\psi_{tp^+} y_p - \psi_{tp^-} y_p - m_t) \leq B_t \qquad \forall t \in T \tag{18}$$

$$y_p \in \{0, 1\} \tag{19}$$

$$e_t > 0 \tag{20}$$

$$m_t > 0 \tag{21}$$

Where c_{et} is the unit penalty for having less empty containers at terminal t and c_{mt} is the unit penalty for having more empty containers to terminal t than the required balance B_t. The variables e_t and m_t are respectively the number of empty containers less than B_t and the number of empty containers more than B_t at terminal t.

4   Computational Results

Five days of real-life data have been collected with the following characteristics:

- 275-329 orders per day
- 19-38 terminal/inland container yard locations
- 56-82 customer locations

All orders consist of one container (export or import). The day has been divided into time units of 5 minutes intervals in the planning period from 6 am to 6 pm. Customer time windows are given as one time unit, i.e., the time windows are very tight in the collected data. Distances and travel times were not available in the data set, so we have calculated the distance based on the Haversine formula used for distance measures on a sphere. The travel time is calculated based on an estimated average travel speed of 70 km/h for the trucks. Note, that in this experiment we do not consider handling costs, the path cost is related only to the distance traveled. Note that in the experiments done here we do not consider minimizing the number of trucks used. The container type is not considered. Moreover, the empty container can be taken from or delivered to any terminal and costs for waiting are not included in these preliminary tests.

The experiments carried out perform an optimization on the collected data and on a modified data set where the customer time windows have been changed such that all import orders must occur in the interval 6 am - 12 pm and all export

Table 1. Results. Setting t1 refers to tight time windows and setting t2 refers to import in the morning and export in the afternoon time windows.

	TW setting	dist	# routes	box triangulation
10242011	t1	116760	260	25
	t2	116339	248	37
	diff	321	12	12
10252011	t1	124450	245	30
	t2	123953	239	36
	diff	497	6	6
10262011	t1	102380	262	45
	t2	100130	226	77
	diff	2250	36	32
10272011	t1	159643	305	31
	t2	158903	302	34
	diff	740	3	3
10282011	t1	133403	303	34
	t2	132829	297	46
	diff	574	6	12

orders are in the interval 12 pm - 6 pm. The modified time windows should allow for a larger amount of box triangulations. Table 1 summarizes the results of the instances for the five days. Setting t1 refers to tight time windows and setting t2 refers to time windows where import is in the morning and export is in the afternoon. It is noticed that although the number of triangulations increases for all instances (between approx. 10-70%) the decrease in travel distance is not that much larger (only between approx. 0.5-2.2%). This is a little discouraging but, we must take into account that handling costs are not considered in this experiment. Therefore, it is to be expected that the actual savings by the increased number of box triangulations is much greater than what is indicated by the reduced travel distance. The number of trips to be made decreases accordingly with the increase of box triangulations which is to be expected.

5 Conclusion

In this paper we have considered an intermodal transportation problem in the liner shipping industry. We have proposed a mathematical model for optimizing the planning of a one-day schedule for covering all import and export orders. The model is based on a set of all feasible truck patterns which is found by enumeration. In the experiments we have considered single-location paths and box triangulation paths. The model has been tested on five real-life instances and we have analyzed the solution quality when considering the very tight time windows of the real-life data compared to time windows with import orders in the morning and export orders in the afternoon. The results show that although the total travel distance was not decreased by more than 0.5-2.2% the amount of box triangulations increased by 10-70%. The increased number of box triangulations indicates that there is a large saving in handling costs which was not considered explicitly in this model.

In future work waiting costs will be introduced and different restrictions on terminals for the deposit or delivery of empty containers as described in the different models. Moreover, we shall look into minimizing the number of trucks needed for a day's operations.

Acknowledgments. We wish to thank the three anonymous reviewers from whom we have received many valuable comments.

References

1. Caris, A., Janssens, G.K.: A local search heuristic for the pre- and end-haulage of intermodal container terminals. Computers & Operations Research 36(10), 2763–2772 (2009)
2. Imai, A., Nishimura, E., Current, J.: A Lagrangian relaxation-based heuristic for the vehicle routing with full container load. European Journal of Operational Research 176, 87–105 (2007)
3. Mingozzi, A., Giorgi, S., Baldacci, R.: Exact method for the vehicle routing problem with backhauls. Transportation Science 33, 315–329 (1999)
4. Osman, I.H., Wassan, N.A.: A reactive tabu search meta-heuristic for the vehicle routing problem with back-hauls. Journal of Scheduling 5, 263–285 (2002)
5. Parragh, S.N., Dörner, K.F., Hartl, R.F.: A survey on pickup and delivery problems: Part I: transportation between customers and depot. Journal für Betriebswirtschaft 58(1), 21–51 (2008)
6. Parragh, S.N., Dörner, K.F., Hartl, R.F.: A survey on pickup and delivery problems: Part II: transportation between pickup and delivery locations. Journal für Betriebswirtschaft 58(2), 81–117 (2008)
7. Toth, P., Vigo, D.: An exact algorithm for the vehicle routing problem with backhauls. Transportation Science 31, 372–385 (1997)

Multi-item Simultaneous Lot Sizing and Storage Allocation with Production and Warehouse Capacities

Cagatay Iris and Mehmet Mutlu Yenisey

Department of Industrial Engineering, Istanbul Technical University, 34367,
Macka, Istanbul, Turkey
{ciris,yenisey}@itu.edu.tr

Abstract. This paper addresses simultaneous capacitated lot sizing and storage allocation in a multi-item manufacturing environment. The Capacitated Lot Sizing Problem (CLSP) is a very crucial tactical level decision making problem resulting in production amounts and replenishment cycles in a dynamic demand environment. Regarding the capacity aspect, there may be different kinds of sources. Capacity bounds may be set on production capacity, and there may also be another upper bound on the units-on-hand inventory due to limited warehouse capacity which is a direct outcome of an adapted storage allocation policy in warehouse activities. Solving such an extended CLSP is proved to suffer from NP-hardness properties. Hence, heuristic algorithms are required to simultaneously solve lot sizing and pre-defined storage allocation problems. The aim of the study is to present a two-stage metaheuristic algorithm to solve related problems in polynomial time under different storage allocation policy boundaries on inventory. The proposed algorithm utilizes transfer of lots between consecutive periods. Results show that storage allocation policies which are primary drivers of inventory boundaries directly affect the results obtained. The algorithm is also applied to a shop floor planning problem.

Keywords: Lot Sizing, Storage Allocation, Capacity Management, Simulated Annealing.

1   Introduction

Due to the fact that there is a tremendous increase in competition in industry, companies are looking forward to obtain low-cost production activities via efficient planning and management techniques. In this sense, production planning and control which includes lot sizing, scheduling, and storage allocation correspond to emphatic importance. Optimizing these activities simultaneously brings remarkable advantage on cost reduction. Results indicate that holistic perceptions and integrated analyses are advantageous on the strategic, tactical and operational level.

The multi-item dynamic lot sizing problem pertains utilization of sources and aims to obtain minimum cost production plans with pre-defined parameters. In this paper, we focus on how to obtain a multi-item dynamic lot sizing strategy with production and warehouse capacities with different storage allocation policies. The difficulty in

H. Hu et al. (Eds.): ICCL 2012, LNCS 7555, pp. 129–141, 2012.
© Springer-Verlag Berlin Heidelberg 2012

optimizing planning of production relies on three tight constraints. Solutions found should be feasible with production and warehouse capacities and inventory balance between consecutive periods [16]. In this context, capacitated lot sizing and storage allocation policies are extensively discussed.

The Capacitated Lot Sizing Problem (CLSP) has many variations regarding product structure, setup time, overtime, backlogging, lead times, time windows, planning horizon etc. Recently, related problems are also extended to relevant research areas such as scheduling, lot streaming, storage allocation, vehicle routing etc. Hierarchical optimization of these problems may result in some infeasible solutions because decisions taken in previous steps are not made by considering possible infeasible outcomes. However, integrated solution strategies are much more favorable.

Our problem which is denoted as lot sizing with varying storage policies is not widely studied in literature. References [5], [7], [10] focus on inventory boundaries to formulate different dynamic programming recursive functions and algorithms. Most of these studies assume a single-item planning case with uniform costs between periods.

As an integrated coordination study, [6] has proposed a forward algorithm which is based on cost function relaxation. Another forward strategy firstly determines lot sizes and then smoothes them with warehouse capacities via Lagrangean relaxation [3]. Smoothing approaches seem to be popular strategies for solving related problems. However, all of these studies neglect the existence of production capacities, and solve the problem for uncapacitated production cases. Reference [11] has formulated a savings-based algorithm and computationally compared its result with results of [3]. Numerical results show that detailed savings heuristics outperform conventional hierarchical smoothing techniques.

It is deduced from literature reviews that metaheuristic algorithms are not utilized to solve such an extended problem [12]. A prior analysis before metaheuristics is made via fitness landscape analysis [4]. In this study, it is found out that a metaheuristic including staggering operation would fit the problem structure. The approach presented in our paper is based on the simulated annealing metaheuristic with restricted search spaces. Restriction of the solution space is made with dominance properties which conduct relevance between lot sizing and storage allocation parameters.

If the ending period inventories resulting from replenishments should be feasible with the warehouse capacity constraint, allocation of different products should be coordinated within the warehouse system, accordingly. Studies in literature focus on shared storage systems which consider an overall warehouse capacity [4], [11].

This study aims to integrate an efficient applicable lot sizing heuristic (LFL) and metaheuristic search procedure to solve the CLSP with storage allocation decisions. The initial solution neglects capacity constraints (production and storage) while maintaining inventory balance equations is employed to find an initial solution. The results derived from this phase are given as input for an improvement heuristic [8]. The proposed procedure is capable to improve a given initial solution within the restricted search space. The philosophy maintained here is transferring some amounts of lots from one period to another regarding bounds reflected by storage allocation policies. *Simulated annealing* (SA) is utilized not to stuck in local optima [14].

The organization of the paper is as follows. In the second section, a mathematical model of the related problem will be detailed, and dominance properties will be presented separately for each storage allocation policy, then specific steps of the algorithm will be expressed and computational tests will be conducted. Finally, future research directions will be presented.

2   Model Formulation and Dominance Properties

The paper focuses on the CLSP in two further aspects. It assumes two sources of capacity exist as regular production time and warehouse capacity. There are some basic assumptions that are made through the modeling phase. First of all, we assume that demand is projected in SKU parameter. Hence, each unit of demand may be kept in storage as one unit. No shortages are allowed during the planning horizon. Warehouse capacity is a bound on ending inventory of related periods. The warehouse capacity $MaxW$ is a dynamic parameter. However, it changes with different storage allocation policies. The generalized mathematical model for shared storage is:

Mathematical Model 1.

$$z = Min \sum_{\forall t}\sum_{\forall i}(c_{i,t}X_{i,t} + h_{i,t}I_{i,t} + s_{i,t}Y_{i,t} + os_t C_t) \tag{1}$$

$$s.t. \ I_{i,t-1} + X_{i,t} - I_{i,t} = D_{i,t} \qquad \forall i, \forall t \tag{2}$$

$$\sum_{\forall i}(cp_i X_{i,t} + cs_i Y_{i,t}) = C_t \qquad \forall t \tag{3}$$

$$X_{i,t} \leq (\sum_{\forall i}\sum_{\forall t} D_{i,t})Y_{i,t} \qquad \forall i, \forall t \tag{4}$$

$$C_t \leq MaxC_t \qquad \forall t \tag{5}$$

$$\sum_{\forall i}(I_{i,t}) \leq MaxW_t \qquad \forall t \tag{6}$$

$$X_{i,t} \geq 0, \ I_{i,t} \geq 0, \ C_t \geq 0, \ Y_{i,t} \in \{0,1\} \qquad \forall i, t \tag{7}$$

Where $X_{i,t}$ = Lot Size of item i in period t
  $I_{i,t}$ = On-hand inventory of item i at the end of period t
  $Y_{i,t}$ = Binary setup variable (=1 if item i is produced in period t, =0 otw)
  C_t = Consumed regular production capacity in period t
  $D_{i,t}$ = Dynamic demand of item i in period t
  $c_{i,t}$ = Unit production cost of item i in period t
  $h_{i,t}$ = Unit holding cost of item i in period t
  $s_{i,t}$ = Unit setup cost of item i in period t
  os_t = Unit regular time cost of consumed capacity in period t
  cp_i = Unit processing time of item i
  cs_i = Unit setup time required for item i
  $MaxC_t$ = Maximum available production capacity (time) in period t
  $MaxW_t$ = Maximum available warehouse capacity in period t

The model covers multiple-items with single-level product structure to be planned over T periods. The objective (1) aims to minimize total cost of production, holding, setup, regular time activities. Constraint (2) is the inventory balance equation for each product and period. Due to the fact that there are two different production capacity consumers, production limitations are formulated by constraint (3) consisting of production time and setup time with an upper bound of threshold of regular time. Constraint (4) ensures that whenever production takes place of each item, a setup operation is performed. Constraints (5) and (6) are control parameters to limit the maximum available production capacity and bound on the ending-period inventory. Constraint set (7) reflects non-negativity conditions and binary variables of setup activities. Constraint (6) may be modified with dedicated storage allocation technique. In this policy, each product family is assigned to a pre-determined zone. Hence, bounds should be set for each, and Constraints (6) should be updated; $I_{i,t} \leq MaxW_{i,t}$. It should be noted that single-level product structures do not require setup time as an individual parameter in the algorithm because most commonly, setup times are incorporated into unit processing times. Initial inventory level is set to zero at the start of the planning horizon.

The model contains a tradeoff between cost of setup and holding a unit of inventory in stock. The tradeoff occurs because in periods where demand result in idle capacity, it will be logical to produce more and hold inventory rather than making repeating setups [15]. In respect to right hand side values of the mathematical model, there exists another tradeoff which is a result of an adapted storage allocation policy. Whenever production capacity becomes binding, the algorithm should control whether resulted warehouse capacity is infeasible or not. For this reason, the proposed algorithm structure should be based on taking advantageous side of such tradeoffs.

Hence, transferring production lots from one period to another by some inferences may be an appropriate neighborhood structure. In this sense, search for global optima dominates the algorithm.

In an improvement heuristic, a move is generated by forward or backward transferring a lot to another period in order to restore feasibility of capacity constraints or improve the objective function. It depends totally on the constructive heuristic solution whether to improve the objective function or attaining capacity feasibility [15]. Simulated annealing, which deals with acceptance of a taken move by controlling the objective function, seems to be quite proper for such neighborhood structure.

In order to reflect capacity feasibility more precisely, source of tradeoffs should be clarified. Common storage allocation policies are random storage, dedicated storage and class-based storage. Random storage is most commonly applicable for warehouses where warehouse management systems (WMSs) are utilized. In this strategy, all items correspond to one class and may be assigned to any location. Hence, in such a model total unit capacity of warehouse is used as upper bound. However, dedicated storage is more convenient for facilities where data-sharing is a problem. In this strategy, specific zones are set for each product type [9]. An upper bound of the algorithm is set for each unique item. Finally, class-based storage use rate-of-return of item by using cube-per-order index which is the ratio of an item's ending-period inventory to its demand. In this study, the algorithm is modified according to different storage allocation policies to ensure warehouse capacity feasibility, and solved for different storage assignment strategies.

The proposed algorithmic structure starts with an easy-to-implement constructive heuristic which is LFL. Results obtained from this phase are given as input to the improvement heuristic. Since LFL may produce an infeasible solution to production and warehouse capacities, a smoothing mechanism is adapted. Related smoothing mechanism is based on restricting the search space of forward and backward transfers.

There are three fundamental decisions that should be made: determining periods to shift a lot from/to, items that will be shifted and the amount of transfer that will be subtracted and added between consecutive pre-determined periods.

After determining the period and item that will be shifted, the amount of the lot that will be transferred may be determined. Transferring a lot between periods will result in a cost fluctuation by changing the indices of related cost parameter. Forming a dominance property on one-at-a-time lot transferring may be useful for problem structure. These properties help to limit the search space, and result in high efficiency in search procedures [14].

Dominance properties: $Z = f(c_1, c_2, ..., c_n)$ is the value of measure (objective function in our case) that characterizes iteration S and $Z' = f(c'_1, c'_2, ..., c'_n)$ represents the value of the same measure under some different iteration S'. Then a dominance set is applied as long as condition $Z' \geq Z$ implies that $c'_j \geq c_j$ for some parameter j [1].

Property-1: Backward transferring an amount of Δ (Delta) from t_2 to t_1 for item i is dominance as: Starting from the period with highest load and an item with highest gap in total holding and production cost with previous period will form a dominance set for the backward scheduling procedure;

$$t_2 := \text{argmax}_{t=1,2,...,T}\{C_t | X_{i,t2} \geq 0\}, \text{ then } t_1 = t_2 - 1 \tag{8}$$

$$x := \text{argmax}_{i=1,2,...,N}\{\forall i \ (c_{t2} - c_{t1} + h_{t2} - h_{t1}) | X_{i,t2} \neq 0\} \tag{9}$$

if $x \neq \emptyset$
      then := add x to transfer list
else

$$x := \text{argmax}_{i=1,2,...,N}\{cp_i * X_{i,t2} | X_{i,t2} \neq 0\} \tag{10}$$

      then := add x to transfer list

Property-2.1: Transferring the lot in backward (which means transferring a lot from $t+1$ (t_2) to t (t_1)) direction, the maximum quantity that may be shifted depends on the production capacity and the adapted warehouse capacity for ending-period inventory. The maximum quantity of item i to be transferred is totally dependent on the implied storage allocation policy;

For backward transfer with dedicated storage policy;

$$\text{if } Q_{t1}^1 = \delta_{t1}/cp_i \text{ and } Q_{i,t1}^2 = W_{i,t1} - I_{i,t1} \tag{11}$$

$$\Delta_{\max} = \max_\forall \{0, \min_\forall \{X_{i,t2}, Q_{i,t1}^1, Q_{i,t1}^2\}\} \tag{12}$$

For backward transfer with random storage policy;

$$\text{if} \quad Q_{t1}^1 = \delta_t/cp_i \text{ and } Q_{t1}^2 = \Sigma_{\forall i}(W_{i,t1}) - I_{i,t1} \tag{13}$$

$$\Delta_{\max} = \max_\forall\{0, \min_\forall\{X_{i,t2}, Q_{t1}^1, Q_{t1}^2\}\} \tag{14}$$

The maximum quantity that may be shifted from t_2 to t_1 is limited to the amount of product that is produced in t_2, the available production capacity in t_1 and available storage space. The defined Q_{t1}^1 is calculated by dividing available time in (C_{t1}) which is δ_t to unit processing time of determined item i which is cp_i. However, calculation of $Q_{i,t1}^2$ differs with storage allocation policies. For dedicated storage, a parameter is calculated by subtracting ending-period inventory of item i from specific available storage capacity of the related item. For random storage policy, calculation of $Q_{i,t1}^2$ uses total available space (capacity) in warehouse.

Property-2.2: If the decision is to transfer the lot in forward direction (which means transferring a lot from t (t_1) to $t+1$ (t_2)), the maximum quantity that may be shifted depends upon the performance of backward shifting and inventory on-hand in the analyzed period t_1. The maximum quantity of item i to be transferred is also depending on the storage allocation policy;
    For forward transfer with dedicated storage policy;

$$\text{if} \quad Q_{t2}^1 = \delta_{t2}/cp_i \text{ and } Q_{i,t2}^2 = W_{i,t2} - I_{i,t2} \tag{15}$$

$$\Delta_{\max} = \max_\forall\{0, \min_\forall\{I_{i,t1}, Q_{t2}^1, Q_{i,t2}^2\}\} \tag{16}$$

For forward transfer with random storage policy;

$$\text{if} \quad Q_{t2}^1 = \delta_{t2}/cp_i \text{ and } Q_{t2}^2 = \Sigma_{\forall i}(W_{i,t2}) - I_{i,t2} \tag{17}$$

$$\Delta_{\max} = \max_\forall\{0, \min_\forall\{I_{i,t2}, Q_{t2}^1, Q_{t2}^2\}\} \tag{18}$$

The maximum quantity that may be shifted from t_1 to t_2 is limited to the amount of product that is on hand in t_1 and the available production capacity in t_2.
    Due to the fact that ending inventory of period t_1 may be hold during period t_2, warehouse capacity of period t_2 is also reflected with storage allocation policies. Limitations here are directly related to the initial performance of lot-for-lot schedule. The quantity that will be shifted is determined by using random integer generators between 0 and $\Delta_{\max}$ values [14].

3   Solution Method

As mentioned above, the algorithm consists of two consecutive stages. In the first, there is an "easy to implement" constructive heuristic which is a lot-for-lot technique. The solution set obtained in the first phase (Step 0) gives inputs for the improvement heuristic. The proposed algorithm utilizes a neighborhood strategy of [2]. In this paper, a multi-item lot sizing problem is considered for multi-level product structures with production capacities. The solution algorithm assumes single source of capacity (production) and a constructive solution is generated by using different types of

Lagrangean relaxation schemes. Four different neighborhood structures are tested for the CLSP by using simulated annealing solution procedures. Obtained results show that starting with an inventory-balance feasible solution yields better performance. For this reason, simulated annealing moves and neighborhood structure of [2] are adapted into algorithmic structure with modification defined in Property-2.

The following pseudo code gives information about the flow of the algorithm:

Algorithm 1.

1: **begin** { set all I_j=0;

2:     $X_{i,j} = D_{i,j}$, LFL; Calculate all C_t, I_t, W_t; }

3: **begin** { input = : an initial solution

4:     $t_2^{(1)} = t_2$ by using Eq.(8), $t_1=t_2-1$;

5:     find i by using Eq. (9)

6:     **if** $(t_2^{(1)}=1)$, Update t_2+=rand(0, t_{max});

7:         **go to** 5;

8:     **else**

9:     **calculate** ava_cap$(t_1)^{(1,2)}$ and $Q_{i,t1}^{(1,2)}$;

10:     **calculate** Δ_{max} by using Eq. (12) or (14); (Depending on Storage allocation)*

11:     $\Delta \leftarrow$ U[0, Δ_{max}]; make necessary backward shift;

12:     **calculate** Φ_{cost};

13:     **if** $(\Phi_{cost}>0)$, **calculate** β, ΔT; (Simulated annealing parameters)

14:     **if** $(\Phi_{cost}<0)$ or $(\Phi_{cost}>0)$&(SA accept); transfer Δ ; Update C_t, I_t, W_t, Φ_{cost};

15:     **if** $(\Phi_{cost}>0)$&(SA reject); **calculate** ava_cap$(t_2)^{(1,2)}$ and $Q_{i,t2}^{(1,2)}$;

16:         **go to** 5;

17:     (Apply **calculate** Δ_{max} by using Eq. (16) or (18))*;

18:     $\Delta \leftarrow$ U[0, Δ_{max}]; make necessary forward shift;

19:     **return** $X_{i,j}$;

The algorithm starts with calculating initial values by using a constructive heuristic. There is no involvement of storage allocation policies in this phase. Initially, lot sizes are determined, and they are given as input to the simultaneous assignment and planning algorithm.

The improvement heuristic conducts an accumulation strategy regarding all feasible capacities (both warehouse and production capacities), because assumptions are based on no-shortage policy. The procedure may not work forward since in the initial step there is not any on-hand inventory at the end of each planning period.

Some nervousness may occur in backward shifting. First nervousness of Dominance property-1 reveals whenever the most loaded period (regular) t_2 is 1. Then, there would not be any convenient period prior to t_2. Therefore, a random t should be assigned to update t_1 and t_2 [8]. The step taken by this command need not yield a better solution, but this will help to search for a global optimum without getting stuck in a local optimum. After that, available capacity for period t_1 is calculated, and then the maximum quantity of item i which can be shifted without violating feasibility of available capacities is calculated [8].

The calculation of maximum transferable lot sizes requires determining available production and warehouse capacities. Whenever a move is generated, updated values of W and δ should be set in order to calculate amount bounds.

After determining an amount to be transferred, the cost of transfer is calculated. If it is negative, then the move is directly applied. However, if shifting yields an increase in the objective function, rejection of the move is not directly applied. In this situation, parameters of simulated annealing are calculated by using formulas in [2]. If a uniformly selected random number between zero and one is greater than a calculated threshold value, the move is directly rejected. Otherwise, although backward shifting causes a worse objective, the move is applied, and parameters are updated [2].

If the move is rejected, lots are transferred forward to overcome problems derived from backward shifting. The adjustments made by forward shifting are not directly applied without assessment. The algorithm goes back to the stage where new items are determined for forward shifting, and continues until a termination criterion is met.

Once the algorithm obtains an initial solution, the improvement heuristic is applied for n times. The number of n is determined as a function of actual stopping criteria.

4   Computational Analysis

In this section, we present the description and analysis of computational results. We performed all runs on a personal computer with Intelcore i5, 2.53 GHz, 64 bit.

Performance of the algorithm is controlled with different characteristic measures. Most commonly the results may be evaluated according to total cost and optimality performance. All of these variants are involved in this study. In addition, for large test instances, the algorithm should be analyzed for run time, and actual termination criterion. In addition to all of these, we have also integrated parameters to test performance of lot sizing and storage allocation together. The authors have also controlled the overall utilization of warehouse capacity under different allocation scenarios.

The small-sized problems are used to control optimality, while large-sized instances are intended to reflect characteristics of the algorithm for computation measures. The performance of the heuristic also depends on robustness of structure. If it is possible to show that algorithm results are not affected by fluctuation in test data, then the structure may be called as a robust algorithm. The analyzed problem extension is not studied in previous literature. Hence, data is produced with special pre-determined characteristics to check some features. [15] is utilized to create the new experimental test bed. Parameters are modified by regarding differences in problem and solution procedures.

Generation of data requires setting some coefficients for each characteristic. Parameters which are related to lot sizing are separated from storage allocation parameters. Demand pattern, the ratio of production cost to holding cost, and the available production capacity are lot-size based parameters. These values are generated by using exact probability distribution functions which are reliable according to literature studies [15]. However, warehouse capacity is a storage allocation dependent parameter. In real manufacturing systems, warehouse capacity with rack systems is most commonly calculated by multiplying expected demand of each period with a coefficient. For random storage, overall capacity is imposed as a tight constraint. For dedicated storage, the problem becomes more complicated, because assigning a fixed percentage of capacity for each item requires a dynamic review interval to reflect fluctuations in demand. In this study, dedicated area percentage for each item is determined by considering item's overall demand over the planning horizon [13].

The small-sized test instances are composed of 4 items to be planned over 4 periods planning horizon. Hence, the optimizing mathematical model may not take enormous time. By having the higher planning periods, the algorithm will be more capable to shift a lot between periods and this decreases the probability of nervousness in execution. For larger-sized problems, a real manufacturing system data that produces cable harness is gathered. The large-instance test bed is divided into two basic sets. In Class-1, 20 periods (5 months in company's MRP system) are planned for 7 different basic products. In Class-2, 35 different items have been scheduled in 6 production periods.

For small-sized problems 30 different data instances are produced. The dynamic demand of each item is drawn from a normal distribution as $D_i \sim N(140,70)$, and we have analyzed different levels of demand variability where the coefficient of variation $(cv_i = \sigma_i/\mu_i)$ is set to $\{0,5;1;1,5\}$. These values are embedded in the parameter generation phase. Another parameter is the ratio c_i/h_i which reflects the change of production and holding cost rates between periods. All of these variables are produced for each unique period.

To reflect different types of products in the data set, 4 different levels of c/h are imposed in each period. Item1 has a c/h with a mean of 12 and a standard deviation of 8. Item1 represents products with higher production cost in respect to the holding cost. Item2 has a c/h ratio with mean 14 and a standard deviation of 12. These types of products have huge deviations in each period in c/h level. That means for item2, there is a great fluctuation in its data for each period. For item3, the ratio is normally distributed with a mean of 7 and standard deviation of 3. Item4 has a c/h with a mean of 2 and standard deviation of 1. These types of products represent the items with high holding costs [15]. Random values of holding cost and unit production costs are generated with pre-determined ratios. Unit processing time (cp_i) of each item is another input parameter; most commonly it is assumed that a single machine manufacturing system is applicable. Otherwise, a more detailed scheduling approach should have been incorporated into the algorithm. A related parameter is assumed to show a discrete distribution with different values between 3 and 20 minutes. Since, processing time will be used in capacity consumption, upper bound of given period's production capacity is generated accordingly. Due to the fact that setup times are not sequence dependent and there is no application of setup carryover, setup times are embedded in unit processing time depending on each item type [10]. Additionally, setup costs are obtained as a function of attained holding cost which is relatively steady between periods. In real manufacturing systems, setup costs are not very sensitive to variations as in other components. Hence, values have been smoothed.

Apart from lot-size relevant parameters, the algorithm requires warehouse capacity of each planning period. The tradeoff between warehouse capacity and system throughput needs to be analyzed in the earlier stage of system design [9]. In this study, it is assumed that the overall capacity of the warehouse has only variation within a range of 5% between periods. However, determination of exact warehouse capacity is more complicated. In order to sustain a tight-constraint criterion, overall warehouse capacity is set at most twice of the average demand of each item randomly for each case. Using this parameter as an input for random storage is adequate. However, it should be justified for dedicated storage. Adjustment is made proportional to total demand of each item. Percentage of each item in dedicated warehouse system;

$$k_i = \left. \frac{\sum_{t=1}^{T} D_{i,t}}{\sum_{t=1}^{T} \sum_{i=1}^{N} D_{i,t}} \right. \tag{19}$$

Variation within-range of %5 rule is still kept for this system. The overall results including those obtained by the rule of thumb approach are directly used in the algorithm structure. Assumption of SKU-based demand, inventory and warehouse capacity helps us not to convert such units to another.

For the small-sized problem instances, the performance of the algorithm is evaluated by using five different performance measures in Table 1. (Z is the objective function value of given alternative (H: Heuristic, O: Optimal, C: Lot-for-Lot)).

The parameters of outputs that show us performance of the algorithm should be clarified in detail;

$GAP_1 = [(Z_H - Z_O)/Z_O]*100$ (distance of heuristic from optimal)

$GAP_2 = [(Z_C - Z_O)/Z_O]*100$ (distance of constructive from optimal)

$GAP_3 = [(Z_C - Z_H)/Z_C]*100$ (distance taken from constructive to heuristic solution)

$GAP_4 = [(Z_H - Z_O)/(Z_C - Z_O)]*100$ (distance taken by heuristic according to the constructive solution)

$GAP_5 = [Z_H - Z_O]$ (cost gap of heuristic from optimal solution)

$UTL_1 = av. [(\Sigma I_{i,t})/W_t]$ (average utilization of warehouse capacity-overall)

$UTL_2 = av. [av. (I_{i,t}/W_{i,t})]$ (average utilization of dedicated warehouse capacity)

Table 1. Relative performance parameters for small sized problem instances

	N, T	Random Storage			Dedicated Storage		
		Mean	Std. Dev.	Max*	Mean	Std. Dev.	Max*
GAP_1	4, 4	3.68	2.85	6.78	4.41	3.21	9.42
GAP_2	4, 4	21.12	18.16	42.14	22.14	16.35	52.12
GAP_3	4, 4	54.45	25.58	86.12	52.16	20.22	82.45
GAP_4	4, 4	65.12	21.64	75.16	58.14	17.16	66.12
GAP_5	4, 4	4092 $	3707	9752	4876 $	4005	9866
UTL_1	4, 4	%88	%12	%100	%65	%30	%100
UTL_2	4, 4	--	--	--	%82	%13	%100

The results obtained show that the algorithmic performance is quite satisfactory in terms of optimality tests and warehouse utilization performance. Deviation from optimal solution is acceptable in terms of literature equivalents. It may be also deduced that whenever the number of periods is increased finding a near optimal solution becomes more challenging. Mean values which are reflected gives reasonable results, but constructive heuristic lacks such a well-performing characteristics.

Due to the fact that there is no guarantee that the constructive heuristic yields a feasible solution, the algorithm first obtains a feasible solution and then tries to improve it. Second criterion which is about performance of LFL may be misleading in this phase [8]. The improvement obtained by applying simulated annealing is tremendous. It may be observed that approximately 50% improvement has been achieved via improvement heuristic.

There is an obvious difference in performance characteristics between dedicated and random storage policies. Main differentiation may be observed in the utilization of the warehouse. Whenever random storage allocation is used, overall utilization is comparatively high. On lot sizing aspect; difference between allocation policies is valuable. Because of the fact that random assignment does not set a strict bound on ending inventory, the capability of the algorithm to obtain a better search area is increased in this strategy.

For small problem instances, the algorithm approximately takes 1 CPU second to solve the problem. For this type the total number of iterations has not exceeded 80 in each run.

If the problem size is increased to the large-sized set gathered from industry, the problem gets more complicated and finding an optimal solution via the MIP solver requires too much time, hence computational performance of such set is presented to be controlled. Due to the fact that the company does not use upgraded WMS, the facility applies a dedicated storage system.

Results obtained are evaluated with two different characteristics. One of them is the actual termination criterion and the other is CPU seconds. For Class-1, the algorithm is mostly stopped by a maximum number of iterations which is fixed at 5000 for each run to facilitate a fair comparison. Approximate time to obtain a result is 15-20 CPU seconds for Class-1. The company plans to schedule its production based on 70% of its product mix. Hence, the other class contains more products. Most runs in Class-2 stopped by losing forward move capability because of high number of products within short planning horizon, because of the lack of movement in forward/backward direction under warehouse capacity. For this set of problem instances, the approximate solution time is 20-27 CPU seconds. These results show that the algorithm performs quite well in big problem sets as well. Another critical performance criterion is robustness of algorithm. Given high fluctuations in data with item2, results obtained have low standard deviations in optimal solutions [8].

In the point of applicability of the proposed method, the company has initiated the algorithm as a supporting tool. After this phase, related code is planned to be embedded into an ERP system and the integrated version of MRP may yield better results.

5   Conclusion

Combined treatment of storage allocation and lot sizing is a promising research area which may result in good performances and increase the efficiency of both planning and warehouse systems.

In this paper, we have proposed a metaheuristic based solution procedure for this problem. A two-stage heuristic algorithm is presented to solve related problems in reasonable time. As a future research aspect, we are planning to construct a heuristic model based on a class-based storage system which dynamically plans production lot sizes and allocates items in the warehouse simultaneously. Another future research topic is to focus on the proposed algorithm and improve performance of heuristic.

References

1. Baker, K.R.: Introduction to Sequencing and Scheduling. Wiley, New York (1974)
2. Barbarosoglu, G., Ozdamar, L.: Analysis of solution space-dependent performance of simulated annealing: the case of the multi-level capacitated lot sizing problem. Computers & Operations Research 27(9), 895–903 (2000)
3. Dixon, P.S., Phol, C.L.: Heuristic procedures for multi-item inventory planning with limited storage. IIE Transactions 22(2), 112–123 (1990)
4. Grahl, J., Radtke, A., Minner, S.: Fitness landscape analysis of dynamic multi-product lot-sizing problems with limited storage. In: Gunther, H.O., Mattfeld, D.C., Suhl, L. (eds.) Management Logistischer Netzwerke, pp. 257–277. Physica, Heidelberg (2007)
5. Gutierrez, J., Sedeno-Noda, A., Colebrook, M., Sicilia, J.: An efficient approach for solving the lot-sizing problem with time-varying storage capacities. European Journal of Operational Research 189(3), 682–693 (2008)
6. Günther, H.-O.: A heuristic solution procedure for lot sizing under production and storage capacity constraints. In: Ahn, B.-H. (ed.) Asian-Pacific Operations Research: APORS 1988, pp. 349–362. Elsevier, Amsterdam (1990)
7. Hwang, H.C., van den Heuvel, W.: Improved algorithms for a lot-sizing problem with inventory bounds and backlogging. Naval Research Logistics 59(3-4), 244–253 (2012)
8. Iris, C., Yenisey, M.M.: An Efficient Heuristic Algorithm for Capacitated Lot Sizing Problem with Overtime Decisions. In: Frick, J., Laugen, B. (eds.) APMS 2011. IFIP AICT, vol. 384, pp. 107–114. Springer, Heidelberg (2012)
9. Lee, M.K., Elsayed, E.A.: Optimization of warehouse storage capacity under a dedicated storage policy. International Journal of Production Research 43(9), 1785–1805 (2005)
10. Liu, X.: A polynomial time algorithm for production planning with bounded inventory. International Journal of Advanced Manufacturing Technology 39(7-8), 774–782 (2008)
11. Minner, S.: A comparison of simple heuristics for multi-product dynamic demand lot-sizing with limited warehouse capacity. International Journal of Production Economics 118(1), 305–310 (2008)
12. Mishra, N., Kumar, V., Kumar, N., Kumar, M., Timari, M.K.: Addressing lot sizing and warehousing scheduling problem in manufacturing environment. Expert Systems with Applications 38(9), 11751–11762 (2011)

13. Muppani, V.R., Adil, G.K.: A branch and bound algorithm for class based storage location assignment. European Journal of Operational Research 189(2), 492–507 (2008)
14. Ozdamar, L., Barbarosoglu, G.: An integrated Lagrangean relaxation-simulated annealing approach to the multi-level multi-item capacitated lot sizing problem. International Journal of Production Economics 68(3), 319–331 (2000)
15. Ozdamar, L., Bozyel, M.A.: The capacitated lot sizing problem with overtime decisions and setup times. IIE Transactions 32(11), 1043–1057 (2000)
16. Tempelmeier, H., Derstroff, M.: A Lagrangean-based heuristic for dynamic multi-level multi-item constrained lot sizing with setup times. Management Science 42(5), 738–757 (1996)

Planning Maritime Logistics Concepts for Offshore Wind Farms: A Newly Developed Decision Support System

Kerstin Lange[1], André Rinne[2], and Hans-Dietrich Haasis[1]

[1] Institute of Shipping Economics and Logistics (ISL), Bremen, Germany
{lange,haasis}@isl.org
[2] University of Bremen, Chair of Business Administration, Production Management
and Industrial Economics, Bremen
arinne@uni-bremen.de

Abstract. The wind industry is facing new, great challenges due to the planned construction of thousands of offshore wind turbines in the North and Baltic Sea. With increasing distances from the coast and rising sizes of the plants the industry has to face the challenge to develop sustainable logistics concepts in order to implement projects in the planned cost and time frame.

In a research project a simulation tool that considers various logistical specifications of maritime supply chains in offshore wind energy such as weather dependant transport and installation at sea was developed.

The whole supply chain can be simulated – starting with the manufacturers and ending with the construction of the wind farm at sea. Different logistical strategies have an essential impact on the realisation time and the costs of a wind farm. With the aid of the simulation tool different scenarios can already be analyzed in the planning process.

Keywords: Offshore wind, installation, simulation, maritime supply chain, logistics concepts, logistics strategies, assembly, production, installation vessel.

1 Introduction

1.1 Importance of Offshore Wind Power for Energy Supply in Europe

Today, a growing economy and a rising prosperity of the population is accompanied by an increasing consumption of energy. Energy is the fuel for the world economy.

The increased burning of fossil fuels and the use of nuclear resources for power generation induces a rise in the external costs of energy supply, such as the emission of greenhouse gases as CO_2 and the risk of nuclear accidents. Moreover, the excavation of oil, coal and natural gas is hampered by regional distribution, limited access and the finiteness of resources. In the long run, fossil fuels like oil, coal or nuclear energy will become too expensive, too scarce or too harmful to the environment.

The European commitment to reduce CO_2 emissions, as well as Germany's exit from power generation by nuclear energy and rising oil prices lead to an increasing importance of renewable energy as an alternative energy source. In particular, wind

H. Hu et al. (Eds.): ICCL 2012, LNCS 7555, pp. 142–158, 2012.

energy is one of the most important renewable energy sources. The Renewable Energy Law by the German Federal Government proposes the increase of renewables in the share of electricity supply in the amount of 35% by the year 2020 and 50% by the year 2030.[1] With this, an important contribution to the objectives of European energy policy shall be provided. [2]

However, it is already evident that onshore the number of additional annually installed wind plants will decrease as the repowering potential in the countryside limited. [3] Therefore, the development of wind farms at sea is pushed – not only in Europe but on a global scale. The strategy of the German Federal Government for the use of offshore wind energy aims to achieve 25.000 MW installed wind power capacity in the North and Baltic Sea by the year 2030 [4]. Nevertheless, the installation of the first wind farms was delayed considerably – the influence of restricted time windows for transport and mounting processes was notably underestimated.

1.2   Scientific and Technical Background of the Research Project

The motivation for the research proposal arose from the discussion on the impacts of climate change and the increasing demands for the use of renewable energies. Wind plants play an important role, as they currently represent the only industrially applicable and economically operable facilities for energy conversion from renewable energy sources in several European countries.

The wind energy industry is currently facing big new challenges posed by the planned construction of 4,000 offshore wind plants in the German North and Baltic Sea until the year 2020. These challenges arise from the financial, technical and logistical dimensions of the wind farm projects. To be economically advantageous, plants have to grow in size (≥ 5 MW). As a consequence, the entire process of production, mounting and operating offshore wind plants has to be optimized.

The development of new transport chains and sustainable logistics concepts is required, taking into account long distances and the special challenges of maritime transport. The logistics costs of an offshore wind energy plant are estimated at 15% of the total cost. In contrast to other industries, e.g. automobile, there is hardly any transparency in logistics costs in the wind energy industry.

Novel logistical problems for the control of supply chains arise from the influences of specific parameters like campaign-based planning, short-term scheduling due to meteorological influences and constraints on scarce and costly resources.

Research on offshore wind plants, which until now has been carried out by different institutions, was mainly based on the technical challenges in the design, manufacture, installation and operation of the facilities. [e.g. 3, 5-8] With regard to logistical problems in production, installation and especially maintenance (spare parts logistics) and disassembly (reverse logistics) of offshore facilities only little research has been carried out up to now. [9-12]

This young industry is characterized by mainly medium-sized manufacturers and suppliers, who are forced to adjust their production and logistics concepts to the specific requirements in the maritime supply chain. Modern planning and control instruments are required, in which the experience of long-term projects can be embedded.

1.3   Research Goal and Approach

The scientific and technical challenge is the modeling of campaign-based supply chains by a simulator that can be integrated into a planning and control tool for logistics service providers. The simulation model has to take into account disturbances on the offshore wind supply chain and has to allow the assessment of logistics concepts with respect to planned goals and use of scarce and expensive resources. An important aspect is the transparency of logistics costs.

Ideally, the supply chain includes all production and manufacturing stages of the creation of a product development process - from raw materials to customers of a product. The supply chain often has a tactical and strategic character. Between companies, stable business partnerships are established, creating a more intensive exchange of information. A common goal formulation and the planning for the whole supply chain can be enabled with new planning tools.

In this project, the described long-term dimension of the supply chain is replaced by a campaign dominated dimension. This includes a temporary design of corporate relations as a function of changing external factors. This characteristic can be found in industries such as wind energy, plant engineering and construction (project business) or agriculture and forestry, which are subject to strong seasonal fluctuations. Here, supply chains are only of a temporary character and their structure depends on varying external factors.

The identification of the essential requirements for these specific offshore networks was done primarily in expert discussions in which information about the processes in the network was gathered. In addition, it was necessary to understand the product structure and assembly processes of wind turbines to derive the necessary requirements of the model. These restrictions were complemented by other characteristics of the logistics chain. One particular focus were disturbances like weather conditions and breakdowns which were integrated in the tool according to the experts prioritization.

As a methodological approach, the discrete simulation of the supply chains is selected. The simulation program was development by the Institute of Shipping Economics and Logistics. It is based on the tool Plant Simulation (formerly eM-Plant or SIMPLE + +) from Tecnomatix, distributed by Siemens PLM Software.

2   Logistical Challenges

Numerous offshore wind farms are being built in Europe. In Germany, the turbines are commonly constructed in comparatively high water depths (20 to 50 meters) and far distances (30 to 100 kilometers) from the coast. Facing these constraints, plants have to grow in size and output in order to be profitable. This implies serious financial, technical and logistical effort. Thus, the offshore wind industry is facing the following challenges:

- How is it possible to use the available weather windows at sea optimally, to deploy the expensive installation units efficiently?
- How is it possible to implement projects in the planned cost and time frame using comprehensive logistical concepts?

- What is the effect of different supply chain designs on the construction and energy costs?

Due to the ever-growing components, the challenges for manufacturers of wind plants and all other stakeholders in the supply chain are increasing. Although the installation of wind plants in different variants usually takes place at sea, components are firstly transported to the assembly areas on the *road*.

Due to the size of the offshore components logistical challenges arise, which often induce immense costs. This results in costs and risk factors that require an optimal management of service delivery. In particular, the interface problems along the supply chain represent an important field of research: cost and risk factors at the construction site, the transport chain, production and storage and the control of risk transfer have to be identified.

At *sea*, the scope of *installation work* and the necessary equipment are determined by the type of foundation (see Figure 1). For example, monopile foundations require heavy hydraulic hammer works to ram steel pipes with diameters of 4 meters up to 20 meters into the seabed. Even with the tripod, tripile and jacket designs three or four ramming procedures for each wind plant are required.

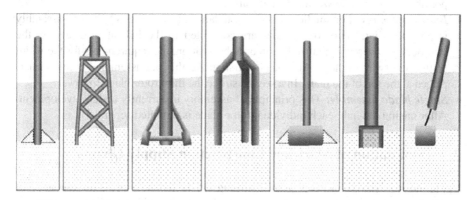

Fig. 1. Technical Concepts of Foundation Structures: Monopile, Jacket, Tripod, Tripile, Gravity Base, Bucket Foundation and Floating Foundation (Source: dena)

Here, weather is a major risk factor, which plays a meaningful role in the preparation and installation of wind plants at sea. All currently known mounting techniques can only be performed in calm sea. In this context, important criteria are wave height and wind speed. With significant wave heights of more than one meter, works become extremely difficult or even impossible. A temporary suspension of the work must be taken into account in logistics concepts.

The weather-related accessibility of offshore plants can also be a major problem for the maintenance and repair procedures of offshore wind farms. The consequences can be long shutdowns, when defects cannot be corrected immediately due bad weather conditions.

For the multi-megawatt wind plants *transport* is a technical and organizational challenge, which also has to be considered from an economic point of view. For large components the transportation problem which arises by the dimensions and the weight is an important challenge. To keep transportation costs low, the design of the plant with respect to length and size of the components is an essential factor. For the planned offshore wind farms in the North and Baltic Sea wind plants with rotor diameters of more than 120 meters are provided. One of the main current transport problems are scarce crane capacities and spatially limited transport permits. New large components often cannot be transported properly. Sometimes total weight exceeds the capacity of the vehicles.

A special logistical problem arises in the transport of the rotor blades. Due to the immense length of these components, different logistical concepts for transport and assembly at sea have been developed:

- *Star assembly:* State of the art is a star assembly. Here, the hub and the three rotor blades are pre-assembled on land. Depending on rotor blade length, this star has a diameter of about 120 meters. In the future, blade lengths will rise up to 90 meters, which would result in a star diameter of about 180 meters. This preassembled component is transported in a horizontal position on a suitable boat or pontoon out to the wind farm at sea. The assembly process at the head of the plant is only possible with suitable weather conditions.
- *Bunny assembly:* For smaller offshore installations (up to 3 MW) a bunny assembly is possible. Here, two rotor blades are connected to the hub at landside. As the transport on a vessel is realized in an upright position, the requirements for the width of the waterway are less. At sea, in a first stroke this pre-assembled component is placed at the top of the plant. In a second stroke the third rotor blade follows.
- *Single blade assembly:* This principle of assembly is currently under development. After raising the hub, each individual rotor blade is mounted separately.

3 Simulation of Maritime Construction Supply Chains

Up to now, research projects were focusing on technical aspects in the area of construction, development, erection and operation of offshore plants. Regarding logistical aspects in production, installation and maintenance (spare part logistics), only few studies have been realized [9-12].

To close this gap, a simulation tool was developed which considers various logistical specifications of supply chains in offshore wind energy such as:

- *Weather dependant* transport and construction of power plants at sea.
- Modeling of *production- and transport networks*, which are composed of user-defined sites for production, assembly, transshipment, ports and wind farms (see Section 3.1.).
- Definition of *land and sea transport* and handling resources.
- Simulation of wave heights and wind forces which delay transport- and production- orders by a *weather generator*.
- Representation of *disturbing factors* in the transport chain by stochastic breakdowns (total breakdowns, delays etc.).

As distances from the coast and the size of plants increases, the offshore wind industry is facing the challenge to implement projects in the planned cost and time frame using comprehensive logistical concepts. The simulation of different supply chain designs can support the planning process of wind farms. With our tool, the effects of possible deviations from planned time schedules on due-dates and costs can be seen in advance. Logistics strategies can be adapted with regard to the planner´s preferences.

After a process analysis, different scenarios and transport networks can be simulated, analyzed and compared, considering variable constraints and requirements. Hence, the decision process of finding the appropriate logistics concept for the offshore wind industry is assisted. Finally, conclusions about possible savings in the logistical system can be made.

3.1   Structure of the Model

The model is characterized by a tripartite structure (see Figure 2). Firstly, all requirements and restrictions concerning the logistics network such as the product and network structure and the process parameters have to be defined using the input tool. For the systematic identification of all needed data, an intuitive graphical interface has been developed. This interface allows the user to create logistical scenarios, to use stored catalog information and to adjust necessary changes for the analysis of varying logistical concepts.

In the next step, a masterplan proposal which provides a planning basis for the network is automatically generated by the tool and can be customized by the user. Based on this data, the simulation model is started via an interface and the simulation is carried out. Finally, the results of the simulation runs are evaluated and prepared for further analysis.

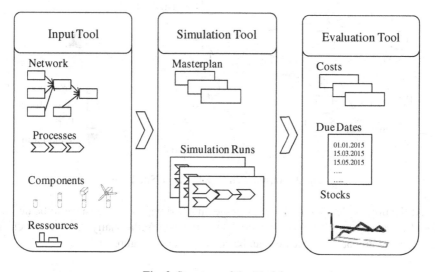

Fig. 2. Structure of the Model

Following the structure of Figure 2, the topics of Input Data, Simulation and Evaluation will be described in the next sections.

Input of Required Data. The required input data consists of the production network, the components of the wind plant, the transportation, transshipment, production and storage processes and the resources needed for these processes. Finally, disturbances like breakdowns and weather restrictions have to be defined.

Network and Processes. First of all, the logistics network that is to be analyzed has to be composed. Therefore, two layers have to be distinguished – a site-level and a process-level. In the site-level, four different sites can be drawn up (see Figure 3): In *production sites* the parts of component suppliers (like control boxes, unmachined parts or generators) and their due-dates can be defined. In *assembly sites* manufacturers assemble all incoming parts to bigger components. These finally reach the *ports* via land or sea transport. Depending on the weather, they are craned on specialized sea going vessels or installation units and shipped to the *wind farm*.

For a clear presentation, the network structure is represented based on graph theory as nodes and edges. Production and manufacturing sites as well as ports and wind farms are illustrated as nodes. These sites have to be linked with a **transport network** (road, rail, inland waterway, sea transport). The nodes are interconnected with edges which define the corresponding transport relations between the sites. Thus, the logistics network is a combination of the above mentioned types of sites that are linked with transport connections. Transport resources (heavy load vehicles, barges, installation units etc.) and handling resources like cranes and possible disturbing factors have to be defined later.

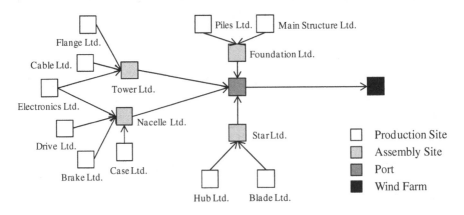

Fig. 3. Construction Supply Chain: Site-Level

At the process-level at each site, storage and retrieval processes have to be defined for the transport of the parts within the network. Additionally, for each vehicle loading and unloading processes can be considered (see Figure 4).

The logistics processes begin at the components supplier´s sites. Here, the starting points are input storages at each site in which the input materials for the production are stored. These may be raw materials, semi-finished products, components or assemblies which are stored until they are needed. For the production of components or modules which are made from one or more input materials resources such as personnel, machinery and equipment are used. After manufacturing, the product is stored in a warehouse until the transport to the next manufacturing or assembly facility begins. The necessary storage area must be adjusted regarding storage duration and size of the parts.

To be processed at the next site, a transport of the product between the nodes is necessary. Therefore, the component has to be removed from stock and to be loaded on a vehicle. Since most segments and components for offshore wind turbines usually are large, bulky and very heavy, these transports are mostly special and heavy transports which require additional approval and monitoring procedures. After the authorization of a transport, the components are loaded individually or in batches on a vehicle. For the loading process (as well as the unloading process at the destination) resources like cranes, slings or self propelled modular transporters might be necessary. These are often specific resources that are only available in limited numbers and that generate high costs for the period of use. This can lead to delays and additional costs in transshipment processes, when scheduled resources have to wait for other scheduled resources which are still occupied with other tasks.

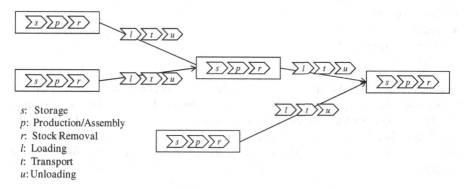

s: Storage
p: Production/Assembly
r: Stock Removal
l: Loading
t: Transport
u: Unloading

Fig. 4. Logistics Network: Process-Level (Source: Petri, R./Schuett, H.)

After the completion of the loading process the transportation of the goods to the next site is started. These shipments are usually heavy load transports which require appropriate special equipment and which can only be carried out on a limited number of transport routes. At the destination, the goods are unloaded and stored in the next warehouse. For this process the same statements as for the loading process are relevant. Here, the components are stored until all required materials are available and the next assembly process starts.

Finally, the main components arrive in one (or more) port(s), where additional storage and assembly processes can be realized. In the end, the installation vessels are loaded (considering the assembly in the wind farm) and the sea transports to the wind farm start.

Depending on the logistics strategy, there are different possibilities for the deployment of the installation vessels (see Section 3.2). Having arrived in the wind farm, the installation units start to install the wind plants. For the transport and construction processes, weather restrictions have to be taken into account. In this model, the installation of the wind plants´ components is the last step in the logistics chain.

Product Structure. For the structure of the main components (tower segments, nacelle, rotor blades) parts lists have to be defined. On this basis the production- and transport-orders are determined. Moreover, the sequence of the installation of the components at sea has to be clarified.

In several interviews the characteristics of the logistics network, the product structure, the resulting assembly steps and the dependency of subsequent assembly processes and transports between locations within the network were elaborated. The examination of the offshore wind turbine structure was limited to the currently used systems with a horizontal axis rotor.

This usually consists of the following components: three blades, rotor hub, drive train, generator, wind measurement systems, measurement and control unit, tower, foundation, a variety of auxiliary equipment and the grid connection. For the simulation of the logistics concepts the following main components and their composition can be defined:

- Foundation
- Tower segments
- Nacelle (machine house)
- Rotor hub (hub) and
- Blades

For the production and construction of foundations for offshore wind turbines a much larger effort for the production and installation is required compared to onshore wind plants. Among the various types of foundation concepts for offshore wind turbines the gravitation foundation, the monopile, the tripile, the tripod and the jacket represent the classical concepts which are derived from the conventional offshore industry (see Section 2.

Resources. The definition of resources is quite comprehensive: technical equipment for the processes of loading/unloading, production, assembly and transport can be defined. These have to be allocated to the sites in the network. Probabilities of failures as well as different types of costs (costs of mobilization and demobilization, variable and fixed costs, rental costs etc.) can be included in the tool.

Resources are essential for the realization of the logistical processes. Thus, if technical equipment is not available, processes are delayed until the needed resources are at hand. There are two reasons why needed equipment is not obtainable:

First, several resources are *scarce*. For loading big components usually special lifting equipment such as special cranes with higher lifting capacity, special slings and beams are required. Also, the used transport vehicles are mostly representing particular designs, which are specially adapted to the components. These special resources often only exist in small numbers or even are unique. If they are needed at different sites these resources and their availability may have a decisive influence on the logistics chain. This applies especially to the assembly of the plants at sea. Floating cranes and installation vessels are only available to a limited extent and might be the bottleneck resources in the network. The consideration of these resources is of great importance in the planning process. [13]

Secondly, resources – as well as processes – can be sensitive to *disturbances* like breakdowns, delays of previous processes or weather conditions.

Disturbances for Processes and Resources. An identification of the major disturbances was conducted mainly with the help of experienced staff of offshore related businesses. Using the input tool of the developed decision support system, identified disturbances can be assigned to specific resources and processes in the model. A disturbance is characterized by a name, the failure probability and the duration, which is defined in the form of a triangular distribution. This includes information regarding minimum, maximum, and normal breakdown duration. As no adequate records of the occurrence of faults that could be used for statistical analysis are available, we relied on expert knowledge to assign probabilities to the disturbances considered.

Influence of the Weather on Logistics Processes. For the installation of offshore wind turbines a calm sea and low wind are required. In general, the work is stopped at a swell of 1.5 meters for safety reasons. Considering the weather conditions at the offshore site, wind farms are installed in areas with relatively high wind levels to achieve a high efficiency in the operation phase. Since wave height and wind speed are directly related, high waves have to be expected in these areas. Thus, time windows for the installation of the turbines at sea are relatively limited.

These weather-related interruptions in the maritime part of the supply chain lead to challenges in the network. On the one hand, 1st- and 2nd-tier suppliers in the hinterland produce their parts following the planned masterplan, on the other hand, the processes at sea and thus in the ports are delayed due to the weather conditions. This leads inevitably to the formation of stocks within the chain, since a continuous assembly of the components throughout the year is not possible and since long production times of the components impede a just-in-time delivery.

A further special condition which aggravates the situation is the fact that in the offshore wind industry we are dealing with components which are large, heavy and expensive as well. As a consequence, for the storage of the parts a large area specially prepared for these heavy weights is required. Thus, the cost of storage is an important factor to be considered when analyzing logistics costs.

In our model, we rely on statistical weather data. As it is a tool to assess different logistics concepts for the installation of wind farms in the planning phase, no real time data and no interface for actual forecasts is needed. The data of the investigated site is revised on a detailed level and can be simulated by using Markov chains. Then, it is imported into the simulation tool. Wind and significant wave height are the most important weather restrictions. Furthermore, currents, wave periods, temperatures or ice conditions can also be relevant aspects that could be integrated in the model.

During the simulation of a logistics concept for the installation of a wind farm the weather is checked continuously. Before a process can be started, the weather is checked in two ways: First, the current simulated weather is checked to see if the process is allowed to start. However, this is not sufficient. Moreover, the weather development for the required time window for the whole process has to be acceptable to start the process.

Weather restrictions can be defined for resources, processes and components in the model. For example, seagoing specialized vessels like jack-up barges or other installation units are characterized by weather constraints. Depending on wind force or wave height (or both), the vessel might not be allowed to leave the port and start its journey to the wind field although the loading processes are completed. Having arrived at its destination at sea, processes like the installation of each component of a plant can be delayed, too.

Simulation. After entering all the required data a first masterplan is generated. It proposes dates for all production and transport orders for every site and transport vehicle. This masterplan has to be checked and adjusted by the user. The simulation of the designed scenario is repeated several times to demonstrate the impact of the disturbing factors and the weather, as these influencing factors are characterized by stochastic behavior. In order to show the effects of these disturbances not only on the basis of average values but also in terms of variances, the simulation technology is used. Thus, the sensitivity of the results with respect to the input data can be evaluated.

Masterplan. The masterplan is the key element for the user to interact with the simulation. It defines the start dates of all assembly and transport processes and determines which products are produced and transported at what time and in what quantity. It reflects the project plan.

According to the user´s specifications, the input tool generates a masterplan, which is imported by the simulation tool automatically. In this way, the simulation tool gets the required movement data for the strategy to be simulated. To "make the parts move" in the simulation model, jobs are needed, which are sequentially executed in the model. The masterplan consists of production orders and transfer orders, which have to be distinguished:

- For the manufacturing of parts *production jobs* are defined. These determine when and where which number of components is to be produced or installed.
- For the subsequent transport of the finished parts and components additional *transportation orders* are needed. These determine when which number of components is to be transported via which means of transportation using which route to be transported to which node.

The masterplan for the installation of 80 wind turbines can be very extensive. In principle, the number of nodes can be used as an indicator for the number of rows (number of production and transport orders) in the plan. Since almost all parts are transported to and from a node, that number must be multiplied by two. Thus, an estimator of the number of lines can be derived, which is calculated as follows.

$$lines \approx 2 \times n_{nodes} \times n_{turbines}$$

For a wind farm with 80 wind turbines, for each node 160 lines are created. The small example network shown in Figure 3 consists of 16 nodes. Thus, the corresponding masterplan would contain about 2600 lines. Since in some nodes several parts are produced, this number may increase considerably. For the user, this number is difficult to overlook, a manual creation of a plan hardly feasible without major errors.

For this reason, we developed an algorithm which generates a masterplan, based on the entered network information. The user can choose between a forward and a backward scheduled masterplan. After entering the planned number of wind plants the tool automatically generates the masterplan, considering the duration of the processes. The user can choose whether he wants to take into account the downtimes of resources or not.

The starting dates are displayed as text as well as graphically, similar to other project planning tools as Gantt charts. This allows the user to compare dates and move production and transport orders manually. The possibility to export the masterplan to Microsoft Project could be added.

Simulation Runs. The simulation tool imports the information which was entered in the input tool and constructs the network that is to be analyzed. Additionally, it is also possible to define presettings of stocks with the input tool which are imported by the simulation tool. Next, the simulation is started. Following the masterplan, production and transport processes are carried out – considering weather restrictions and other disturbances.

In the first run, it has to be checked, if the simulation can be completed. If not, the masterplan might have to be adjusted for further simulation runs. This is done manually, considering the expertise of the user. Our tool is a decision support system which is supposed to support the planner – it is not the aim to replace the human decision-maker.

After simulating the construction of the wind farm several times, it can be seen, where delays occur and what the possible bottlenecks in the network are. The planner is interested in the impact of disturbing factors to the entire logistics chain, and thus the total logistics costs. By altering restrictions, adding resources or changing assembly concepts, different logistics strategies can be compared.

It must be mentioned that simulation cannot be equated with optimization. The result of the simulation is not an optimized masterplan. This simulation model provides the results of the imported simulation data, which are then evaluated by the user and can be improved if necessary, by manual adjustments of the input data or the masterplan. In this way it is possible to approach an optimal result for the user gradually.

The duration of the simulation runs depends on the detail level of the network to be analyzed and if the simulation runs are carried out with or without the simulation of the weather. Without the consideration of weather influences, the duration of the runs is in the range of minutes. With the simulation of the weather the running time is much longer. For example, it took about four hours to complete 50 simulation runs of a wind farm consisting of 80 plants. This can be explained with the necessary time-consuming scanning for suitable weather windows, when weather dependant processes are waiting for their release. Nevertheless, this run time is acceptable, as this is a tool designed for the planning phase. Our experience with wind farm planning shows that the gathering of the input data and the coordination of the processes in the planning phase is very time consuming and extensive, as no standardized processes (like e.g. in the automotive sector or container logistics) exist. Thus, the run time of the tool implies no problem for the evaluation of real logistics concepts for offshore wind farms.

Evaluation. For the evaluation of a logistics scenario, detailed data is logged in the course of each simulation run. Since disturbances are based random numbers, it is not sufficient to rely on the results of a single simulation run.

In order to obtain useful results, it is necessary to simulate a scenario several times to identify extreme values and to be able to consider the influence of random variables. Therefore, to ensure the transferability of results to reality, several simulation runs are performed. As the results of each run are always different, the user needs a presentation, which depicts the results quickly and clearly.

The data generated during the simulation can be analyzed in many ways. In our project, we identified the project costs and the compliance of due dates as the most relevant parameters. Consequently, the evaluation tool was designed to reflect these values. A suitable representation is needed, which gives an overview of the bandwidth of total costs and completion dates of all simulation runs. The user should further be able to get a closer look at individual runs.

To give the planner a first overall picture, an evaluation of multiple runs is helpful. For this, the two key variables total costs and schedule variances are shown in a table and next to it in a scatter plot. Thus, the user can immediately get a visual impression on the costs and delays to be expected. He can see where points accumulate and where the over all average run lies. An example of the results of the simulation runs of a fictitious wind farm is shown in Figure 5. The high impact of breakdowns, delays, the weather and further disruptions on the realization time (abscissa) and on logistics costs (ordinate) in the installation phase is obvious.

The points near the mean value represent simulation runs, which are considered particularly relevant. Therefore, a closer examination of these runs is recommended. In addition to the scatter plot the user is given the opportunity to look at the values in tabular form. Here, minimum, maximum and average costs are given. These are broken down to stock, resource and overall costs. Furthermore, the masterplan offers the possibility to analyze schedule variances. Here the user can look for the minimum, maximum and average schedule variances of the processes. For all values of standard deviations are also indicated. This facilitates the assessment of the results.

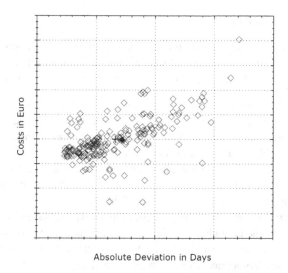

Absolute Deviation in Days

Fig. 5. Scatter Plot of Simulation Runs (Source: Petri, R./Schuett, H.)

Not only the overall costs and the schedule variances are of importance. There are different possibilities to evaluate the simulation runs. Some examples are:

- *Resources:* Depending on their deployment, vehicles, installation units and other resources can have different status: Different cost rates are assigned to active times, waiting times and down times. Moreover, it is possible to distinguish own resources, which generate variable costs per time unit used and resources like e.g. installation vessels or floating cranes, which have to be chartered for a period of time. For the latter, different costs might be relevant: Costs for mobilization and demobilization (which can amount up to several million Euro), charter costs per day (which amount up to 500.000 Euro) and standby costs, which are generated when the installation vessel is available but cannot work due to delays in previous processes.
- *Stocks:* When evaluating stocks and the use of storage capacities the development of stock levels during the installation phase can be important. If the planned capacities are not sufficient, additional buffer areas have to be defined or other logistics strategies have to be tested (e.g. the use of a second installation vessel). Storages and buffers generate logistics costs.
- *Components of the plants:* When disruptions occur, the analysis of the progress of single components might be a way to evaluate the logistics concept. Each component can be tracked individually, so the information when, where and in which status a component was is available. Storage times, processing times and transportation times can be checked for each part.

An increase in costs can be caused by waiting times of resources because of weather influences, breakdowns of technical equipment or other failures in the simulated scenario. Depending on the system to be analyzed and the question to be solved different key figures will be relevant.

3.2   Possible Scenarios

In a planning process not all of the possible features will be relevant. It is also common to concentrate on selected parts of the network which are to be simulated in detail. Hereby, different logistics strategies can be represented, evaluated and compared:

- *Assembly strategies:* Different assembly strategies at the wind farm can be realized. On the one hand, a separate installation of the tower segments, the nacelle, the hub and the three rotor blades is possible. On the other hand different strategies to reduce installation time at sea are investigated: The transport and assembly of the blades as "bunny" or "star". A future idea is the complete assembly of the whole plant at the quay side and the transport of it to the wind field.
- *Logistics strategies at sea:* Here, the pendulum and the feeder system have to be distinguished. In the pendulum system, the installation vessel carries out the transport of the components itself. It is loaded at the base port and takes the parts to the wind field. There, the components of the plants are installed successively by the same installation vessel. No unloading processes are needed. After the installation process the vessel turns back to the port to pick up the next components.

  In the feeder system, the installation unit stays in the wind farm. It is supplied by "smaller" feeder vessels or barges which bring the necessary components from one or more ports to the field. As there are no travel times for the installation unit, the productivity can be higher. However, the coordination of this system is more complicated.
- *Consolidation versus accumulative transport:* Following the consolidation strategy, all components produced in different sites are shipped by different smaller vessels to one base port, where all transports to the wind farm start. The strategy of accumulative transport represents a case, where one installation vessel has to stop at different ports to collect components which have to be brought directly to the wind farm.

Depending on the question to be solved, the simulation can be run with/without the breakdown of equipment and with/without the influence of weather.

4   Conclusion

At the current stage of development in the branch of offshore wind energy, in particular logistics costs represent an important risk factor. Mainly due to the lack of experience, weather risks and restricted time windows for logistics processes at sea, planned wind farms in Germany have to cope with considerable delays.

The innovative contribution of the project is the development and use of a new tool for planning and controlling logistics processes in the wind energy industry. Economic results are reflected in the improvement of the predictability and transparency of logistical processes, both on land and at sea. Existing management tools can be supported by simulation to assess possible disturbances and project risks.

With the aid of a simulation tool different logistics concepts can be tested and compared in the field of offshore wind energy – before starting to implement a logistics concept in reality. A multitude of different scenarios can be analyzed, beginning at the manufacturer´s site and ending at the installation processes at sea. The impact of various logistical strategies on the required realization time of such a complex project can be evaluated. Risks of delay and total costs can be estimated beforehand.

Investigated scenarios for real wind farms show, that especially in the final part of the network, which is the transport of the main components to the wind farm and the installation at sea, disturbances due to weather restrictions can lead to an explosion of logistics costs. This is the starting point for further research: In a following paper selected transport and installation strategies shall be compared, using realistic assumptions for the parameters and restrictions for the resources and processes, as far as officially accessible. Moreover, first O&M-concepts have been compared – a highly topical field in offshore wind energy. Another field of interest is the further development of the planning tool to use it in the operational phase of constructing or operating a wind farm. In our model, we rely on statistical weather data. As it is a tool to assess different logistics concepts for the installation of wind farms in the planning phase, no real time data and no interface to actual forecasts is needed. This would change when using a tool for real-time decisions.

Acknowledgements. The model was developed in cooperation with the Fraunhofer Institute for Factory Operation and Automation IFF in Magdeburg and the Logistics Service Agency (LSA) in Bremerhaven.

References

1. Bundestag: EEG 2012, Gesetz für den Vorrang Erneuerbarer Energien (Erneuerbare-Energien-Gesetz – EEG), Berlin (2012)
2. Paschedag, U.: Offshore Wind Energy Use. In: Köller, J., Koeppel, J., Peters, W. (eds.) Offshore Wind Energy. Research on Environmental Impacts, pp. 3–7. Springer, Heidelberg (2006)
3. Hau, E.: Windkraftanlagen – Grundlagen, Technik, Einsatz, Wirtschaftlichkeit. Springer, Heidelberg (2008)
4. BMWi, BMU: Energiekonzept für eine umweltschonende, zuverlässige und bezahlbare Energieversorgung, Federal Ministry of Economics and Technology (BMWi) together with Federal Ministry for the Environment, Nature Conservation and Nuclear Safety (BMU), Berlin (2010)
5. Frandsen, S., Barthelmie, R., Pryor, S., Rathmann, O., Larsen, S., Højstrup, J., Thøgersen, M.: Analytical modelling of wind speed deficit in large offshore wind farms. Wind Energy 9(1-2), 39–53 (2006)
6. Burton, T., Jenkins, N., Sharpe, D., Bossanyi, E.: Wind Energy Handbook, 2nd edn. John Wiley & Sons, Ltd., Chichester (2011)
7. Barthelmie, R.J., Courtney, M.S., Højstrup, J., Larsen, S.E.: Meteorological aspects of offshore wind energy: Observations from the Vindeby wind farm. Journal of Wind Engineering and Industrial Aerodynamics 62(2-3), 191–211 (1996)

8. CA-OWEE: Offshore Wind Energy – Ready to power a sustainable Europe. Final Report of
    the CA-OWEE project (Concerted Action on Offshore Wind Energy in Europe), Delft (2001),
    http://www.offshorewindenergy.org/ca-owee/indexpages/
    downloads/CA-OWEE_Complete.pdf
9. Gabriel, S.: Prozessorientiertes Supply Chain Risikomanagement: Eine Untersuchung am
    Beispiel der Construction Supply Chain für Offshore-Wind-Energie-Anlagen. Peter Lang,
    Frankfurt am Main (2007)
10. Haasis, H.-D., Heidmann, R.: Untersuchung der Logistik als Wettbewerbsfaktor in der
    Offshore-Windenergie, Bremen (2010)
11. Kolmykova, A., Haasis, H.-D.: Simulation of logistics processes for offshore wind farms.
    In: Ivanov, D., Lukinskiy, V., Sokolov, B., Kaeschel, J. (eds.) Logistics and Supply Chain
    Management: German-Russian Perspectives, Proceedings of the 5. German-Russian
    Logistics Workshop, St. Petersburg (2010) (in Russian)
12. Lange, K.: Mehr Sicherheit durch Simulation. In: Deutsche Verkehrs-Zeitung,
    Internationale Fachzeitung für Transport und Logistik, (DVZ), vol. 64(119), p. 9. DVV
    Media Group, Hamburg (2010)
13. Wiersma, F., Grassin, J., Crockford, A., Winkel, T., Ritzen, A., Folkerts, L.: State of the
    Offshore Wind Industry in Northern Europe. Lessons Learnt in the First Decade, Ecofys
    Netherlands, Utrecht, The Netherlands (2011)
14. Dena: Foundations for offshore wind turbines, Deutsche Energie-Agentur (2012),
    http://www.offshore-wind.de/page/index.php?id=10236&L=1
15. Petri, R., Schuett, H.: Verbesserung der Planungsgrundlagen für kampagnengeprägte
    Supply Chains (SC) am Beispiel von Offshore-Windenergieanlagen (OWEA),
    Magdeburg/Bremen (2010)

Application of Cycle-Based Simulation to Estimate Loss of Logistics Productivity on Construction Sites

Feng Xu, Yuanbin Song, and Hao Hu

School of Naval Architecture, Ocean and Civil Engineering
Shanghai Jiao Tong University, 1954 Huashan Road, Shanghai, PRC, 200030,
{F.Xu,ybsong,hhu}@sjtu.edu.cn

Abstract. Logistics management is a critical factor that determines the successful delivery of a construction project. The logistics activities have close connection with other logistics/construction activities, often producing hazards on site. Moreover, the policies and measurement taken to prevent these hazards often decrease the productivity of logistics activities. Therefore, quantitative evaluation of the influence of dynamic hazardous interactions between logistics/construction activities is critical for estimating the logistics productivity on situ. Unfortunately, previous research is inadequate in evaluating the contribution of dynamic hazardous interactions to the logistics productivity loss. This study develops a cycle-based simulation model for abstracting dynamic hazardous interactions between two logistics/construction activities, and then presents an algorithm for computing productivity loss. Consequently, the work delay of logistics activities can be better estimated and understood by site planners. In particular, the results of the case study indicate that the fluctuating characteristics of both logistics and construction activities in the same cycle significantly affect the logistics productivity loss.

Keywords: Logistics Productivity Loss, Hazardous Interaction, Safety, Hazard Prevention, Cycle-Based Simulation.

1 Introduction

It was estimated that poor logistics results in at least £3 billion unnecessary expenditure in the construction industry a year, and the unsatisfied logistics management on construction sites also significantly increases the risk to health and safety of operators and often delays the delivery of projects [14]. Many logistics activities are concurrently scheduled with construction activities due to various reasons like early delivery, critical resource sharing, and implementation of concurrent engineering philosophy. The application of concurrent scheduling approaches further exacerbates the difficulty of logistics management on sites.

The concurrency between logistics/construction activities is frequently a major course of hazards on construction sites. The execution of a logistics/construction activity may produce dangerous objects or energy that may hurt the operators of other adjacent activities. For example, when pipes are lifted by a crane concurrently with

H. Hu et al. (Eds.): ICCL 2012, LNCS 7555, pp. 159–170, 2012.

the earth moving, the crew of the latter may be hit by pipes dropped off from the crane hook. Another example is that when the polyurethane foam panels for thermal insulation is being transported under a roof with truss welding, the foam panels can be ignited by spark. Thus, site managers should re-sequence such logistics/construction operations for preventing hazards [8]. Simply, the truck for transporting earth should stop beyond or bypass the dangerous area when the bundle of pipes is being lifted. Otherwise, the pipe lifting operation should wait until the coming truck travels through the restricted area. Likewise, the flammable hazard can also be prevented by disjointing the trusses welding with transportation of polyurethane material. In general, such safety management inevitably decreases the production rates of the associated logistics/construction activities, thus delaying their finish times. However, few studies provide tools for quantitatively estimating the loss of productivity arising from the hazardous interaction between overlapped logistics/construction activities, resulting in unreliable schedule of construction programs. Although many studies have been conducted in the field of construction logistics, their focuses are often on the network configuration and supply chain management [12, 15].

The concurrency relationship between logistics/construction activities has been explored in a number of aspects. Some studies focus on resource-constrained scheduling where concurrent logistics/construction activities compete for common resources. Such approaches as ant colony algorithm [6], integer linear programming [7] and Multi-heuristic approach [13] have been developed for optimizing construction schedules. Later, the sharing of workspace resource is incorporated into schedule evaluation for identifying various types of conflicts, including hazardous interaction [1, 2]. Furthermore, the hazard space is defined as the boundary space where harmful energy or dangerous substance can reach [16, 17]. Some studies indicated that the intersection between the hazard space and the workspace of the potential victims results in the hazardous interaction between concurrent logistics/construction activities [2, 16]. Many research studies attribute hazardous interaction between concurrent logistics/construction activities to many safety problems, which is one of the major causes of the logistics/construction productivity loss [2, 5, 11]. In addition, some studies suggested rescheduling approaches to disjoint the concurrent logistics/construction activities in order to deal with the hazardous interaction between them [8]. In this regard, evaluating the operators' exposure degrees to hazardous space [9, 10] is crucial for estimating the duration of overlapped activities. However, the productivity loss in relation to hazardous interaction between concurrent logistics/construction activities is inadequately studied.

A construction schedule often consists of a collection of logistics/construction activities, and each should be executed with a number of repetitive cycles of low-level operations. A cycle herein defines a closed chain of operations, simulating the repetitive nature of logistics/construction operations [3, 4]. Since the execution of logistics/construction operations is often affected by many site factors, the durations of executing such operations are fluctuating instead of constant, resulting in dynamic interactions between cycles. Accordingly, the cycle concept has been used for simulating construction activities with the development of CYCLONE by Halpin [3, 4]. After that, cycle-based discrete event simulation has become an effective approach for modeling the random of both construction and logistics operations, This simulation approach can also be borrowed for modeling the hazardous interactions between activities/cycles.

This study utilizes the cycle-based discrete event simulation to evaluate logistics productivity loss resulting from hazardous interactions. The hazard prevention rules are firstly designed for preventing logistics/construction operators from access to dangerous areas, and then these rules are incorporated into the cycle-based simulation model for deriving the delay of the affected logistics/construction activities. Furthermore, the algorithm for calculating logistics productivity loss is detailed. Finally, a case study with hazardous interaction between earth moving and pipe lifting is modeled and simulated with discussion of the simulation results.

2   Hazardous Interaction and Coordination Modeling

2.1   Hazardous Interaction between Cycles

As described earlier, each logistics/construction activity can be regarded as a set of consecutive cycles of low-level operations. Using the cycle-based discrete event simulation approach, it is possible to simulate the interruption between a hazardous operation and its potential victims by incorporating the hazard prevention rules. In this way, the decrease of logistics production rate can be further derived using the simulation data.

A logistics/construction activity is often executed by utilizing multiple units of resources. For simplifying the problem, this study only considers one unit of resource for each activity. Accordingly, Fig. 1 illustrates a typical cycle of earth moving, consisting of five sequential operations. It starts with earth being loaded on the truck by an excavator, and then hauled to and dumped at the unloading place. Subsequently, the empty truck will go back to the loading place, waiting for the next cycle. Before reloading earth, the truck may wait for some time until the earlier arrived truck finishes its loading operation. In this case, the excavator only serves one truck, so the waiting can be assumed to be zero. In this regard, the cycle that is a sequence of operations repeats itself a number of times to make up an activity. Moreover, Fig. 1 also describes a pipe-lifting cycle, composing a sequence of 7 operations: prepare, fasten, lift up, rotate forward, put down, unfasten, and rotate backward. It depicts the workflow that pipes are transported from its storage place to the installation workface by the tower crane, and then the boom rotates horizontally back to its origin place, preparing for its next cycle.

Additionally, Fig. 1 further shows the dynamic hazardous interactions between two cycles, i.e. earth moving and pipe lifting. An accident may occur during the interval from the 120th to 122th minute when the pipe bundle, being rotated forward to its installation destination, drops from the crane hook and then hurt the driver for dumping since the dumping workspace is just beneath the rotating area required for transporting pipes.

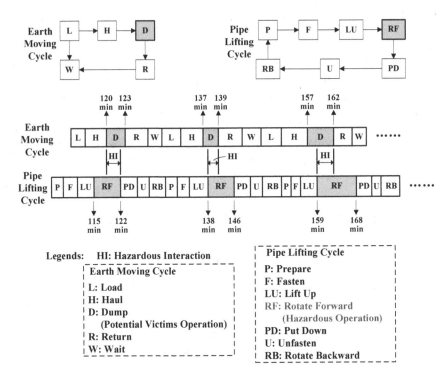

Fig. 1. Hazardous Interaction between Truck Dumping and Crane Rotation

2.2   Temporal Coordination for Preventing Hazardous Interactions

In order to prevent the harmful interactions as shown in Fig. 1, the hazardous operation should be prevented from overlapping against the potential victims operation. In this case, the truck used for dumping cannot avoid the space beneath the rotating boom of the crane. Thus, only temporal coordination is available. In detail, either operation start later, its commencement will be delayed until the earlier finishes. The example shown in Fig. 2 illustrates the condition of non-overlap between the operation "Dump" (potential victims operation) and the operation "Rotate Forward" (hazardous operation). Although the operation "Haul" finishes on the 120th minute, its successor "Dump" (potential victim operation) in the cycle still need to wait for 2 minutes until the end of the operation "Rotate Forward", the hazardous operation in the pipe lifting cycle. Otherwise, the potential victim operation will overlap with the hazardous operation, which is a highly risk factor for the truck driver. Obviously, the dormant gap between "Haul" and "Dump" means the productivity loss of earth moving. Fortunately, the inter-cycle interaction mechanism can be used to model the coordination between two concurrent logistics/construction activities for avoiding hazardous interactions.

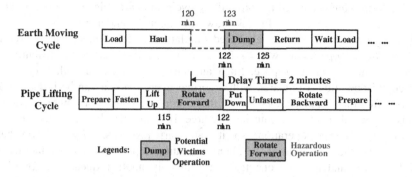

Fig. 2. Temporal Coordination between Two Cycles for Preventing Hazardous Interaction

3   Cycle-Based Simulation Model for Temporal Coordination

As mentioned previously, a logistics/construction activity can be abstracted with many cycles modeling the repetitive operations. Moreover, the fluctuating duration of each repetitive operation can be modeled using a stochastic variable. This makes it possible to stochastically simulate logistics/construction activities and schedule using cycle-based discrete event simulation. In this way, the effect of non-overlap constraints for preventing accidents can be simulated, and then the extension of the associated activities can be evaluated. Fig. 3 illustrates the same simulation model as Fig. 2. The Safe Space herein denotes the space beneath the rotating boom of the tower crane that can only be exclusively occupied by the operation "Dump", or "Lift Up", or "Rotate Forward".

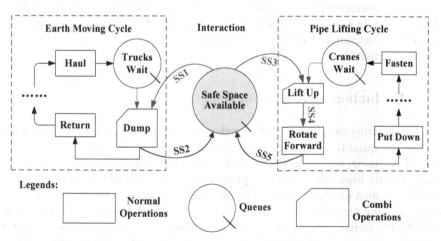

Fig. 3. Cycle-based Temporal Coordination Simulation Model between Two Simultaneous Cycles

The earth moving cycle and the pipe lifting cycle shown in Fig. 3 follow the same case as Fig. 1. The center of Fig. 3 shows the queue component *Safe Space* for coordinating two cycles. In the cycle-based simulation model, a queue can be used to model the linked operations waiting for such a logistics/construction resource as operator, equipment or workspace. Such an operation connected with a queue is called combi operation. Compared with a normal operation that can be immediately triggered after their predecessors finish, the commencement of a combi operation depends on whether the prerequisite resource is available. For instance, *Rotate Forward* is a normal operation, so it can start just when *Lift Up* finishes. Comparatively, the execution of the *Dump* operation depends on the availability of the *Safe Space*, and at least one truck available in another queue *Trucks Wait*. Likewise, the triggering conditions for *Lifting Up* are both available, the *Safe Space* and the idle Crane in the *Cranes Wait* queue (See Fig. 3).

Furthermore, the exclusive occupation of the *Safe Space* can be represented by three links *SS1*, *SS3* and *SS4*. Likewise, two links *SS2* and *SS5* indicate the occupation of the *Safe Space* is released. The link *SS1* means that the *Dump* operation can only start when the *Safe Space* is available, i.e. not being used by the *Lift Up* operation. Similarly, the link *SS3* means that the *Lift Up* operation can be triggered only when the truck is not engaged in the dumping operation that needs to exclusively occupy the *Safe Space*. It is also mentioned that the occupation of the *Safe Space* is not released when the *Lift Up* operation finishes, but released until the *Rotate Forward* operation finishes (See the links *SS4* and *SS5* in Fig. 3). In this way, the *Dump* operation (potential victim operation) has no opportunity to overlap with the *Rotate Forward* operation (hazardous operation), and the disjoint relationship between the hazardous operation and its potential victim can be semantically depicted. Additionally, this will ensure that continuous performance of both operations will not pause. Otherwise, if the *Safe Space* is released just after the *Lift Up* operation finishes, it is possible that the *Dump* operation arrives earlier than the *Rotate Forward* operation in the queue for the *Safe Space*, and executes between the operations *Lift Up* and *Rotate Forward*, which is an unreasonable and unsafe situation.

4   Evaluation of Simulation Data

When initializing the simulation, the number of earth moving cycles can be estimated by moving quantity and average execution productivity for acquiring earth. For a normal operation, its start time is often the same as the finish time of its predecessor since it starts immediately after its predecessor finishes, while the start event of a combi operation can be triggered when none of its immediate predecessor queues is empty. During the simulation, since the durations of operations are generated using Box–Muller formula, the finish time of each operation can be calculated by the sum of its start time and duration. Thus, alone the simulation, the dynamic time stamps of the start and finish events of each operation are captured and recorded into the database for further analysis.

Using the aforesaid temporal data along the simulation, the *delay time* (D) of the earth moving activity and the pipe lifting activity can be calculated using the following equation:

$$D = T' - Q/P \tag{1}$$

Then, the *productivity loss rate* (PLR) of either activity can be derived using Equation 2.

$$PLR = (P - Q/T')/P = D/T' \tag{2}$$

Where T' = activity duration acquired from simulation with the non-overlap constraint between the hazardous operation and the potential victim operation, Q = work quantity of the affected activity, and P = productivity of the affected activity without safety coordination being considered.

Consequently, the extension of the activities affected by the safety coordination for exclusive utilization of the safety space can be quantitatively evaluated, and moreover the fluctuating characteristics of the affected can also be calculated using the time stamp data. Such evaluation is explained in detail with the following case study.

5   Case Study

Following the model depicted in Fig. 3, the authors coded a simulation program using Visual C++ and SQL Server. Two activities, i.e. moving earth and lifting pipes scheduled for a chemical engineering project, are selected as *potential victim activity* and *hazardous activity*, respectively. Two cycles associated with these two activities, as well as dynamic hazardous interactions, have been illustrated in Fig. 1. To simplify the simulation case, only one truck and one tower crane are considered. Hence, the waiting operation in earth moving cycle can be neglected.

The variable durations of all operations in the earth moving cycle and the pipe lifting cycle were measured via a three-day site survey. The histogram in Fig. 4 shows the frequency distribution of 81 rounds of the operation "Rotate Forward" measured on site, while Fig. 5 provides the frequency histogram of 47 rounds of the operation "Dump". These two histograms indicate that the distribution of both the hazardous operation and the potential victim operation is roughly normal. The resultant μ and σ^2 of both operations are listed in Tables 1 and 2, respectively. In addition, the distributions of other operations measured are also approximately normal $N (\mu, \sigma^2)$. Due to the limited space, the duration data of those operations are omitted in this paper.

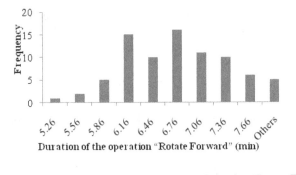

Fig. 4. Frequency Distribution of 81 Rounds of the Operation "Rotate Forward"

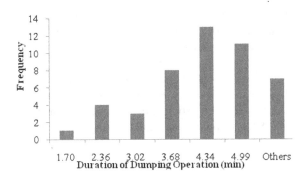

Fig. 5. Frequency Distribution of 47 Rounds of Dumping Operation

Table 1. Normal Distribution Parameters of Operations in Pipe Lifting Cycle

Operations	μ(min)	σ
Prepare	1.43	0.27
Fasten	2.44	0.31
Lift Up	1.18	0.18
Rotate Forward	6.66	0.68
Put Down	1.31	0.19
Unfasten	1.87	0.36
Rotate backward	2.73	0.22

Table 2. Normal Distribution Parameters of Operations in Earth Moving Cycle

Operations	μ(min)	σ
Load	5.34	0.98
Haul	10.63	0.41
Dump	4.18	0.79
Return	8.35	0.47

The construction schedule indicates that the activity Earth-Moving overlaps with Pipe-lifting from Day 204 to 211, and there is average 118 cycles required for moving earth during this overlap interval when average 205 pipe-lifting cycles can be concurrently simulated. In this case, altogether 3000 rounds of simulation have been executed by the aforesaid simulation program within 5 seconds.

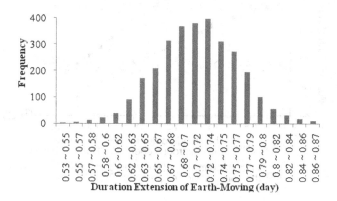

Fig. 6. Frequency Distribution of Duration Extension of Earth-Moving with the non-overlap constraint

Fig. 6 presents the frequency distribution of the duration extension of Earth-Moving collected in 3000 rounds of simulation, indicating that the extension of Earth-Moving duration follows a normal distribution with mean of 0.71 day and variance of 0.05^2. On the other hand, the distribution of the duration extension of Pipe-Lifting is also normal $N\ (0.06,\ 0.02^2)$. Accordingly, the productivity loss rate of Earth-Moving and Pipe-Lifting can be derived, using Equation 2. The former follows a normal distribution with mean of 9.24% and variance of 0.006^2, while the distribution of the latter is normal $N\ (0.91\%,\ 0.0027^2)$. Accordingly, construction managers should give enough attention to such extension that may result in delivery delay of a project.

In order to explore the relationship between the duration extension of a logistics/construction activity and the standard deviations of the duration of hazardous/victim operation, three groups of simulation tests have been designed, while each group contains 21 tests with different standard deviation of the duration of the potential victim operation "Dump". In each group, the standard deviation of the duration of the hazardous operation "Rotate Forward" was assigned 0.34, 0.68 and 1.36 minutes, respectively; and the standard deviation of the duration of "Dump" for those 21 tests in each was evenly increased from 0.395 to 2.095 with the step of 0.085, which is a reasonable fluctuation range of dumping operation. The other temporal data of the associated operations keep constant, following the setting describe in Tables 1 and 2.

Each curve in Fig. 7 and Fig. 8 indicates correlation between the average extension of Earth-Moving/Pipe-Lifting and the standard deviation of the duration of "Dump" interval. In detail, the increase of the latter variable causes the decrease of the mean of Earth-Moving delay and the increase of the mean of Pipe-Lifting delay. In these two

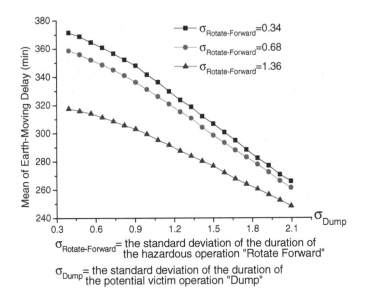

Fig. 7. Average Extension of Earth-Moving in Relation to σ_{Dump}

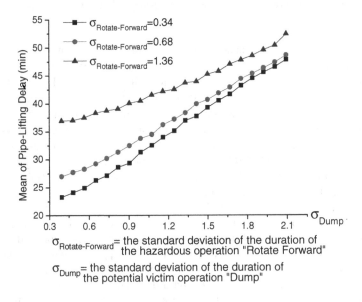

Fig. 8. Average Extension of Pipe-Lifting in Relation to σ_{Dump}

figures, $\sigma_{Rotate\text{-}Forward}$ and σ_{Dump} denote the standard deviations of the durations of "Rotate Forward" and "Dump", respectively. On the other hand, in order to further explore the relationship between the average extension of Earth-Moving/Pipe-Lifting and the interval of the standard deviation of the duration of "Rotate Forward", three values of $\sigma_{Rotate\text{-}Forward}$ (0.34, 0.68, 1.36) were tested, which produces respectively three curves in Figures 7 and 8. These curves mean that larger standard deviation of the duration of "Rotate Forward" results in less extension of Earth-Moving and more extension of Pipe-Lifting. Accordingly, the standard deviation of duration of hazardous/victim operation keeps positively correlative with the average extension of hazardous activity, and negatively correlative with the average extension of potential victim activity.

However, high variation of the duration extension of a logistics/construction activity, which often arises from high fluctuation of the hazardous operation and the potential victim operation, frequently implies harder management and higher cost. Therefore, construction managers should work with site managers and foremen to control the variation of durations of the identified operations.

6   Conclusion

Concurrent logistics/construction activities on a construction site may produce dynamic hazardous interactions, often leading to duration extension and productivity loss of the associated activities, but the construction industry still lacks a quantitative evaluation tool for evaluating the productivity loss in relation to dynamic hazardous interactions between logistics/construction activities, resulting in difficulty of rescheduling logistics/construction programs and of estimating the manpower expenditure for claims. Additionally, the dynamic and variable nature of logistics/construction activity exacerbates this difficulty. This study uses cycle-based discrete events simulation as a vehicle to quantitatively analyze the productivity loss, and provides a quantitative analysis approach for temporal coordination of concurrent operations. Furthermore, the simulation results indicate that not only the waiting time is a major cause of the productivity loss of the affected activities, but the fluctuating characteristics of activities also play a critical role in the extension of their durations. It also shows that these findings provide rich information for remedying the productivity loss of the affected activities.

Additionally, this study is only in its initial stage with the limitation of only allocating one unit of resource for each activity, but the simulation framework, especially with the queue and combi operation constructs, allows allocating multiple units of resources for a number of operations. In addition, the operation durations may not be normally distributed, and further site survey is required to further the distribution study of various types of construction/logistics operations.

Acknowledgement. The writing of this paper is partially supported by the Shanghai Natural Science Foundation (Grant No. 12ZR1415100).

References

1. Akinci, B., Fischen, M.: Four-dimensional Workplanner—A Prototype System for Automated Generation of Construction Spaces and Analysis of Time-space Conflicts. In: Fruchter, R., et al. (eds.) Computing in Civil and Building Engineering, pp. 740–747. ASCE, Reston (2000)

2. Akinci, B., Fischen, M., Levitt, R., et al.: Formalization and Automation of Time-Space Conflict Analysis. Journal of Computing in Civil Engineering 16(2), 124–134 (2002)
3. Halpin, D.W.: CYCLONE-method for Modeling Job Site Processes. Journal of Construction Division, ASCE 103(3), 489–499 (1977)
4. Halpin, D.W.: MicroCYCLONE User's Manual. West Lafayette, Division of Construction Engineering and Management, Purdue University, Indiana (1990)
5. Howell, G., Ballard, G.: Factors Affecting Project Success in the Piping Function. In: Alarcon, L. (ed.) Lean Construction, Rotterdam, The Netherlands, pp. 161–185 (1997)
6. Kuang, Y.-P., Xiong, Y., Zhang, M.-F.: Ant Colony Algorithm for Construction Resource Leveling. Journal of Zhejiang University (Engineering Science) 42(7), 1194–1198 (2008) (in Chinese)
7. Mattila, K.G., Abraham, D.M.: Resource Leveling of Linear Schedules Using Integer Linear Programming. Journal of Construction Engineering and Management 124(3), 232–244 (1998)
8. Panagiotis, M., Manoj, N.: New Method for Measuring the Safety Risk of Construction Activities: Task Demand Assessment. Journal of Construction Engineering and Management 137(1), 30–38 (2011)
9. Ophir, R., Rafael, S., Yehiel, R.: 'CHASTE': Construction Hazard Assessment with Spatial and Temporal Exposure. Construction Management and Economics 27(7), 625–638 (2009)
10. Sacks, R., Rozenfeld, O., Rosenfeld, Y.: Spatial and Temporal Exposure to Safety Hazards in Construction. Journal of Construction Engineering and Management 135(8), 726–736 (2009)
11. Sanders, S.R., Thomas, H.R., Smith, G.R.: An Analysis of Factors Affecting Labor Productivity in Masonry Construction. PTI#9003, Pennsylvania State Univ., University Park, PA, Pennsylvania (1989)
12. Serra, S.M.B., Oliveira, O.J.: Development of the Logistics Plan in Building Construction. In: Bontempi (ed.) System-based Vision for Strategic and Creative Design, pp. 75–80. Lisse, Swets&Zeitlinger (2003)
13. Son, J., Skibniewski, M.J.: Multi-heuristic Approach for Resource Leveling Problem in Construction Engineering: Hybrid Approach. Journal of Construction Engineering and Management 125(1), 23–31 (1999)
14. Strategic Forum for Construction Logistics Group (2005). Improving Construction Logistics, Technical Report, p. 5 (August 2005)
15. Veiseth, M., Rostad, C.C., Andersen, B.: Productivity and Logistics in the Construction Industry. In: Conference Proceeding, Nordnet 2003, Oslo, September 26 (2003)
16. Xu, F., Song, Y.: Spatio-Temporal Analysis of Hazards to Achieve Safer Schedule. In: Proceedings of the International Conference on Information Management, Innovation Management and Industrial Engineering, pp. 513–516. IEEE Computer Society's Conference Publishing Services, Xi'an (2009)
17. Xu, F., Song, Y.-B., Hu, H.: Hazard Space Modeling for Falling from Edge of High Places on Construction Site. China Safety Science Journal 21(4), 102–108 (2011) (in Chinese)

Benchmarking European Airports
Based on a Profitability Envelope
A Break-Even Analysis

Branko Bubalo

German Airport Performance (GAP) Research Project
at Berlin School of Economics and Law, Berlin-Schöneberg, Germany
branko.bubalo@googlemail.com

Abstract. In this paper a simplified benchmarking methodology is presented. This new approach is based on the computation of a discrete envelope over distributed data points. Financial and operational data from 139 European airports in 10 countries was collected for the years 2002 to 2010. For reasons of comparability financial data is deflated to a reference price level, currency and point in time. The data requirements are reduced to the two core variables of the production process, passenger demand and profits or deficits (before interests and taxes) per year. Such data is used to isolate airport industry benchmarks based on minimum passenger levels and maximum profitability. Benchmarking can guide supranational decision-making and regulation on airport subsidy policy by stating maximum feasible profits per passenger and by estimating critical demand levels at the break-even point. In conclusion, scenario-based calculations about potential efficiency gains for underperforming airports are outlined.

Keywords: Airport benchmarking, profit maximization, break-even analysis.

1   Introduction

To this day large-scale financial or operational comparisons of airports across countries are rare and far from sufficient in guiding decision makers in a simplified manner. Given the importance of airports in a globalized economy regarding the linking of national and international destinations and the magnitude of daily travelers and shipped cargo, current research undervalues careful empirical observation and numerical description in favor of theoretical modeling. Frequently the results and implications from models for decision-making in management can only be validated with large efforts, if ever. A deeper understanding of the real processes would lead to better predictions of "what if?" scenarios compared to "what is?" baselines. However, full comprehension requires many observations until the underlying interrelationships become obvious. In our case the preliminary plotting of performance ratios from the collected data leads to the discovery of regular patterns. Access to information and full knowledge of today's mathematical techniques allow the replication of the described model on another dataset. For the first time such vast collection of financial

H. Hu et al. (Eds.): ICCL 2012, LNCS 7555, pp. 171–189, 2012.

and operational data from 139 European airports has been holistically analyzed. This article represents only one in a line of articles [2, 4].

Independent of type of ownership (public, partially private or fully privatized) airports should strive for a financial breakeven. Managerial feasibility of maximizing profitability and performance is limited by existing demand. Similar to most (private) businesses economic losses need to be minimized in order to limit subsidies or other compensations, e.g. debt from credits. It should be a common goal for airport management to maximize profits and to reach breakeven, so corporate taxes, benefitting the whole society, may be paid. There is no clear reason why the society should constantly 'pay' for subsidies benefitting few passengers travelling to or from loss-making airports frequently found in remote locations.

It is obvious that loss-making airports would not be able to survive in a competitive and fully private market [8]. Airports rarely or never achieving a breakeven must therefore receive subsidies to some degree. Often this is achieved by the mechanism of cross-subsidization between profitable and non-profitable airports inside an airport portfolio of a *multi-airport operator*. To individual airports these subsidies come directly in form of public funds (taxpayer's money), (low interest) grants, national capital expenditure programs or other non-operating sources of income. This article follows the definition by [1] who define 'an airport as a private [or public] production system in which society maximizes social welfare by encouraging airport management to maximize profits.' A loss of social welfare is suspected, when public funds support air transport infrastructure through subsidies, which could instead be spend on local transport, infrastructure, hospitals or schools [5].

A new partial factor productivity (PFP) approach in airport benchmarking and performance measurement [14] is developed driven by the collected panel data. From earlier research it was found that it is sufficient to strictly focus only on a few core variables of the production process in order to pinpoint best-practices. Reducing the data requirements has many advantages, such as better ability of data handling, extending, updating and adjusting. It is a key task in performance measurement to find the right level of aggregation of the data for any specific analysis. For this study, demand as a given *Input* of the production process (although passengers have Input and Output characteristics) is measured in number of total (arriving and departing) passengers. Unit profits (or losses) as an *Output*, on the other hand, are measured in 'earnings before interests and taxes' (EBIT) per passenger (PAX). In many cases this kind of data can be directly extracted from income statements and airport operational statistics [5], [6], [11], [14]. However, there exist understandable *ressentiments* against the publication and sharing of financial data in the airport industry, which requires personal appeasements, non-disclosure agreements or the usage of carefully coordinated questionnaires.

The trend and shift of the profitability frontier and function will be observed for the 139 airports over a time-frame of nine years, answering questions such as: Which benchmark or range of profits could *a priori* be expected for any airport given the local level of demand? Or, how does 'my' airport perform over time relative to the best-practices? Where is the break-even point for the airport-industry located in a particular year, and in which direction does the break-even point and the profitability envelope shift over the years?

The paper is structured in five parts, starting with this introduction. In part two the discussion continues with the theoretical background including the review of literature, overview of different methodologies and description of the dataset. The third part will show the application of the profitability envelope over the collected data points. The fourth part will look at some possible gains in profitability, if the identified benchmarks would be reached. The final part will draw some conclusions and will give an outlook on further research.

2   Theoretical Background, Methodology and Data Description

In the discussion on measuring the profitability or 'cost efficiency' of airports one goal with this study is to draw parallel conclusions to more sophisticated linear programming and optimization techniques, such as Data Envelopment Analysis (DEA), but with less restrictive data requirements. These techniques frequently make use of multiple inputs and outputs with strict requirements on multi-dimensional data. However, in the research community it is increasingly difficult to justify and defend straightforward and simple approaches, where the analyst preserves full control over his or her data. In recent analyses there is little progress in reducing the number of variables to only a few explanatory variables, which are convenient to communicate to practitioners and which offer intuition of the internal processes. It is common that the consequences of the results are neither appreciated nor implemented by the parties for which these are aimed for. Science has shown that even in the broad field of mechanics for practical purposes it is sufficient to work with only a few variables, such as force depending on mass and acceleration (or gravity). The suitability of some core variables is discussed in the following paragraphs.

Figure 1 exhibits a clearly recognizable correlation pattern with the elementary variables costs, revenues and EBIT. However, many benchmarking studies are trying to explain differences in efficiency or profitability by additional variables, such as type of ownership or capacity utilization [3], which both suit only a selected peer group of larger airports and have little relevance for smaller unprofitable airports. The previous benchmarking study involving Norwegian airports operated by the state-owned company Avinor has led to the conclusion that a public entity is indeed capable of successfully managing a system of close to 50 airports. Since the operations of Avinor are closely monitored by the auditor general office in Norway greater transparency towards the public spending is guaranteed, which is reflected by frequently published public reports about the activities of Avinor and the level of subsidies per passenger [12]. To the contrary in Germany, where a large degree of airports are privatized as limited companies, yet, partly owned by local authorities, it is increasingly difficult to obtain detailed financial information.

In supplement regression analyses for this recent benchmarking study including Norwegian airports it was found by [2] that there exists a sufficient correlation between DEA relative efficiency scores and the PFP measure of unit profits, measured in 'EBIT per PAX.' However, it is evident that airports need the 'critical mass' [10] in number of passengers and consequential revenues in order to operate self-sufficiently. Therefore, deeming loss-making airports to be inefficient and *vice versa* profit-making airports to be efficient would not allow for a fair comparison among different sized entities. Similar to the DEA we aim at revealing and computing the 'relative efficiency' compared to other similar sized peers [1, 2]. Accordingly, the ratios of outputs over inputs are related to the size of airports, thus relative to comparable peers. An airport is deemed the more inefficient the further the calculated ratio is located from the related profitability benchmark.

One reason of not using EBIT or other profit measures in the DEA is the inability of the method to deal with variables which could be either negative or positive such as profits. This drawback could be circumvented in all linear programs by adding a 'sufficiently large constant' to the profit figures in order to make them all positive, thereby not changing the 'optimum strategies' [7]. A DEA study using EBIT or another measure of profitability has yet to be conducted. Most existing studies focus on the input-output balance of costs and revenues and make use of additional traffic or capacity data [1, 2].

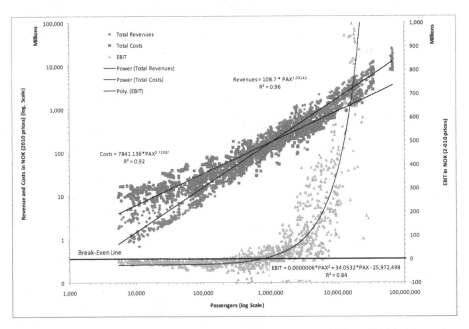

Fig. 1. Revenues, costs and EBIT for sample airports in the years 2002 to 2010 in Norwegian Kroners (PPP-adjusted base Norway in 2010 prices) (Source: Own survey data)

When plotting the adjusted and cleaned dataset of the 139 European airports (see the table in the appendix), it is observed that especially small and regional airports lie below the break-even line of (unit) profits and usually do not report any profits in subsequent years (Figure 1). There are very few airports which are *volatile* with regard to their profitability, showing deficits as well as profits in subsequent years.

Another main observation are decreasing returns to scale on a unit profit basis (i.e. EBIT per PAX), but constant (or even increasing) returns to scale on absolute profits (i.e. EBIT). With increasing output these returns to scale pick up below the break-even line at volumes of 300.000 to 400.000 PAX per year, which can be observed in Figure 1 and subsequent Figures 4 and 5 in Section 3. With the approximation functions in Figure 1 the *average* industry break-even point is calculated at 1.06 million PAX when total operating costs equal total operating revenues, and is about 750.000 PAX, when EBIT is equal to zero.

In the literature one can find different assumptions regarding the airport industry break-even point. For example, in the 1970's Doganis and Thompson [6] have calculated the break-even point for British airports to be around 3 million passengers. This might be a result of a much smaller sample and different distribution of airport sizes. They also used a different definition of profits, hence breakeven, which includes interest expenses. Heymann [10] (citing an unavailable study by the European Commission) estimates the break-even point for European airports to be in the broad range of 500.000 to 2 million passengers. Our figures support this estimation, since the calculated break-even point falls into that range. Certainly the break-even point estimates vary with the definition of 'profits' and which costs or revenues are included in it. Our data is cleaned from 'outside' revenue sources such as state grants or 'government transfers.'

Koopmans [11] has empirically tested the correlations between the closely related profitability measure 'earnings before interests, taxes, depreciation and amortization' (EBITDA) per workload unit (WLU = 1 PAX or 1/10 tons of cargo) and found it a good descriptor of 'operational airport performance.' Hence, this strongly implies that 'EBIT per PAX' could be a sufficiently good descriptor of airport managerial efficiency. This is a similar result as shown by Vogel and Graham [14] who found that 'profit per WLU' correlates significantly and highly significantly to ten of fifteen of the studied airport performance measures, such as return-on-investments, EBITDA margin and asset turnover. Doganis and Thompson [6] have used absolute 'surplus and deficits' (including interests) relative to the output level in WLU as a descriptor of 'managerial effectiveness' and for determining the break-even point. Their work focused mainly on the structure and balance of revenues and costs. Gritta, Adams and Adrangi [9] have chosen EBIT and its variation over time as a measure to quantify the 'business risk' of a firm and to construct financial performance measures in their study 'of the effects of operating and financial leverage on [...] Major U.S. Air carriers' rate of return.' In conclusion sufficient evidence was collected to support the claim that annual 'EBIT per PAX' serves as an adequate approximation of airport productivity and relative efficiency.

However, Gillen and Lall [8] dispute the usefulness of profitability measures and state that these are 'totally misleading,' 'given the unique position of airports.' In light of our graphical and numerical analysis of data from 139 airports over a period of nine years this judgment may not be accurate, since we observe strong 'industry-wide' [6] trends in profit generating ability with regard to the output level. Hence, we consider for the 'unique position' related to airport size. It should be noted that our results only relate to European airports. The situation may look differently for

North-American airports or airports on other continents, which may exhibit contrasting cost and revenue structures.

Firstly, we argue that using EBIT as a single aggregate output measure has the advantage that this figure includes all required operating costs, generated income and necessary investments in infrastructure and provision of capacity. In a simplified sense annual (positive or negative) EBIT is defined as revenues minus costs minus depreciation of assets. In our case, certain types of non-operating revenues or costs have been deducted from the EBIT figures, e.g. earnings from trading or government sources or costs for air traffic control services. For many airports EBIT (net result, EBITDA or some other definition of profits) is generally published in profit-and-loss statements as part of annual reports or financial statements, because it represents a common figure in finance. For reasons of comparability, the collected nominal figures are adjusted for currency, purchasing power parity (PPP) and inflation. As base currency Norwegian Kroners (NOK) was chosen. The financial data has been PPP-adjusted relative to Norway to account for different price and wage levels between countries, as well as inflation adjusted to 2010 prices.

Second, we limit the operational variables only to the input number of passengers, as this figure represents the original (origin, transfer and destination) demand, and is usually easily available. Divisions by passenger characteristics, such as international, domestic, business or leisure, have not been made, since these ultimately reflect groups of people with different spending behavior, service requirements and associated costs, which need to be targeted commercially by the airport business and charges model.

In Doganis and Thompson [5, 6] it was emphasized that airport management has only limited control over 'externally defined' factors, such as demand, i.e. level of passengers departing from or arriving at a particular location, and indivisible costs. Therefore, the airport managements' prime function is to balance (expected) revenues and cost, and to maximize output (EBIT) given the level of input (PAX). To generate demand for certain destinations is understood as a major function of airline marketing and route development, but should be closely coordinated with the airport management in a collaborative decision-making (CDM) setting.

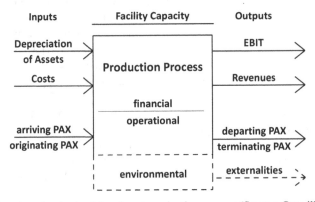

Fig. 2. Core inputs and outputs of the airport production process (Source: Own illustration)

Figure 2 exemplarily shows the main inputs and outputs of the airport production process, yet, it is not so clear which side needs to be maximized or minimized in an optimization program. Typically, the inputs are minimized and the outputs are maximized, for example in an output-oriented DEA. In Figure 2 one may define all costs, including depreciation, as a financial input, and all revenues as a financial output. On the operational side of the production process arriving or originating passengers, who request to be served by the airport, may be viewed as an operational input, and all departing and terminating passengers, who have been served by the airports may be viewed as an operational output. Therefore, total PAX show input and output characteristics, in our case these are defined as inputs. Externalities, such as noise and delay, may be viewed as 'undesirable output' [1] and its *reciprocal* (i.e. inverse) may be maximized. Additionally all passenger related facilities place a limit on the technical capacity in relation to a minimum level of service [3].

The data points can have five characteristic locations in relation to the profitability envelope and the break-even line. Figure 3 shows theoretically the different stages of development of an airport with regard to increase in size and profitability. For example Reinhard [13] has used a similar function for the break-even analysis of the 'Tri-star' aircraft development program of Lockheed in 1970's, where the amount of future sales of aircraft determine the financial feasibility (i.e. positive net present value) of the project.

Group 1 would represent loss-making airport, which data points lay below the reference profitability benchmark. The second group would include loss-making airports which define the profitability envelope and represent a benchmark. The third group consists of one (or more) airports, which break exactly. More realistically it is this airport in the data set, which is first making profits in EBIT per PAX, with minimum demand in terms of number of passengers.

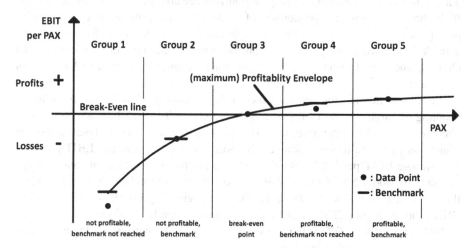

Fig. 3. Data points in relation to break-even line, (industry) profitability envelope and break-even point (Source: Own illustration)

The fourth group consists of profitable airports, which are relatively inefficient with regard to their position below the (maximum) profitability envelope. Similar to the first group, it is possible to calculate productivity gains, if the benchmarks would be reached (see Section 4). The fifth group represents superior airports, which are profitable and define the profitability envelope. These airports show maximum profitability with regard to their output level and comparable peers; therefore, these truly represent best-practices. It is this group of airports, where one could expect the largest interest from private investors, as these promise the highest dividends and return on investments (ROI). Under the assumption of future air traffic growth at different locations one can assume that airports will 'mature' over time and will place themselves in different groups. Through streamlined management activities they may switch from group 1, the underperformers, to the peer group of best practices in group 2. At this stage it is not expected for them to operate profitably. As growth continues they may pass the break-even point and become member of group 4. Eventually these airports may set the benchmark regarding their passenger level and profits, hence become members of superior group 5. In summary, the members of groups 2, 3 and 5 represent the 'cornerstones' of the discrete profitability envelope.

The strategies behind the required number of total flights measured in annual air transport movements (ATM) have not been analyzed here. It is assumed that frequencies of flights and available seats per route are under the control of carriers which try to match capacity to demand on each flight on a particular route by maximizing load factors. Subsidized public service obligation (PSO) route networks are certainly an exception, where whichever operating costs of the commissioned airline are covered by the state to serve a particular network and frequency [4]. Certainly, the aircraft sizes in each carrier's fleet put a significant limitation to matching air transport demand exactly, since the ability of a flight breaking even and economies of scale must be considered by the airline management. Therefore, we find that the applicability of ATM as a holistic operational variable for airports is not given, since this measure is related only to *airside* Inputs and Outputs. The airport management has very limited control over the actual number of movements.

In order to account for airports which make a majority of their turnover with the handling of cargo the use of the aggregate measure WLU may be considered as an alternative operational measure, i.e. EBIT per WLU. Sensitivity analyses across the sample only showed minor differences between the trends of average EBIT per PAX and average EBIT per WLU. For the full data sample the average amount of cargo accounts for about 5% of the total WLU, with eight airports having shares of more than 20% of the total WLU (Table 1). The Norwegian airports Hasvik (HAA), Rost (RET) and Svalbard (LYR) are the only ones having significant shares of cargo of up to 10% cargo of total WLU. For reasons of clarity we do not discuss the alternative measure WLU any further in this article.

Table 1. Airports with relevant average share of cargo >20% of total Workload Units (WLU) across the years 2002 to 2010 (Own survey data)

Airport	IATA Code	Share of Cargo of total WLU
Leipzig	LEJ	> 60%
Cologne	CGN	41%
East-Midlands	EMA	38%
Bergamo	BGY	30%
Benbecula	BEB	28%
Brussels	BRU	27%
Rennes	RNS	23%
Billund	BLL	21%

Note: One WLU equals one passenger or 100 kg of cargo. In the literature the usage of this combined measure and the equivalence of passengers to cargo is disputed, especially in terms of different handling costs, revenues and infrastructure requirements.

3   Application of the Profitability Envelope on the Dataset

In our heterogeneous sample of airports across different countries, time and sizes we relate average units of output to average units of input. This gives us the *profitability ratio* between the surpluses or losses in EBIT divided by the number of passengers, namely 'EBIT per PAX.' It is state-of-the-art in current research to divide the airport sample into sub-sets, classes or 'clusters' [5, 6] by certain characteristics, such as 'hubs' above 2 million or 'regional airports' below 2 million passengers. Since this kind of division is always arbitrary we chose to present the ratio on a continuous scale. The distribution of passenger demand covers a large range of airports different in size, therefore, a logarithmic (base 10) scale has been chosen for displaying the data points.

We observe in Figure 4 that growth in number of passengers is a strong driver of more than proportional increases in EBIT per PAX. However, the chosen profitability ratio stagnates at a certain level of saturation, after which it appears the average EBIT per PAX can only marginally be increased any further. The maximum profitability benchmark has been observed at London-City (LCY) airport with 144 NOK per passenger at a level of 3.3 million passengers in 2008. LCY defined the maximum benchmark for the years 2007 and 2009 as well, with passenger levels of 2.9 or 2.8 million passengers and a related EBIT per PAX of 133 and 99 NOK, respectively. LCY airport is operating a short take-off and landing (STOL) runway and has very limited terminal and aircraft parking stand capacity, which makes this achievement of high average profitability even more special. This example shows that the airport management at LCY airport has reached a high value-added productivity by fully exploiting its available resources.

It can be concluded that airports with a critical level around the break-even point of more than, say 300.000 to 1 million passengers, are becoming increasingly interesting for investors, but also request less regulation for achieving maximum profitability.

A marginal increase in annual number of passengers directly leads to increasing absolute profits and returns to scale at this high level of output (see Figure 1). However, from a welfare state point of view, the application of price-cap regulation to profitable airports (group four and five) may be an advantageous instrument. This regulation limits monopoly power and decelerates growth. Therefore, it could balance airport revenues from charges and from non-aeronautical sources against true (societal) costs.

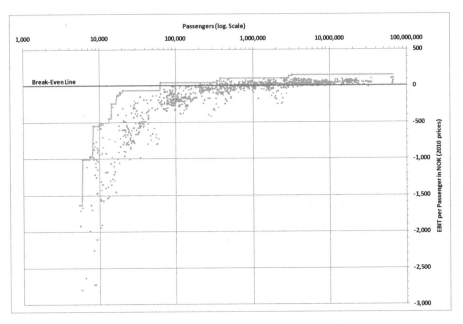

Fig. 4. Profitability and profitability envelope by airport size for the years 2002 to 2010 (all airports in the DEA sample, PPP-adjusted base Norway in 2010 prices; 2010 without Italy and France) (Source: Own survey data)

For loss-making airports (in groups one to three) a laissez-faire approach may be appropriate, if social obligations for transportation services are not of public interest. Otherwise, there is a lack of incentives and degrees of freedom for airport management to change the revenue and cost structure in order to become profitable. Similar to private entrepreneurs, the state may provide start-up funds or low-interest grants in initial stages of airport development. Even airport closures should remain as a last option, if an airport has no financially sustainable strategy.

To derive the *profitability envelope* exemplarily shown in Figure 4, we made use of a fairly simple algorithm, which plots the envelope over the maximum data points. The result of the algorithm provides profitability benchmarks for each level of passengers, thus giving a feasible *strategic target* for the airport management at underperforming airports. Trying to reach the benchmark should be the main motivation of all management efforts.

```
Program Profitability_Benchmarks
DIM n, PAX(n) as NATURAL
DIM EBIT_per_PAX(n), BENCHMARK(n) as REAL
n = Number of airports in the sample
i = 1 to n
# Sort table by PAX column in ascending order
PAX_i < PAX_{i+1} < ... < PAX_n
# The first entry in the 'EBIT_per_PAX' column is equal to the
initial starting point for the Envelope.
i = 1
BENCHMARK_i = EBIT_per_PAX_i
# From the second entry onwards, the new entry is compared, if
it is larger than the last stored Benchmark in third column. If
yes, it is set as new Benchmark. If not, the last Benchmark
remains.
FOR i = 2 TO n STEP 1
        IF   EBIT_per_PAX_{i+1} > BENCHMARK_i
        THEN    BENCHMARK_{i+1} = EBIT_per_PAX_{i+1}
        ELSE    BENCHMARK_{i+1} = BENCHMARK_i
NEXT
END.
```

[The algorithm outlines the required steps to create the 'profitability envelope' in Pseudo-code. Three table columns are required for PAX, EBIT per PAX and the running benchmark]

4   Break-Even Analysis

We want to get clearer answers on where the best-practice break-even point lies in each year. More particularly, we ask at which level of demand the observations surpass the break-even line. Thus, at which critical level of demand full coverage of operating cost could possibly be managed. We have not attempted to calculate the break-even points exactly by interpolation between the last observation below breakeven and the first observation above breakeven, because we recognize when working with real data, the quality is commonly mixed and certain limitations of accuracy exist. Therefore, all presented figures and thresholds are 'real' and accurate, given the resources. For a more mathematical and theoretical treatment in the future, such as the derivation of the profitability envelope or an approximation of an exact function, a smoother construction of the curve by interpolation seems appropriate.

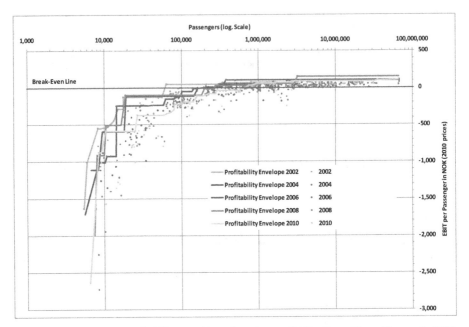

Fig. 5. Sample airports profitability trend by selected years (PPP-adjusted base Norway in 2010 prices; 2010 without Italy and France) (Source: Own survey data)

By dividing the sample under study into years we are able to derive more precise benchmarks for particular years which can be related to the observations. Figure 5 gives an overview of the profitability envelope change for even years between 2002 and 2010. As it can be seen the part of the envelope below the break even line shifts downwards. It could be interpreted, that, in general, the profitability worsened for the low-demand airports. The break-even point moves right suggesting that a higher level of passengers is required to increase the chances of breaking even on the EBIT level, while the top part of the envelope stagnates at average EBIT levels of 60 to 100 NOK per PAX, with London-City (LCY) airport with 144 NOK per passenger being the exception.

   In 2002 airports on the lower tail were more profitable than in the following years. The break-even point is located between such low passenger volumes as 17,680 and 63,000 defined by French airports Aurillac (AUR) and Bergerac-Roumaniere (EGC). Already in 2003 the break-even point significantly shifts to the right towards larger passenger volumes and is then situated somewhere between the observations Pescara (PSR) airport with about 300,000 passengers and an average EBIT of -3 NOK per passenger and Forli (FRL) airport (both in Italy) with about 350,000 passengers and an average EBIT of 4 NOK per passenger.

   In the years 2004 to 2009 the break even point lies between top performing French airports in the range of 180,000 - 290,000 passengers. In 2010, where Italian and French airport data is missing, the break even point is shifted even more significantly to the right and lies approximately between German airport Friedrichshafen (FDH) with 590,000 passengers and an average EBIT of -23 NOK per PAX and British airport Exeter (EXT) with 737,000 passengers and an average EBIT of 12 NOK per PAX. This leads to the conclusion that France is managing its low-demand airports very effectively, while achieving break even with around 200,000 passengers.

Table 2. Airports frequently defining the profitability envelope (2010 without Italy and France)

Benchmark Airports	IATA Code	Country	2002	2003	2004	2005	2006	2007	2008	2009	2010	Number of Times defining the Envelope
Tiree	TRE	UK	1	1	1	1	1	1	1	1	1	9
Aurillac	AUR	France	1	1	1	1	1	1	1	1		8
Barra	BRR	UK		1	1	1	1	1	1	1	1	8
Dinard-Pleurtuit-Saint-Malo	DNR	France		1	1	1	1	1	1	1		7
London City	LCY	UK	1				1	1	1	1	1	6
Bournemouth	BOH	UK			1		1	1		1	1	5
Bergerac-Roumaniere	EGC	France	1	1	1	1		1				5
Southampton	SOU	UK	1	1			1	1			1	5
Graz	GRZ	Austria					1	1	1	1	1	5
London Heathrow	LHR	UK			1	1	1				1	4
Stavanger	SVG	Norway	1	1			1				1	4
Fagernes	VDB	Norway	1						1	1	1	4
Caen-Carpiquet	CFR	France		1	1	1						3
Berlevåg	BVG	Norway	1	1	1							3
Svolvær	SVJ	Norway		1	1					1		3
Rennes	RNS	France		1	1	1						3
Exeter	EXT	UK	1	1						1		3
Hasvik	HAA	Norway	1	1	1							3
Bristol	BRS	UK	1	1								2
Lorient-Lann-Bihoue	LRT	France				1		1				2
Stokmarknes	SKN	Norway				1				1		2
Røst	RET	Norway	1	1								2
Ørsta-Volda	HOV	Norway				1				1		2
Calvi-Sainte-Catherine	CLY	France							1	1		2
Vadsø	VDS	Norway			1	1						2
La-Rochelle-Ile De Re	LRH	France				1	1					2

The 'Ebit per PAX' benchmarks back the argument, that volatile airports, which achieve profitability in certain years, but make losses in other years, should receive special attention from the airport operator, mainly towards increasing profitability or demand (for example by pushing route development) in order for the airport to reach breakeven or remain profitable in the long-term. The observed trend of the profitability envelope is clearly downwards for low demand airports below one million passengers and upwards for the profitable airports above the break-even point. Obviously, profitability on the EBIT level could mainly be achieved either by reducing operating costs, such as staff costs, or by increasing charges by 'Ramsey-Pricing' in cases of high elasticity of demand. Furthermore, profitability may be increased by a higher degree of commercialization, such as revenues from non-aeronautical sources, or by reducing depreciation, through postponing investments or extending economical lives. The ideal balance of these factors should ideally be under the responsibility of the airport management, in order to set incentives. In such cases where the airports lie below the profitability benchmarks (groups two and four), we do not expect the airports to have positive EBIT per se, but rather to achieve the respective benchmark by analyzing the business model of its best-practice peers.

Furthermore, we calculated the potential relative *efficiency gains* for each airport in a hypothetical scenario, if the according profitability benchmarks of other European airports would be reached. Reaching these gains means that increasingly fewer transactions would be made in form of cross-subsidies to loss-making airports in the system and increasingly more profits could be paid in dividends (or would be subject to taxes, hence would increase social welfare). We highly recommend a long-term sustainable efficiency policy, 1) by continuously benchmarking with comparable peer airports, 2) by analyzing business models of national and international best-practices and 3) by trying to adjust profits (hence, finding the ideal balance between revenues and costs) to the best-practices. As a consequence, cross-subsidizations from profitable to loss-making airports will be reduced, particularly in a national system or in a multi-airport organization. This effect is exemplarily shown by a cumulative *Lorenz*-like curve for a sub-sample of 139 European airports, showing cumulative EBIT (ordered from smallest to largest).

In Figure 6 it can be observed that 80% to 90% of the European airports are not profitable. In 2009 only the top 13% of the airports made a profit after depreciation. Overall the 139 airports made a substantial system profit of 12 to 22 billion Kroners (1.5 to 2.75 billion Euros[1]). This picture changes significantly, if we account for the potential efficiency gains, which amount to about 28 to 38 billion Kroners (3.5 to 4.75 billion Euros) in absolute terms, or increases of between 233 to 317%. The order of magnitude of these calculations shows that efforts to increase efficiency are a worthwhile endeavor, especially for larger systems of airports.

When including the feasible profitability gains in the cumulative distribution curves in Figure 6, the immediate relief on the loss-making airports underneath the break-even line can be seen. With the gains included in the 2009 figures, significantly less overall cross-subsidies would be required for the loss-making airports. In this case the proportions are much different and about 50% of the 139 airports report profits. In more detail the results for the 139 European airports are as follows: In 2005, 54% of the airports report losses, which are compensated by the profits of the next 36% higher ranked airports. The break-even point lies at the rank of the top 18% of

---

[1] Average nominal exchange rate in 2010: 1 Norwegian Kroner ≙ 0.124921205 Euro (Source: OECD).

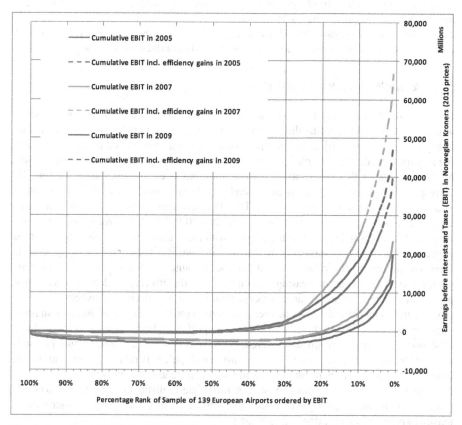

Fig. 6. Cumulative EBIT (in NOK, 2010 prices) with and without potential efficiency gains for 139 European Airports 2005, 2007, 2009 (Source: Own survey data)

the airports. With efficiency gains in place the proportions would change significantly and 33% of the airports would report losses. These losses are compensated by the next 22% higher ranked airports; therefore, the break-even point lies at 55%. The top 45% airports in this case contribute to the system profits of 41.3 billion Kroners (~5.15 billion Euros).

In the strong financial year of 2007 the efficiency gains have also the most significant impact on the feasible cumulative profits. In this year, 55% of the airports report losses, which are offset by 25% higher ranked airports which are reporting profits. We find the break-even point at around the top 20% of the sample, which generate the system profits of around 23.2 billion Kroners (~2.9 billion Euros). If the efficiency gains are included in the 2007 data, we could expect the largest increases in system profitability. Again, 33% (100% – 67%) of the lowest ranked airports would report just losses, which are compensated by profits of the next 13% of airports to reach the system equilibrium. In 2007, 50% of all airports, if managed efficiently, could contribute to the total system profit of 67.4 billion Kroners (~8.42 Billion Euros). The system profits would almost *triple* by these profitability improvements.

In this sense, large airport operators could *ex-ante* postulate clear strategic management targets, whereas its achievements may *ex-post* be evaluated, e.g., in cost-benefit analyses regarding policy changes such as changes in the structure of airport charges schemes. These efforts should be continuously conducted and closely monitored.

5   Conclusions and Outlook

It is the aim of this article to present a method of comparison and to spot best-practice airports with regard to profitability. We wanted to give some numerical evidence of 'managerial effectiveness' [6] and airport performance. It was recognized that a benchmarking approach needs the right choice of peers to give meaningful results, therefore a continuous scale rather than an arbitrary classification has been chosen, where we find the corresponding peers along the scale. Thereby particular justice is done towards small airports, especially in the region below 100.000 passengers, which have very different characteristics compared to airports with, say, 100.000 to 1 million passengers and above. As it was shown with empirical data, airports with more than 1 million passengers can be expected to operate above breakeven, thus making profits. These profit making airports show sharply increasing returns to scale on the absolute EBIT level, although the marginal returns to scale are decreasing. This means that the effort to exploit each additional passenger is much higher at large airports, than it is at small airports, where it may be much easier to increase the revenues per passenger. However, any small increase in revenues per passenger leads directly to increasing profits at large airports, because fixed costs and depreciation are already covered. With the construction of a maximum possibility frontier, which here is named 'profitability envelope', it is relatively straightforward to generate appropriate benchmarks and to recognize trends and shifts of the curve over time. In this way, airport management can formulate realistic strategic targets towards profitability. It can for example be calculated which level of profits per passenger may be feasible given a passenger demand forecast.

To be able to replicate this analysis, large amounts of data are needed, which mostly do not lie in the public domain. This is a major drawback of the presented method, because in practice the viewpoint may be one-dimensional. However, from the airport management perspective just peers with comparable passenger figures are required, which lowers the data collecting effort drastically. Therefore, our method is more suitable for large airport system operators, regulators or other large scale decision-makers. If the fundamental effects, which are presented in this paper, are understood, it may seem reasonable for future research to aggregate the numerical evidence further (as was exemplarily shown with the cumulative curves in Figure 6 towards even fewer control variables, such as the *Gini*-coefficient, to measure the changes over time in the distribution of airport profits in a multi-airport environment.

References

1. Adler, N., Liebert, V., Yazhemsky, E.: Benchmarking airports from a managerial perspective, Omega (2012), doi: 10.1016/j.omega.2012.02.004, http://userpage.fu-berlin.de/~jmueller/gapprojekt/downloads/gap_papers/bmarking.pdf (accessed on June 4, 2012)

2. Adler, N., Ülkü, T., Yazhemsky, E.: Small regional airport sustainability: Lessons from Benchmarking. Presented at the G.A.R.S. Junior Researchers Workshop at University of Applied Sciences Bremen (June 2012), http://userpage.fu-berlin.de/~jmueller/gapprojekt/downloads/SS2012/ulku-yazhemsky-adler_final2.pdf (accessed on July 17, 2012)
3. Bubalo, B., Daduna, J.R.: Airport capacity and demand calculations by simulation – the case of Berlin-Brandenburg International Airport. Netnomics (2012), doi: 10.1007/s11066-011-9065-6
4. Bubalo, B.: How to break the vicious circle? Monopoly bidding for public service obligation route networks in Norway, German Airport Performance Working Paper, Presented at the GAP Workshop, Berlin School of Economics and Law (June 2012), http://userpage.fu-berlin.de/~jmueller/gapprojekt/downloads/SS2012/PSO_Route_Networks_in_Norway_Branko_Bubalo_rev13052012.pdf (accessed on July 15, 2012)
5. Doganis, R.S., Thompson, G.F.: The Economics of British Airports-Report of an Investigation, Transport Studies Group, Department of Civil Engineering, Polytechnic of Central London (1973)
6. Doganis, R.S., Thompson, G.F.: Airport Profitability and Managerial Effectiveness. The Manchester School 43, 331–352 (1975), doi:10.1111/j.1467-9957.1975.tb01236.x
7. Dorfman, R.: Application of the Simplex Method to a Game Theory Problem. In: Koopmans, T.C. (ed.) Activity Analysis of Production and Allocation - Proceedings of a Conference, pp. 348–358. Wiley, Chapman & Hall, New York, London (1951), http://cowles.econ.yale.edu/P/cm/m13/m13-22.pdf (accessed on June 3, 2012)
8. Gillen, D., Lall, A.: Developing measures of airport productivity and performance: an application of data envelopment analysis. Transportation Research Part E: Logistics and Transportation Review 33(4), 261–273 (1997), doi:10.1016/S1366-5545(97)00028-8
9. Gritta, R., Adams, B., Adrangi, B.: An Analysis of the Effects of Operating and Financial Leverage on the Major U.S. Air Carriers' Rates of Return: 1990-2000. 47th Annual Transportation Research Forum (TRF). New York University, New York (2006), http://www.trforum.org/forum/downloads/2006_8A_FinLeverage_paper.pdf (accessed on June 3, 2012)
10. Heymann, E., Vollenkemper, J.: Expansion of regional airports: Misallocation of resources, Deutsche Bank Research, Frankfurt am Main (2005), http://www.dbresearch.com/PROD/DBR_INTERNET_EN-PROD/PROD0000000000193311.PDF (accessed on June 4, 2012)
11. Koopmans, J.-P.: The Impact of Commercial Activities on Airport Financial Performance (An Analysis of 35 Airports), Master Thesis submitted to the Faculty of Economics and Business Administration, Maastricht University, Netherlands (2008), http://arno.unimaas.nl/show.cgi?fid=15656 (accessed on May 19, 2012)
12. Norwegian Ministry of Transport and Communications (Samferdselsdepartement). St.meld. nr. 48 (2008-2009): Om verksemda i Avinor AS, Oslo, Norway (2009)
13. Reinhardt, U.E.: Break-even analysis for Lockheed's Tri Star: An application of financial theory. The Journal of Finance 28, 821–838 (1973), doi:10.1111/j.1540-6261.1973.tb01408.x
14. Vogel, H.-A., Graham, A.: Airport valuation: an alternative driver-based approach. Journal of Air Transport Studies 1(1), 20–47 (2010), http://www.airtransportnews.aero/content/jats/jats11.pdf (accessed on June 4, 2012)

Appendix

Country	Airport Name	IATA	Airport Name	IATA	Country	Country	Airport Name	IATA
Austria	Graz	GRZ	Cagliari	CAG	Italy	Norway	Sandane	SDN
Austria	Salzburg	SZG	Catania	CTA	Italy	Norway	Sandnessjøen	SSJ
Austria	Vienna	VIE	Florence	FLR	Italy	Norway	Sogndal	SOG
Belgium	Brüssel	BRU	Forli	FRL	Italy	Norway	Sørkjosen	SOJ
Denmark	Billund	BLL	Genoa	GOA	Italy	Norway	Stavanger	SVG
Denmark	Copenhagen	CPH	Lamezia Terme	SUF	Italy	Norway	Stokmarknes	SKN
France	Ajaccio	AJA	Naples	NAP	Italy	Norway	Svalbard	LYR
France	Aurillac	AUR	Palermo	PMO	Italy	Norway	Svolvær	SVJ
France	Bastia	BIA	Pescara	PSR	Italy	Norway	Torp	TRF
France	Bergerac-Roumaniere	EGC	Pisa	PSA	Italy	Norway	Tromsø	TOS
France	Biarritz	BIQ	Trapani	TPS	Italy	Norway	Trondheim	TRD
France	Brest	BES	Turin	TRN	Italy	Norway	Vadsø	VDS
France	Caen-Carpiquet	CFR	Venice	VCE	Italy	Norway	Vardø	VAW
France	Calvi-Sainte-Catherine	CLY	Ålesund	AES	Norway	Switzerland	Geneva	GVA
France	Dinard-Pleurtuit-Saint-Malo	DNR	Alta	ALF	Norway	Switzerland	Zürich	ZRH
France	Figari,Sud-Corse	FSC	Andøya	ANX	Norway	United Kingdom	Aberdeen	ABZ
France	Grenoble-Isère Airport	GNB	Banak (Lakselv)	LKL	Norway	United Kingdom	Belfast International	BFS
France	La-Rochelle-Ile De Re	LRH	Bardufoss	BDU	Norway	United Kingdom	Birmingham	BHX
France	Lille	LIL	Båtsfjord	BJF	Norway	United Kingdom	Bournemouth	BOH
France	Limoges-Bellegarde	LIG	Bergen	BGO	Norway	United Kingdom	Bristol	BRS
France	Lorient-Lann-Bihoue	LRT	Berlevåg	BVG	Norway	United Kingdom	Durham Tees Valley	MME
France	Lyon	LYS	Bodø	BOO	Norway	United Kingdom	East Midlands	EMA
France	Marseille	MRS	Brønnøysund	BNN	Norway	United Kingdom	Edinburgh	EDI
France	Montpellier	MPL	Evenes (Harstad-Narvik)	EVE	Norway	United Kingdom	Exeter	EXT
France	Nimes-Garons	FNI	Fagernes	VDB	Norway	United Kingdom	Glasgow	GLA
France	Pau-Pyrénées	PUF	Florø	FRO	Norway	United Kingdom	Humberside	HUY
France	Perpignan-Rivesaltes	PGF	Førde	FDE	Norway	United Kingdom	Leeds/Bradford	LBA
France	Rennes	RNS	Hammerfest	HFT	Norway	United Kingdom	Liverpool	LPL
France	Tarbes-Lourdes-Pyrénés	LDE	Hasvik	HAA	Norway	United Kingdom	London City	LCY
France	Toulon-Hyères	TLN	Haugesund	HAU	Norway	United Kingdom	London Gatwick	LGW

Country	Airport Name	IATA	Country	Airport Name	IATA	Country	Airport Name	IATA
Germany	Bremen	BRE	Norway	Honningsvåg	HVG	United Kingdom	London Heathrow	LHR
Germany	Dortmund	DTM	Norway	Kirkenes	KKN	United Kingdom	London Luton	LTN
Germany	Dresden	DRS	Norway	Kristiansand	KRS	United Kingdom	London Stansted	STN
Germany	Düsseldorf	DUS	Norway	Kristiansund	KSU	United Kingdom	Manchester	MAN
Germany	Erfurt	ERF	Norway	Leknes	LKN	United Kingdom	Newcastle	NCL
Germany	Friedrichshafen	FDH	Norway	Mehamn	MEH	United Kingdom	Southampton	SOU
Germany	Hamburg	HAM	Norway	Mo I Rana	MQN	United Kingdom	Barra	BRR
Germany	Hannover	HAJ	Norway	Molde	MOL	United Kingdom	Benbecula	BEB
Germany	Köln-Bonn	CGN	Norway	Mosjoen	MJF	United Kingdom	Campbeltown	CAL
Germany	Leipzig	LEJ	Norway	Namsos	OSY	United Kingdom	Inverness	INV
Germany	Muenster	FMO	Norway	Narvik	NVK	United Kingdom	Islay	ILY
Germany	München	MUC	Norway	Ørsta-Volda	HOV	United Kingdom	Kirkwall	KOI
Germany	Nürnberg	NUE	Norway	Oslo Gardemoen	OSL	United Kingdom	Stornoway	SYY
Germany	Stuttgart	STR	Norway	Roros	RRS	United Kingdom	Sumburgh	LSI
Italy	Alghero	AHO	Norway	Rorvik	RVK	United Kingdom	Tiree	TRE
Italy	Bergamo	BGY	Norway	Rost	RET	United Kingdom	Wick	WIC
Italy	Bologna	BLQ						

Solving Vehicle Routing Problems Using an Enhanced Clarke-Wright Algorithm: A Case Study

Buyang Cao

School of Software Engineering, Tongji University,
4800 Cao An Road, Shanghai, China 201804
buyang60@hotmail.com

Abstract. A vehicle routing problem (VRP) is an optimization problem encountered in many applications some of them even not directly related to vehicle
routing. For a given fleet of vehicles (or service personnel) the goal of a VRP is
to seek delivering products or services to various customer doorsteps at minimal
cost (that can be represented by travel time, distances, or some customized
ones) while satisfying the imposed business rules such as the vehicle capacities,
the route length traversed by a vehicle, the working hours (schedules) of a driver or service person. It is known that the VRP is a difficult problem to be solved
to its global optimality within a reasonable computational time. In order to
solve VRPs from the real world more effectively, many algorithms, particularly
heuristics, were designed and implemented to tackle this type of problems. Recently the well-known savings approach of Clarke and Wright was
re-considered and some enhanced versions were proposed aiming to achieve
improved solutions for the VRP. The goal of this paper is to present a business
scenario requiring VRP solutions, and to propose an enhanced Clarke and
Wright algorithm in the spirit of those proposed recently to solve the problems
of this case study. Furthermore, the proposed algorithm aims at eliminating the
human interventions such as parameter setting and tuning during the problem
solving procedures. Computational results demonstrate that the new algorithm
addresses the business needs better in the real applications and the results
obtained by the algorithm are preferred by the end users.

Keywords: Vehicle Routing Problem, Case Study, Decision Support, Savings
Algorithm.

1   Introduction

Since the vehicle routing problem (VRP) was first introduced by Dantzig and Ramser
(1959), VRPs have drawn great attention from academic researchers and practitioners
due to their values in theoretical research and real applications. From a practical point
of view, the goal of a VRP attempts to keep distribution costs as low as possible while
these distribution costs may account for a major portion of the total logistics operation
costs of a company. Today a company wants to offer the best service (delivering
products or services) to its customers with reduced logistics costs whenever it is possible, which raises a challenging problem due to the rapid increase in energy and labor

H. Hu et al. (Eds.): ICCL 2012, LNCS 7555, pp. 190–205, 2012.

costs. The effective solution of a VRP might produce significant economic benefits for a company. From the academic perspective, the VRP has been shown to be an NP-hard problem (Lenstra and Rinnooy Kan, 1981), which means a large VRP from the real world cannot be solved to its optimality within an acceptable computational time. Because of the value of time, a fast solution procedure for a VRP is always favorable, which attracts many scholars to invent algorithms seeking solving this difficult optimization problem efficiently.

The goal of a VRP is to decide how to deploy a fleet of vehicles or service personnel to distribute products or provide services to customers at the lowest costs where travel time, travel distance, or service quality may impact the costs of such operations. The fleet of vehicles or service personnel will start from a depot or central office and return to it after the products or services have been delivered. Some business logic to be considered include the vehicle capacities and the driver or service person's working schedule (lunch or break times). Although an extended version of a VRP might include time windows referred as *vehicle routing problems with time windows* (VRPTW), we will focus on solving the VRP in this paper.

Even though small instances of the VRP or its extended versions could be solved by exact algorithms such as branch-and-bound or branch-and-cut approaches (e.g., Ropke and Cordeau (2009), see also Bodin et al. (1983) and Braysy and Gendreau (2005) for more complete surveys on exact VRP algorithms), heuristics are preferred solution methods in solving VRPs in practice due to their capability of obtaining reasonable solutions within acceptable computational times. Therefore, almost every piece of commercial software for solving VRPs uses heuristics to obtain solutions with reasonably good quality within a short period of time.

Clarke and Wright (1964) presented a greedy heuristic that is widely known as the Clarke-Wright savings algorithm that will be named as *C-W algorithm* in the following discussion. The C-W algorithm starts with an individual route for each customer (or stop) and merges routes iteratively as long as the combination can reduce cost and meet the constraints until no further merge is possible. The C-W algorithm is relatively easy to implement and proven to be an effective approach for solving real VRPs, though the C-W algorithm is not quite suitable to solve VRPTWs. As a matter of fact, the C-W algorithm is the most popular VRP solver and has become the basis for many VRP algorithms particularly in finding reasonable good initial solutions for VRPs. Since the C-W algorithm was proposed, a lot of C-W algorithm based or enhanced methodologies have been presented in order obtain solutions with better qualities. Juan et al. (2011) proposed several solution strategies to improve the Clarke-Wright savings heuristic. In order to consider the "route shape" during the route building procedure, Paessens (1988) implemented a parameterized savings algorithm that takes the asymmetry between customer locations with respect to their distances to the depot. However, the parameters included in the savings formula need to be tuned to yield satisfactory results.

Recently, some researchers revisited C-W algorithm and attempted to invent more efficient VRP solvers. Altinel and Oncan (2005) noticed that at the late phases of the route merge of the C-W algorithm or its enhancements, the customer demands will have a greater impact on the quality of a VRP solution. They added a new item in the cost savings formula reflecting the customer demands with an associated parameter. Unfortunately, the more parameters in the savings formula, the more time needed to tune these parameters. Furthermore, the tuned parameters may be good for one dataset but could be very bad for another one because of different characteristics (geography, vehicle capacities, working schedules, etc.). In order to facilitate the parameter tuning procedures for the parametric C-W algorithm and its enhancements, Battarra et al. (2008) proposed a genetic algorithm based methodology that is able to tune the parameters more efficiently upon the computational experiments. Subsequently Corominas et al. (2010) developed a fine-tuning procedure for a parametric C-W algorithm and its enhancement, which appears to be an effective procedure and is able to achieve desired parameters in shorter time frames. The computational results reported in the paper validate the fitness of those tuned parameters.

However, based upon our project experiences in solving real VRPs, it is hard to obtain an "ideal" parameter set for a parametric C-W algorithm and its enhancements not to mention applying this tuned parameter set universally to all VRP problems and expecting overall better results. Furthermore, the end users of VRP software usually do not have any background in Operations Research; it is very difficult for them to tune the algorithm parameters; not to mention that the parameter tuning is very tedious. We believe it might be more crucial to enhance the C-W algorithm structurally, i.e., adding new steps and logic, rather than merely parameter tuning. In this paper we present an algorithm that is capable to solve VPRs relatively efficiently without too much user intervention and a case study for it, which are the motivation of this paper.

This paper is organized as follows. In the next section, we provide a background of VRPs encountered and to be solved. Then we present the details of the enhanced C-W algorithm. Section 4 contains computational experiments using real application datasets to demonstrate the effectiveness of the proposed algorithm. The paper ends with concluding remarks and directions for future studies.

2   Background

The operations research literature documents rich applications of VRPs. Some examples include Weigel and Cao (1999) for delivering furniture, appliances, and related services to customer homes; Kim et al. (2006) for solving VRPs in a waste collection operation and Spada et al. (2005) for scheduling student bus service. The interested readers are referred to Bozkaya et al. (2011) for more details on these and other interesting VRP applications. The following real problem needs to be solved.

The logistics department of a large consumer product company is responsible for delivering their products daily to their authorized stores where the products will be sold. Each store owner will make his order online according to the expected sales. The day before the delivery is conducted; the logistics department gathers the following information in order to make the delivery decision for the next day's operation:

- the available vehicles and their capacities, and they may not be homogenous
- the drivers' working schedule
- the locations of those customers to be delivered and the demands
- the service (delivery) time at each customer location, which varies upon the demand

Based upon the business needs, the objective of the VRP to be solved is to minimize the total travel time of all routes. On average the logistics department needs to deliver around 1000 customers with approximately 30 vehicles every day. In addition, the logistics department must take the following business logic into account while building the delivery routes:

- Provide delivery truck drivers with consistent routes.
- Stores on the same street segment should be delivered by the same truck whenever it is possible.
- The side of a street to unload products needs to be considered.
- Whenever a truck encounters a store of its route on the way out, it should deliver that store immediately if possible to reduce the weight loaded on the truck; it is referred to as "first-see first-serve" rule.
- Larger trucks should be utilized first.
- Whenever it is possible, one area where several stores are located should be delivered by the same vehicle.

For a more comprehensive mathematical model of VRPs, interested readers are referred to Cao and Bozkaya (2012). It is interesting to note that some of these business rules are very difficult to be presented "mathematically". Besides the business rules listed above, the geographic characteristic may be challenging as well. One of the delivery or service areas is a mountain area; Figure 1 illustrates the portion of the service area and some customer locations.

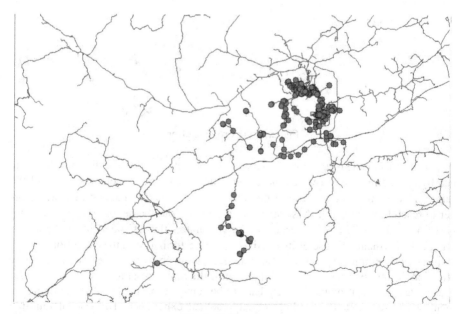

Fig. 1. Delivery area

From Figure 1 it is not difficult to recognize that the street network structure is similar to a "tree" structure because of the nature of mountain roads. Furthermore, some stores are located at some branches of this street network. In this case, there are not so many alternative paths from a depot to a store that is located at a branch. It is conceivable that if a store at one branch is serviced by a vehicle other than the one serving nearby branches, then the majority of the time these two vehicles will traverse the same road segments. If one area is serviced by more than one vehicle, then some vehicle might have to drive extra miles to service the store located on a branch of the street network. We name this scenario as *route crossing over*. From the operational perspective route crossing over is not efficient and that cannot satisfy the business rule listed above stating one area should be serviced by a single vehicle whenever it is possible. Figure 2 presents some route crossing over, which should be avoided whenever it is possible (the number next to each stop is the corresponding route ID).

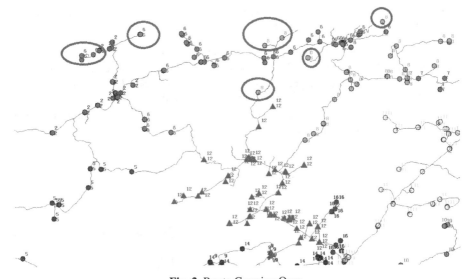

Fig. 2. Route Crossing Over

Those stops inside of red circles are serviced by vehicles that are different from the nearby ones. In order to service these stops more than one vehicle has to travel the same street segments, and some of them have to travel extra time and distance in order to reach those stops. If those stops are far away from the depot, the negative economic impact is severe. This result usually encounters the resistance at the field during the deployment because of its relatively poor performance in the execution.

In order to eliminate the route crossing over as much as possible, we need to pay attention during the route construction phase. If the route crossing over exists after the route construction, it would be very hard to be removed no matter how the improvement steps are applied according to our practical experience. Because of multiple constraints such as time, capacities, etc. it is nearly impossible to utilize improvement steps like transfer/exchange moves to get rid of route crossing over even when metaheuristics are employed. We need to point out that the system we attempted to deploy for this customer has been used by other clients, and the core solver is a meta-heuristics based one which has been evolving over years.

According to the paper of Braysy and Gendreau (2005), there are basically two types of route construction frameworks though there are a number of variants. One is the C-W algorithm that will be discussed further in the following sections and the other is the insertion based algorithm proposed by Solomon (1987). The insertion algorithm starts with a route including a "seed" stop, and sequentially inserts unrouted stops into the route. It restarts a new route when the current route is full (either in terms of time limit of capacity limit). Each time the algorithm inserts a stop with the lowest insertion cost, where the meaning of a cost can be general enough to consider travel time/distance, time window violation, etc. The procedure will repeat until all stops are routed or no route is available for routing. It is not hard to recognize that the insertion framework is able to handle temporal dimension fairly effectively, it has been widely applied to solve VRPTWs (e.g., Bozkaya et.al (2011), Kim et.al (2006), Weigel and Cao (1999)). Nevertheless, the insertion algorithm emphasizes the insertion cost impacted mainly by two neighboring stops at the moment of an unrouted stop to be evaluated for insertion. Unlike the C-W algorithm, the insertion algorithm takes less consideration of the penalty of missing an insertion opportunity for an unrouted stop. Thus, another vehicle may have to travel long time/distance to service this unrouted stop eventually. Actually we experienced some cases where route crossing over occurred at the beginning of the project of building the routing application for this consumer product company as we employed the insertion framework to construct routes.

After careful analyses of the problems, it turns out that we do not need to consider time windows because the stores do not have the imposed time window and usually they can receive the delivery within the business hour of the company. We can take advantage of the C-W algorithm that not only considers the neighboring travel time/distance but also the travel time/distance between unrouted stop and depot during the route construction. We are going to discuss in detail an enhanced C-W algorithm that is able to eliminate the route crossing over at great degree and create more satisfactory results in the next section where the time window is no more a consideration.

3   Enhanced C-W Algorithm

For the purpose of completeness, we discuss the C-W algorithm and its variants briefly here. In a VRP there is a depot d and a set of customer locations $L = (1,...,n)$, where the vehicles start from d and service a subset of L and return to d. The C-W algorithm start with each location or stop being serviced by a vehicle and gradually merges routes until there is no possibility of merging. If we want to use a single vehicle to serve two stops, say i and j, on a single trip, then total travel time/distance is reduced by:

$$s_{ij} = (c_{di} + c_{id} + c_{dj} + c_{jd}) - (c_{id} + c_{ij} + c_{dj}) = (c_{id} + c_{dj} - c_{ij}) \tag{1}$$

where c_{ij} represents the travel distance/time from location i to location j. It is desirable to service two locations that have the larger savings value defined by (1) under the condition that no imposed constraints (capacity, working hour, etc.) will be violated due to the merge. At the beginning of the solution procedure, the list containing savings values is created and sorted in the non-increasing order. At each iteration a pair of stops *(i,j)*, actually a link, is picked at the top of the list, and it considers:

- If both stops are not routed (assigned), then a new route serving these two stops is created. Or,
- If one of the stops is routed, and it is a non-interior stop (a routed stop is called non-interior stop if it is adjacent to the depot in the route), then the unrouted stop may be inserted to the same route if no constraints are violated. Or,
- Both stops are routed, and they are all non-interior stops, then these two routes may be combined if no constraints are violated.

If the saving list is exhausted, the algorithm terminates. Note that at the end some routes may contain a single stop.

Altinel and Oncan (2005) believed that the customer demands impact the overall solution quality, and they proposed the following new savings value:

$$s_{ij} = c_{id} + c_{dj} - \lambda c_{ij} + \mu \left| c_{di} - c_{jd} \right| + v \bar{r} \qquad (2)$$

where $\bar{r}$ is defined by: $\frac{r_i + r_j}{r'}$

Furthermore, r_i is the demand for customer *i*, r' is the average demand. The customer spatial distributions ($\left| c_{di} - c_{jd} \right|$) are taken into account to a certain degree. There are some parameters in the savings value. It is inevitable that these parameters must be tuned in order to achieve satisfactory results. Upon the results reported in the paper, the savings value (2) does obtain better solutions than the native C-W algorithm does after the parameters are carefully tuned.

As we pointed out earlier, based upon our real project experience merely the parameter tuning at times is unable to produce desired results (e.g., route crossing over still occurs) and the parameter tuning is a tedious task that cannot be performed by the end users. We are going to enhance C-W algorithm structurally by adding solution steps to be applied to any VRP without tuning parameters and conduct a case study in which this proposed algorithm is applied. Because in practice there are traversing restrictions for street networks including one-way, divided roads, we assume that the underlying street network is not symmetric, i.e.: we may have $c_{ij} \neq c_{ji}$. The following subsections describe the enhancements for the native C-W algorithm.

3.1   Enhancement on Stop Insertion

In the native C-W algorithm, if one of the pair of stops is not routed or assigned, then this unrouted stop can be inserted to the same route where the other stop is located only if it is a non-interior stop of that route. However, we observed that if this condition must be held to decide if an unrouted stop can be inserted to an existing route, we might miss some opportunities to produce relatively good results. Therefore, when a pair of stops is being evaluated for route assignment, an unrouted stop can be inserted right after (or before) the other stop that has been assigned to the route as long as no constraint is violated. Specifically:

Let $p = (d,...,h,i,k,...,d)$ be an existing route and (i,j) be the pair of stops being evaluated for possible assignment (insertion). If there is no constraint being violated, then the resultant route will be: $p = (d,...,h,i,j,k,...,d)$.

After this strategy is implemented, we find that there are very few routes containing only one real stop comparing to the native C-W algorithm. In this case, we can save the number of vehicles to be used, which in turn saves the operational costs. The combination of native C-W algorithm and this step is called *stop assignment procedure* in the following discussions.

3.2   Enhancement on Route Improvements

The stop assignment procedure presented above alone cannot generate very satisfactory results. The route improvement steps are necessary to bring us solutions with better qualities. We are also going to employ the savings value list or the information gathered during the creation of the savings value list to guide the improvement process. The following route improvement steps are proposed, which are similar to those inter-route improvements presented in Bozkaya et al. (2011) with additional updates:

a)   Stop transfer move: although the application of the C-W algorithm is able to avoid some route crossing over mentioned in the previous section, the results at times contain route crossing over. Regarding the business practice, a route crossing over is usually inefficient and it is desirable to remove any route crossing over whenever it is possible. To this purpose, we create a neighboring list holding neighboring stops for each stop while the saving value list is being created. This neighboring list contains certain number of closest stops (in terms of real travel times/distances) to the underlying one and is sorted in non-decreasing order of travel time/distance. With this neighboring list it is relatively easy to identify the possible route crossing over or the inefficiency of a solution. Fig. 3 illustrates the scenario.

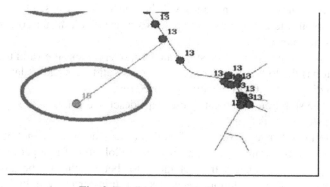

Fig. 3. Possible route crossing over

In Fig. 3 the numbers besides stops represent the route ID. It is not difficult to see, that routes 13 and 18 are crossing since the neighbors of a stop in route 18 are all in route 13. Route 18 has to traverse a lot of street segments that are also traveled by route 13. It is conceivable that it could be more efficient if this stop can be serviced by the route where its neighbors are located. In this example, route 13 will be an ideal route to service the stop currently serviced by route 18. Furthermore, even if the route crossing over cannot be removed completely, we want a stop and its neighboring stops be serviced by the same route whenever it is possible. Here we will perform the improvement move (step) called stop transfer to reach this goal. In order to speed up the entire process, we consider performing the possible stop transfer move for a stop if its first and second neighbors are not at the same route as it does, and the first and second neighbors are serviced by the same route.

Definitions:

- Transfer candidate: a stop that may be transferred
- Source route: the route services a transfer candidate
- Target route: the route can potentially service a transfer candidate, where the first and second neighbors of the transfer candidate are located

Let i be the stop index for the transfer candidate, $ps = (d,...,i-1,i,i+1,...,d)$ be the source route, and $pt = (d,...,j-1,j,...,d)$ be the target route, respectively. The cost for the potential transfer move is determined by (here we will insert the candidate only right after or directly before its first neighbor denoted by $j-1$ in the target route):

$$\Delta_t = c_{i-1,i+1} + c_{j-1,i} + c_{i,i+1} - c_{i-1,i} - c_{i,i+1} - c_{j-1,j} \tag{3}$$

This is the scenario for the candidate being inserted right after its first neighbor; and we can have the similar equation for the case where the candidate is inserted directly before its first neighbor. For each candidate both possible moves are evaluated, and the move with the lowest transfer cost is picked, which is called possible transfer move. Furthermore, for a possible transfer move, the constraints will be checked. If a possible transfer move meets all the constraints and possesses a negative transfer cost, it is a valid transfer move.

At each iteration of the stop transfer move, it picks the valid transfer move that has the lowest transfer cost among all valid ones and updates the corresponding routes after the move is carried out.

The stop transfer repeats these steps described above until no further valid transfer move is found.

b) Route interchange move: it is often that a transfer move cannot be carried out due to the constraint (time, capacity, etc.) violation of a target route. It is not enough to apply merely transfer move for better solutions because the capability of exploring solution space of a stop transfer move is limited. Here we propose a new improvement step called route interchange move, which is described as follows.

An element (a pair of stops) in the saving value list with positive value is called an interchange candidate if they are serviced by two different routes.

According to the principle of the C-W algorithm, it could be beneficial to service two stops of an interchange candidate by the same route. Let (i, j) be the link or stop pair of an interchange candidate, $p1 = (d...,i-1,i,i+1,..., d)$ and $p2 = (d,...,j-1, j, j+1,...,d)$ be the routes serving stop i and stop j, respectively. After the route interchange move is performed, these two routes become: $p1^* = (d...,i-1,i,j,j+1,..., d)$ and $p2^* = (d,...,j-1,i+1,...,d)$, and Figure 4 illustrates the move.

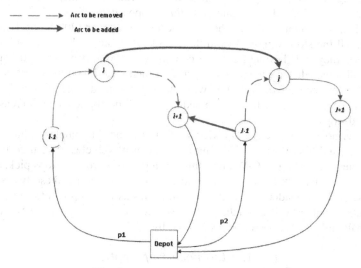

Fig. 4. Route Interchange move

Obviously for each interchange candidate, the corresponding interchange cost is determined by:

$$\Delta_{ri} = c_{ij} + c_{j-1,i+1} - c_{i,i+1} - c_{j-1,j} \qquad (4)$$

If an interchange candidate has the negative interchange cost and it meets all imposed constraints, then it is called a valid route interchange move. Unlike the stop transfer move, the move will be carried out immediately as soon as a valid route interchange move is found and two corresponding routes are updated. Because of using the savings value list, the solution space to be searched is narrowed and the savings value list provides the promising candidates for the route interchange move.

The route interchange move scans the savings value list until no valid candidate is found.

3.3   Enhancement on Route Balance

One of the weaknesses of the C-W algorithm is the route balancing consideration. It is hard to apply the native algorithm to consider the route balancing issue explicitly. Unlike the insertion based framework for the route construction where the routes usually are full and can be built relatively well balanced, the results obtained by the native C-W algorithm contain unbalanced routes, some routes may work until the end of the day while some routes have only a couple of working hours. The solution with unbalanced routes is very difficult to deploy in practice, and it should be fixed. The route balancing procedure described below is invented to reduce the imbalance in resultant routes.

The basic idea of the route balancing procedure is to remove those half-full routes and reassign the stops serviced by these half-full routes to other ones. It employs the methodology called "destroy and re-build" proposed by Cao and Bozkaya (2012), which is also similar to the methods suggested by Glover (2000) and Laporte et al. (2010). All the stops removed from those half-full routes will be treated as unrouted stops and they will be reassigned to certain routes. Based on the solution, we will empty all routes that are working only 40% of their stated working hours and all stops currently serviced by these routes will become unrouted. The stop assignment and route improvement procedures discussed above will be applied again to reassign these unrouted stops.

Furthermore, we have the knowledge of the number of vehicles to handle the customer demand; therefore we can limit the number of vehicles to be used for building new routes (according to C-W algorithms, if a pair of unrouted stops picked from the savings value list, then a new route will be opened to service these two stops). The purpose of this consideration is to build all routes as full as possible and to eliminate the route imbalance. The number (n) of vehicles used for opening new routes after those half-full routes are emptied is defined by:

$$n = \begin{cases} 1; \textit{if the number of emptied route is 1} \\ \lceil (\textit{number of emptied routes})/2 \rceil; \textit{otherwise} \end{cases} \qquad (5)$$

where $\lceil x \rceil$ is the integer that is less or equal to number x.

If we cannot find any route to be emptied, then we believe that the current solution is relatively balanced or most routes are packed, and this step is not necessary to be carried out.

Summary of the enhanced C-W algorithm:
Based on the above discussions we now summarize the enhanced routing algorithm as follows.
Initialization:
Building OD matrix and saving value list.
Main procedure of the algorithm:
Done = false;
Iter (recording the number of iterations) = 0;
While not Done
- Perform stop assignment procedure;
- Perform stop transfer;
- Perform route interchange;
- Iter = Iter + 1;
- If Iter > predefined number of iterations to be performed then
    Done = true;

Else

> Get number of routes to be emptied, n'. If $n' > 0$, set all stops serviced by these routes to be unrouted.

End if

End While

Sequencing all routes:

For each route in route set do

> Perform intra-route improvement (Bozkaya et al. (2011));

End For

Although the stop assignment procedure is included in the loop, it will not be performed if all stops are assigned. If some routes are emptied because they are half-full, certain stops are unrouted. In this case, the stop assignment procedure attempts to reassign these unrouted stops to proper routes with the limited number of vehicles for opening new routes. The number of iterations for the loop in the algorithm is set between 10 and 20 upon the size of a problem.

4   Computational Experiments

We use real datasets to conduct the computational experiment for this case study. The purposes of this experiment are:

- Comparing to the basic C-W algorithm to demonstrate the capability of producing better solutions of the proposed algorithm in this paper, and
- Comparing to the insertion-based algorithm to demonstrate the ability of creating solutions containing non- or nearly non-crossing over routes. As mentioned above, this insertion-based algorithm is not a simple implementation, it has been used by various customers and proven to achieve economic benefits in the past (see Weigel and Cao (1999), Bozkaya et al. (2011) Cao and Bozkaya (2012)).

The data were collected from the real applications, and the delivery area is shown in Figure 1 that contains about 12000 street segments. All computational experiments were conducted on a laptop whose configuration is: CPU - Intel Core 2 Duo P8400 2.26GHz, memory size - 4G. The operating system is Windows 7. The problem sizes vary from 200 stops (customers to be serviced) to 1600 stops. The computational results are listed in Table 1.

In Table 1 we list the results obtained by three algorithms including the algorithm presented in the paper (Our Solver), the basic C-W algorithm (Basic C-W Savings Solver), and the insertion based algorithm (Insertion Based Solver). The results yielded by these three algorithms contain the total travel time in minutes traversed by all routes, the total travel distance in kilometers traversed by all routes, the number of routes to be used, and the CPU time in seconds required to solve a problem. Figure 5 depicts the results (total travel time for each problem).

Table 1. Computational Results (#R: # Routes)

prob-lem size	Our Solver				Basic C-W Savings Solver				Insertion based Solver			
	CPU time (sec.)	#R	total length (km.)	total travel time (min.)	CPU time (sec.)	#R	total length (km.)	total travel time (min.)	CPU time (sec.)	#R	total length (km.)	total travel time (min.)
200	1	5	667.8	1124	<1	5	683.3	1153	2	5	722.0	1227
280	1	6	832.1	1460	1	7	874.71	1513	3	6	884.8	1535
350	2	8	1155.9	1879	1	8	1056.5	1883	5	8	1215.8	2142
420	3	9	1094.1	1957	3	9	1140	2008	8	9	1300.1	2272
490	4	10	1210.3	2187	3	10	1252.2	2233	11	10	1415.3	2548
560	4	10	1305.2	2357	2	11	1326.9	2400	13	10	1472.6	2678
630	6	11	1405.5	2544	5	13	1450.7	2596	16	11	1509.6	2738
700	8	13	1574.9	2815	5	13	1555.2	2791	26	12	1603.1	2928
780	10	14	1679.6	2998	5	15	1692.7	3021	25	14	1761.5	3186
850	9	15	1798.4	3183	4	15	1816.6	3224	24	15	1929.6	3403
920	11	16	1940.9	3421	6	19	2113.2	3672	29	16	2114.0	3731
1000	12	17	2133.1	3692	5	21	2311.5	3969	32	17	2168.5	3798
1200	13	19	2257.5	3912	10	21	2330.7	4025	47	19	2359.2	4087
1400	15	23	2446.3	4219	10	25	2675.4	4548	63	20	2418.6	4224
1600	28	23	2467.0	4278	12	27	2735.9	4719	81	24	2558.8	4442

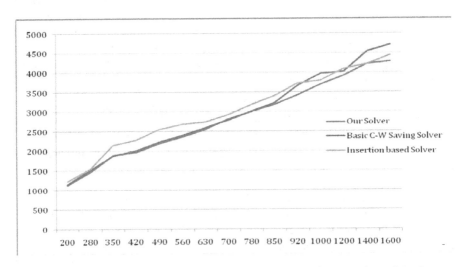

Fig. 5. Computational Results (abscissa: problem size; ordinate: total travel time)

It is not difficult to recognize that the algorithm presented in this paper obtains overall best solutions upon the business logic (minimum total travel time). It is possible that the travel time is shorter but the travel distance is longer. In reality, traveling on a freeway takes shorter time but it may traverse longer in distance compared to traveling on local streets. There is no need to tune the parameters for the algorithm at all. The native C-W algorithm produces consistently more routes than the other two algorithms, because it won't merge two routes if one stop of a pair of stops in the savings value list is not a non-interior node of a route. The enhanced algorithm has the additional consideration to overcome this problem while the insertion based algorithm always makes a vehicle full before a new vehicle is used. Actually using fewer vehicles to handle the same amount of products to be delivered will not only save money but also work more efficiently. Compared to the insertion based algorithm the proposed algorithm is able to solve the problems in shorter computational times and obtain better solutions in this case study. The insertion based algorithm needs longer computational times since it needs to re-evaluate the insertion position of an unrouted stop at each iteration during the assignment procedure (though some implementation strategies can be taken to shorten the time a bit). However, the proposed algorithm scans the sorted list and does not need to perform a complicated evaluation procedure. Furthermore, as we mentioned above, there is no parameter for the solver, and we do not need to conduct comprehensive parameter tuning process. In this case the solver is more suitable for the real applications since an end user usually does not have any idea how to tune the algorithm parameters to fit his problems. The proposed algorithm in this case study provides a very solid alternative for solving VRPs in practice.

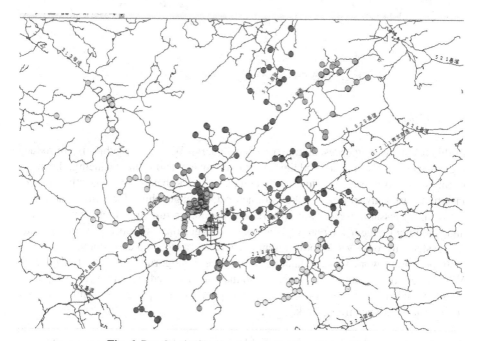

Fig. 6. Results obtained by the insertion based algorithm

Figures 6 and 7 present the results obtained by the insertion based algorithm and the proposed algorithm, respectively. Obviously the routes created by the proposed algorithm have clean route boundaries and have little crossing over while the routes generated by the insertion based algorithm have more crossing over. The end users favor the results created by the proposed algorithm.

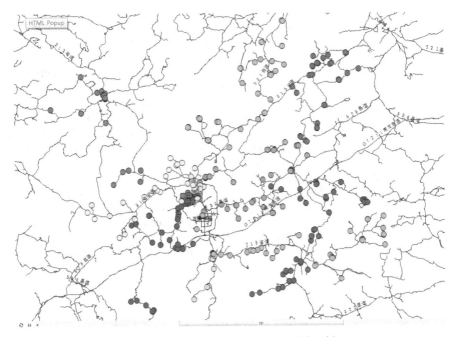

Fig. 7. Results obtained by the proposed algorithm

5   Conclusions

In this paper, we have presented an enhanced Clarke-Wright algorithm. By introducing enhanced steps in route building, stop assignments, and route balancing, the algorithm is able to obtain superior results compared to the basic C-W algorithm and an insertion based algorithm. Unlike parametric C-W algorithms for which parameter tuning is necessary, we do not require any parameter tuning, which facilitates the algorithm deployment for real applications. The algorithm is used in several application systems to solve VRPs for different clients as reflected in a case study.

In our future work we are planning to enhance the algorithm in order to deal with VRPs where time windows are imposed so that the proposed algorithm can be applied to additional applications. Furthermore, we plan to incorporate the approach into some meta-heuristics framework.

Acknowledgements. The author would like to express his gratitude to three anonymous referees for their critics and very useful suggestions to improve the manuscript.

References

1. Altinel, I.K., Oncan, T.: A new enhancement of the Clarke and Wright savings heuristic for the capacitated vehicle routing problem. Journal of the Operational Research Society 56, 954–961 (2005)
2. Battarra, M., Golden, B., Vigo, D.: Tuning a parametric Clarke-Wright heuristic via a genetic algorithm. Journal of the Operational Research Society 59, 1568–1572 (2008)
3. Bodin, L., Golden, B., Assad, A., Ball, M.: Routing and scheduling of vehicles and crews: the state of the art. Computers & Operations Research 10, 63–212 (1983)
4. Bozkaya, B., Cao, B., Aktolug, K.: Routing solutions for the service industry. In: Montoya-Torres, J.R., Juan, A.A., Huatuco, L.H., Rodriguez-Verjan, G.L. (eds.) Hybrid Algorithms for Service, Computing and Manufacturing Systems: Routing and Scheduling Solutions, pp. 46–78. IGI-Global Publishing (2011), doi:10.4018/978-1-61350-086-6
5. Braysy, O., Gendreau, M.: Vehicle routing problem with time windows, Part I: Routing construction and local search algorithms. Transportation Science 39(1), 104–118 (2005)
6. Braysy, O., Gendreau, M.: Vehicle routing problem with time windows, Part II: Metaheuristics. Transportation Science 39(1), 119–139 (2005)
7. Cao, B., Bozkaya, B.: Vehicle routing in service industry using decision support systems. In: Faulin, J., Juan, A.A., Grasman, S.E., Fry, M.J. (eds.) To Appear in Decision Making in Service Industries: A Practical Approach. Taylor & Francis (2012)
8. Clarke, G., Wright, J.: Scheduling of vehicles from a central depot to a number of delivery points. Operations Research 12, 568–581 (1964)
9. Corominas, A., Garcia-Villoria, A., Pastor, R.: Fine-tuning a parametric Clarke and Wright heuristic by means of EAGH (empirically adjusted greedy heuristics). Journal of Operational Research Society 61, 1309–1314 (2010)
10. Dantzig, G.B., Ramser, J.H.: The truck dispatching problem. Management Science 6, 80–91 (1959)
11. Glover, F.: Multi-start and strategic oscillation methods – Principles to exploit adaptive memory. In: Laguna, M., Gonzales-Valarde, J.L. (eds.) Computing Tools for Modeling, Optimization and Simulation: Interfaces in Computer Science and Operations Research, pp. 1–24. Kluwer (2000)
12. Juan, A., Faulin, J., Jorba, J., Riera, D., Masip, D., Barrios, B.: On the use of Monte Carlo simulation, cache and splitting techniques to improve the Clarke and Wright savings heuristics. Journal of the Operational Research Society 62, 1085–1097 (2011)
13. Kim, B.-I., Kim, S., Sahoo, S.: Waste collection vehicle routing problem with time windows. Computers & Operations Research 33, 3624–3642 (2006)
14. Laporte, G., Musmanno, R., Vocaturo, F.: An adaptive large neighborhood search heuristic for the capacitated arc-routing problem with stochastic demands. Transportation Science 44(1), 125–135 (2010)
15. Lenstra, J., Rinnooy Kan, R.: Complexity of vehicle routing and scheduling problems. Networks 11, 221–227 (1981)
16. Paessens, H.: The savings algorithm for the vehicle routing problem. European Journal of Operational Research 34, 336–344 (1988)
17. Ropke, S., Cordeau, J.-F.: Branch and cut and price for the pickup and delivery problem with time windows. Transportation Science 43, 267–286 (2009)
18. Solomon, M.M.: Algorithms for the vehicle routing and scheduling problems with time window constraints. Operations Research 35, 254–265 (1987)
19. Weigel, D., Cao, B.: Applying GIS and OR techniques to solve Sears technician dispatching and home delivery problems. Interfaces 29(1), 112–130 (1999)

An Insertion Heuristic Manpower Scheduling for In-Flight Catering Service Application

San-Nah Sze[1], Ada Ng Suk-Fong[2], and Kang-Leng Chiew[1]

[1] Department of Computational Science and Mathematics, Faculty of Computer Science and Information Technology, Universiti Malaysia Sarawak, Malaysia
snsze@fit.unimas.my
[2] Institute of Transport and Logistics Studies, Faculty of Economics and Business, The University of Sydney, NSW 2006, Australia

Abstract. This paper studies the manpower scheduling for in-flight catering loading operations. Package meals are delivered from a common service centre to aircrafts at apron. All aircrafts must be served within the period upon arrivals and prior to departures using loading trucks. The scheduling process takes into account complex considerations such as meal break allocation, multiple trip traveling and food exposure time limit. Given the aircrafts movement and pre-defined maximum working hours for each loading team, the core puzzle of this study is to assign minimum number of loading teams to the aircrafts and to form a roster. An insertion based heuristic is proposed to generate the solutions in a short amount of time for large instances. Due to the presence of numerous constraints, the insertion heuristic is implemented in stages for constructing trips. Computational results show that the insertion heuristic is more efficient and outperforms the actual roster of a Malaysian in-flight caterer.

Keywords: Multi-trip, Manpower scheduling, Time windows, Vehicle routing.

1 Introduction

The airline industry operates in a time critical mode. All the aircrafts must be served, maintained and well checked within the transit time. Any delay will cost a high penalty. Thus, scheduling is important to make sure the availability of resources. Not only that, the scheduling process is demanded to be efficient and fast to cope with large number of aircrafts and emergency cases such as flight delay or aircrafts swapping. The nature of the problem is complex due to the existence of numerous constraints. Therefore, the manpower planning directly becomes increasingly complex and strategically important.

This research is motivated by airline in-flight catering operations. In the case study, several loading teams are required to deliver and upload packaged meals. The meals are transported by loading trucks travelling from a central kitchen to the aircraft that landed at a nearby apron. Loading trucks can only serve a limited number of aircraft in a single trip; in-flight food has to be stored on aircraft within a certain time period after leaving the kitchen in order to maintain freshness. Furthermore, each loading

H. Hu et al. (Eds.): ICCL 2012, LNCS 7555, pp. 206–216, 2012.

team is given a meal break during their shift. Due to safety reasons, loading teams are restricted to have their meal break in lounge areas. These operational constraints heavily affect vehicle allocation and travelling policies. The fundamental assumption, or constraint, is that all aircraft must be served within their transit time at the apron. Due to tight time windows and different aircraft types, some aircraft require more than one loading team to offload and upload in-flight food on time.

Each vehicle can perform several trips during a shift. There are a few transportation requirements such as the teams must travel back and forth to the depot (the kitchen in our case) in order to provide service. Each trip is subject to a time limit constraint and limited truck capacity. In addition, a mandatory meal break must be scheduled within a predefined time interval. All customers (aircraft in our case) must be visited exactly once, any time within a predefined time window. A certain amount of time is required at the depot and customer sites to load and unload goods. For convenience, this time is included in the travelling times.

Since the problem is motivated by real-life applications, the primary goal is to minimise the total manpower while providing satisfactory service (meeting all deadlines) to all customers. Due to the larger-scale problems demand from industry, this research focuses on developing a computationally bounded heuristic that generates high quality solutions in short time.

Most of the previous studies involve real-life application-based simulations and the problems are solved using heuristics. For example, [1] studies a biscuit distribution problem and [3] considers a petrol station replenishment problem. Both studies report an average 20% improvement by heuristics. In manpower scheduling for airline catering, [6] and [7] suggest a tabu search approach and branch and price, respectively, to achieve the minimum number of unassigned jobs. Other application studies can be referred to in [8], [9], [10], [11], [13], [14] and [15].

2   Formulation and Approach

The model consists of n aircrafts and a group of loading teams. Each aircraft $i \in A$ is associated with an earliest time service that can take place, $r_i \geq 0$, a deadline, d_i, and a servicing time, p_i. The aircraft i cannot be served before r_i and servicing task must be completed by d_i. It is also assumed that $r_i + p_i \leq d_i$, $1 \leq i \leq n$. Each loading team can only serve one aircraft at a time. Preemptions are not allowed.

The *insertion heuristic* was first implemented in 1977 to solve travelling salesmen problems. In the following years, insertion heuristics were widely used to solve variants of the vehicle routing problem (VRP), such as multiple vehicle dial-a-ride problems, VRP with time windows, asymmetric capacitated VRP, and a real-life application of transporting handicapped persons. Furthermore, the insertion technique is also a typical choice in developing an initial solution for metaheuristic approaches, such as tabu search and simulated annealing.

In recent works, Dessouky et al. in [4] embedded an environmental component into the insertion heuristic to solve pickup and delivery problems with time window.

A parallel regret insertion heuristic is proposed in [5] based on a case study at Los Angeles County. [10] present a new measurement criterion, the cost of reducing time window slack into a classical insertion heuristic to solve a multi-vehicle pickup and delivery problem with time windows. Visual attractiveness is also quantified in the proposed insertion heuristic study, Ren et al. in [12], a multi-shift VRP with overtime inspired by a healthcare delivery system. Tabu search is embedded in the insertion heuristic framework for improvement. The empirical results show the improvement in terms of time and cost by the proposed solution.

To the best of our knowledge, no research has been done on multi-trip vehicle routing and scheduling problem with time window and meal break consideration as our case study by an insertion heuristic. The most related paper [2] provides a brief description model of multiple trips per vehicle. This problem is different from our problem because they predefined the number of trips in a route and meal break is not considered. Furthermore, the trip time limit in our model complicates the classical insertion implementation. Traditionally, the insertion heuristic schedules a set of customers in sequential order. In our problem, we need to break the traditional sequence into multiple trips with additional tasks in between, such as meal break and multiple travelling to the depot. Therefore, basic insertion heuristics will not necessarily produce a feasible solution in our case.

In the classical insertion approach, there is only one trip. Therefore, a decision has to be made on which new customer (aircraft, in our case) is to be inserted and where to insert this customer. However, in our case, since there is more than one trip in a route and a meal break has to be inserted, additional factors need to be considered. The number of trips (a complete travelling cycle from service centre to apron) is not fixed which complicates the implementation further. An extra question that needs to be answered in such scenario is when to define a new trip? To overcome this, there seem to be two options: (a) insert all the customers in a trip, then pack the sequential customers into trips; (b) sequentially construct the trips by insertion. Both options can potentially provide the maximum savings by aggregating the customers in each trip, and achieve minimum trips required. However, option (a) could easily make the previous schedule become infeasible because customers' time windows would not be met by adding the travelling tasks of newly defined trips at the packing stage. For option (b), we need to consider if the customer to be inserted into a partial trip or to form a new trip. This makes the evaluation process more complex and creates either too few trips or too many trips in a route. Furthermore, when a customer is proposed to be inserted into any trip of the route, the feasibility check needs to go through every element/task from the first trip to the last trip on the route. This is because an insertion will push the precedent trip to an earlier time unit and forward the following trip to a later time unit. By doing this, the computational effort will be greatly increased. On top of that, when the number of trips is not fixed, travelling tasks (between apron and service centre) can only be allocated along with the first aircraft insertion in a newly added trip. Therefore, potential insertion slots have become another important factor in our case study.

In addition, in our case, there are extra task requirements (the meal break and a few travelling tasks between apron and service centre) that need to be allocated; whereas, previous studies only schedule a sequence of customers. A meal break must be allocated between two consecutive travelling tasks, as they must be conducted at depot, within a given time window. Here, we need to consider when to insert the meal break appropriately. For example, if we only insert the meal break after constructing the trips, it will easily make the previous partial solution impractical due to time window constraints. On the other hand, it will have either too many or too few trips before the meal break if it is allocated before constructing trips for a route.

In this study, the *insertion heuristic* is proposed to construct a shift in three stages to cope with multiple travelling requirements. Initially, all aircraft are sorted in increasing order according to their arrival times, a_i, followed by their laxity, $b_i - p_i$.

Then a new pair of decision variables, e_i and l_i, are defined as the earliest time to start service and the latest time to start service, respectively, to ensure feasibility of the solution.

The three stages of the insertion heuristic to form a route are defined as follows:

(a) *Define new shift*

A new shift is initiated by the aircraft on the top of the sorted list. A pair of travelling tasks is allocated together with the aircraft, travel to apron with truck and return to service centre as one complete trip. The first aircraft to be served, the shift time, the meal break, and the timeline for the first trip are defined accordingly. The shift time limit is set by using a dummy aircraft with zero maintenance processing time; meanwhile, the timeline for the first trip is set by the returning travelling task. A *time window table* (TWT) is created to keep track of each task allocated associated with e_i and l_i. Then, the aircraft chosen in the TWT will be removed from the sorted list. Fig. 1 shows the components to define a new shift and the implementation of it.

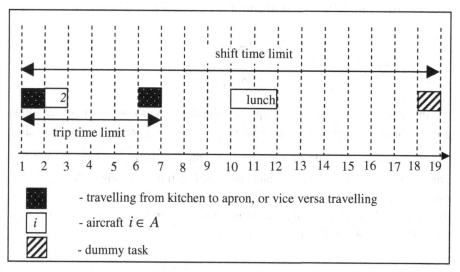

Fig. 1. Components to define a new shift

(b)   *Expand trip*

In this stage, the remaining aircraft in the sorted list will be evaluated for insertion into the newly defined trip. The potential insertion slots are restricted to slots after the scheduled aircraft on the particular trip. In other words, the remaining aircraft are not allowed to be inserted after any travelling tasks, meal breaks or dummy tasks. The best insertion slot, C_1 for each remaining aircraft, u, is selected by using the following equations:

$$C_1(u) = \min[\alpha c_1(u) + \beta c_2(u) + \gamma c_3(u)];\qquad(1)$$

$$\alpha + \beta + \gamma = 1;\qquad(2)$$

$$0 \le \alpha \le 1, 0 \le \beta \le 1, 0 \le \gamma \le 1;\qquad(3)$$

Equation (1) evaluates the maximum savings caused by the insertion, which includes distance reduction, c_1, shorter absolute waiting, c_2, and wider width of new time window, c_3. The time window cost, c_3, tends to offer the aircraft a wider time window due to the insertion. By adding this, it allows more aircraft insertions in future iterations. Parameters α, β, and γ are used to represent the weight of each "saving" criteria, based on the different objective functions or scenarios, as managerial parameters for managerial preferences. For example, the greater value of α on the objective function of minimising the total travelled distance, or the smaller value of β in the single travelling trip.

Next, the equation to evaluate the optimum aircraft, C_2 to be inserted is defined as follows:

$$C_2(i(u^*), u^*, j(u^*)) = \text{optimum}[\mu d_{0,u} + 2\theta p_0 - C_1(u)];\qquad(4)$$

$$\mu + \theta = 1;\qquad(5)$$

$$\mu \ge 0, \theta \ge 0;\qquad(6)$$

The first and second terms in (4) represent the distance and new pairs of travelling tasks required if the aircraft is served on a new trip. $d_{0,u}$ represents the travelling distance in time between depot to customer u; meanwhile p_0 refers to the standard setup processing time at the depot plus the travelling time returning to the depot. The managerial parameter weight of each criterion is given as μ and θ, respectively. This stage will be repeated until no more feasible aircraft in the sorted list can be inserted into the particular trip.

(c) *Insert new trip*

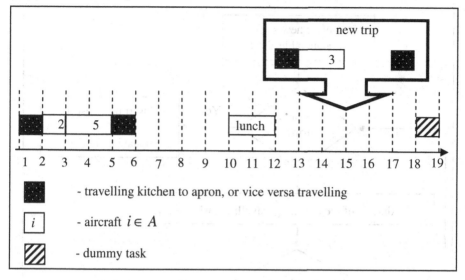

Fig. 2. Components of new trip to be inserted

A travelling time is defined as the travelling activity between depot and the customer's site plus the standard setup time in the kitchen. The meal break, the dummy task and the travelling task are considered as non-aircraft tasks. A new trip is defined as a "block" of tasks including the best feasible aircraft and a pair of travelling tasks. The potential insertion slots for this new group of tasks are restricted to any slot between two non-aircraft tasks, as shown in Fig. 2. An evaluation equation similar to Equation (1) is used to obtain the best feasible aircraft to initiate a new trip. Then, go to stage (b). These stages will be repeated until no more feasible aircraft in the sorted list can be inserted into the route.

The e_i (earliest time to start service) and l_i (the latest time to start service) of each task in the route will be updated after each insertion, except l_i of the returning travelling task of the particular newly defined trip. This is due to its function which consists of setting the time limits of a trip. However, it will be updated at the end of stage (b) by $l_i = l_{i-1} + p_{i-1}$. The time window update of other tasks is as follows:

- Update the l values for all prior tasks from the new insertion backwards by,

$$l_i = \min(l_i, l_{i+1} - p_i) \qquad (7)$$

- Update the e values for all subsequent tasks from the new insertion forwards by,

$$e_i = \max(e_i, e_{i-1} + p_{i-1}) \qquad (8)$$

The Insertion heuristic is presented as flowchart below:

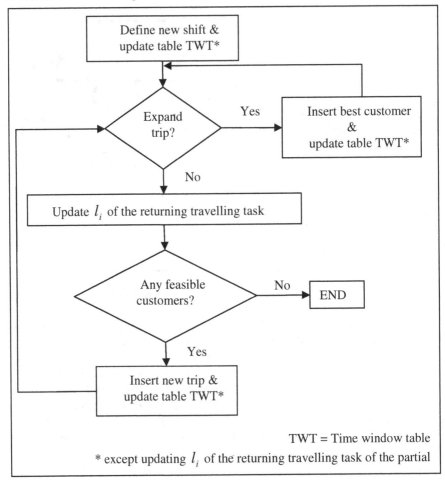

3   Performance Analysis

In this case study, the weekly aircraft movement is fairly static, except for peak seasons. A five day data set from [10], which is based on an in-flight caterer from Malaysia, is studied to evaluate the performance of the proposed solution. The data can be concluded as below:

   Day 1: 234 aircraft tasks
   Day 2: 267 aircraft tasks
   Day 3: 252 aircraft tasks
   Day 4: 278 aircraft tasks
   Day 5: 259 aircraft tasks

The heuristic experiment was coded in C# and all experiments were carried out on a Dell Pentium 4 1.8GHz computer. All experimental tests can be computed in less than five seconds. Computational results with different parameter settings are given to demonstrate the robustness and efficiency of the proposed insertion heuristic.

Table 1. Comparison of the number of loading teams required between real roster and insertion heuristic solution

	Real Roster	Insertion Heuristic			
		Multi-trip with time window and lunch	With-out lunch	Single trip	Lower Bound
Day 1	76	64	60	46	49
Day 2	76	72	68	53	57
Day 3	75	70	64	51	58
Day 4	79	71	67	54	60
Day 5	78	71	62	53	58

The in-flight caterer needs 75-79 loading teams each day, within the five day period. By giving the same simulation setting as real roster: 8-hour working shift, 1-hour meal break, 2-hour trip time limit, 2 aircrafts per trip and 15 minutes kitchen-apron traveling, Table 1 (second and third column) shows that the insertion heuristic is able to reduce the number of loading teams needed. On average, the insertion heuristic reduces 8 to 10.39% of loading teams each day, with maximum of 12 loading teams on Day 1.

In order to study meal break sensitivity, we ran the same data by disregarding one hour lunch allocation. The number of loading teams required reduces further over the range from 5.55% to 7.46% as shown in Table 1. This result demonstrates that the insertion heuristic is able to handle aircraft task effectively even though a meal break is considered. This result makes sense as each loading team is given an extra hour to handle the services.

When all the operation constraints that require multiple trips traveling are relaxed, the problem is reduced to the *vehicle scheduling problem with time windows* (VSPTW). However, all aircraft must be inspected during their transit times and the maximum working hours constraint is applied. The number of loading teams needed is reduced over 30% by using the insertion heuristic as shown in Table 1 under the column of "Single trip". This result is reasonable as only fewer tasks (i.e., meal break and kitchen-apron traveling) are required to be allocated for the loading teams.

A simple lower bound is computed by relaxing trip traveling limit and truck capacity, but only an hour meal break allocation is given, to estimate the quality of solution. To our best knowledge, even though the lower bound is not valid for this problem but an optimal solution is unlikely to be obtained, too. Table 1 shows the performance of the insertion heuristic and real roster by comparing with lower bound (last column). The insertion heuristic requires a range from 13.56% to 30.16% more loading teams than the lower bound. However, the real roster needs an average 35.42% more than the lower bound, with a maximum of 55.10% on Day 1.

In order to further evaluate the computational performance of the insertion heuristic, we are going to compare it with the two-stage scheduling model (TSS) in [11], which has been proven to perform better compared to the current practice in industry, with an improvement ranging from 5.26%.

TSS is proposed to solve the problem in two stages. In stage I, aircrafts are allocated to form trips by using the sorted order while fulfilling the food exposure time limit and truck capacity. It begins with empty multiple trips. During the construction, a set of partial routes with partial multiple trips is present, the feasible allocation of the aircraft at the end of the partial trips is considered. Each aircraft i is allocated by minimizing the idle time between aircraft or trips. If aircraft i cannot be feasibly aggregated into a partial trip, a new trip or new route will be initialized. The allocation is repeated until all jobs have been assigned. All the trips (treated as new jobs in stage II) will be sorted according to their starting times and followed by the total processing time in an increasing order. A greedy packing heuristic is used in stage II by fulfilling the lunch break constraint. As many trips as possible are packed into routes before lunch and after lunch.

We generated sixteen sets of problems, each consisting of ten test instances, in three different demand sizes: 100 aircraft, 250 aircraft and 500 aircraft. This is to test the robustness and efficiency of the proposed heuristic solutions. Solution quality is measured in terms of the minimum number of servicing teams and the computational time required producing this solution.

Table 2. Comparison of the insertion heuristic and the TSS model

	100 aircraft		250 aircraft		500 aircraft	
	IH	TSS	IH	TSS	IH	TSS
Test Problem 1	20	22	49	67	92	100
Test Problem 2	18	21	45	57	99	119
Test Problem 3	19	26	44	69	83	119
Test Problem 4	19	28	50	59	90	108
Test Problem 5	18	27	45	52	126	158
Test Problem 6	20	21	42	53	97	131
Test Problem 7	18	25	42	57	88	117
Test Problem 8	19	22	43	55	89	101
Test Problem 9	21	24	42	52	83	96
Test Problem 10	21	27	45	54	87	100

Table 3. Computational time for heuristics

Problem Size	Insertion Heuristic	Two-stage heuristic
100 aircrafts	250 - 850 milliseconds	250 - 850 milliseconds
250 aircrafts	2.5 - 3.5 seconds	1 - 2.5 seconds
500 aircrafts	18 - 25 seconds	9 - 15 seconds

Table 2 demonstrates that the insertion heuristic performs better than the TSS in all of the test problems. This result is expected because the insertion heuristic is a more complicated heuristic, compared to the TSS, for evaluating and choosing the best aircraft to be inserted.

In terms of computational time, Table 3 shows the average computing time for generating a solution using each heuristic. The computational time is quite stable in all test problems for each sample size. The result demonstrates that both heuristics are efficient when it comes to handling large problem instances. However, the TSS requires slightly less computational effort than the insertion heuristic, which is explained by the more complicated heuristic procedure of the insertion heuristic.

4   Conclusion

In this study, an insertion heuristic is proposed to solve manpower scheduling for the in-flight catering delivery system. After aircraft tasks are sorted according to time windows, the insertion heuristic is developed by constructing a trip by trip scenario due to multiple trip travelling requirements, while fulfilling the aircraft's time window.

Computational results are compared with manual solutions from an in-flight caterer in Malaysia. It illustrates that the insertion heuristic can handle complex manpower scheduling more efficiently and effectively with maximum up to 10.39% manpower reduction. Furthermore, the insertion heuristic can solve large problem instances in seconds. The insertion heuristic is evaluated further by comparing to the TSS model. The result reports that it outperforms TSS in all instances.

References

1. Brandao, J., Mercer, A.: A tabu search heuristic for the multi-trip vehicle routing and scheduling problem. European Journal of Operational Research 100, 18–91 (1997)
2. Campbell, A.M., Savelsbergh, M.: Efficient Insertion heuristics for vehicle routing and scheduling problems. Transportation Science 38(3), 369–378 (2004)
3. Cornillier, F., Laporte, G., Boctor, F.F., Renaud, J.: The petrol station replenishment problem with time windows. Computer & Operations Research 36, 919–935 (2009)
4. Dessouky, M., Rahimi, M., Weidner, M.: Jointly optimizing cost, service, and environmental performance in demand-responsive transit scheduling. Transportation Research Part D 8(6), 433–465 (2003)
5. Diana, M., Dessouky, M.M.: A new regret Insertion heuristic for solving large-scale dial-a-ride problems with time windows. Transportation Research Part B 38(6), 539–557 (2004)
6. Dohn, A., Kolind, E., Clausen, J.: The manpower allocation problem with time windows and job-teaming constraints: A branch-and-price approach. Computer & Operations Research 36, 1145–1157 (2008)
7. Ho, S.C., Leung, J.M.Y.: Solving a manpower scheduling problem for airline catering using tabu search. The Chinese University of Hong Kong (2008)
8. Kim, B.I., Kim, S., Sahoo, S.: Waste collection vehicle routing problem with time windows. Computers & Operations Research 33, 3624–3642 (2006)

9. Lim, P.S.: Manpower Planning with Time Window and Flexible Shift Pattern. MSc thesis. Malaysia University of Science and Technology, Malaysia (2006)
10. Lu, Q., Dessouky, M.M.: A new insertion-based construction heuristic for solving the pickup and delivery problem with time windows. European Journal of Operational Research 175(2), 672–687 (2006)
11. Oron, D., Sze, S.N., Ng, A.: A Heuristic Manpower Scheduling for In-Flight Catering Service. In: Proceeding of the Transportation and Management Science-13th International Conference of Hong Kong Society for Transportation Studies, Hong Kong, China (2008)
12. Ren, Y., Dessouky, M., Ordóñez, F.: The multi-shift vehicle routing problem with overtime. Computers & Operations Research 37(11), 1987–1998 (2010)
13. Salhi, S., Petch, R.J.: A GA based heuristic for the vehicle routing problem with multiple trips. Journal of Mathematical Modelling and Heuristics 6, 591–613 (2007)
14. Semet, F., Taillard, E.: Solving real-life vehicle routing problems efficiently using tabu search. Annals of Operations Research 41, 469–488 (1993)
15. Yan, S., Yang, T.H., Chen, H.H.: Airline short-term maintenance manpower supply planning. Transportation Research Part A 28, 615–642 (2004)

Author Index